Neolithic Houses
in Northwest Europe and Beyond

Neolithic Studies Group Seminar Papers 1

Edited by
Timothy Darvill and Julian Thomas

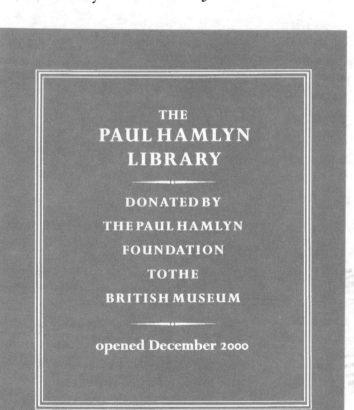

Oxbow Monograph 57

Published by
Oxbow Books, Park End Place, Oxford OX1 1HN

© Oxbow Books, 1996

ISBN 1 84217 076 7

First published 1996
Digital reprint 2002

A CIP record for this book is available from the British Library

This book is available direct from

Oxbow Books, Park End Place, Oxford OX1 1HN
(Phone: 01865-241249; Fax: 01865-794449)

and

The David Brown Book Company
PO Box 511, Oakville, CT 06779
(Phone: 860-945-9329; Fax: 860-945-9468)

or

from our website
www.oxbowbooks.com

*Front cover: Belle Tout, East Sussex. Speculative re-creation of Structure 5 looking southeast.
Drawing by Miles Russell.*

Digital Reprint by
Lightning Source

"Houses and buildings are not only among the most prominent features of contemporary civilization: in their construction and grouping they reflect more clearly than any other material manifestations the economic and social structure of society. And this has been so from the beginning. There is no class of antiquity that affords a closer insight into the life of prehistoric societies than houses." (Clark 1937, 468)

This book is the first proceedings of a meeting of the Neolithic Studies Group to be published. It therefore represents a significant new stage in the evolution of the Group, and further volumes arising from other meetings are planned.

The Neolithic Studies Group is a loose-knit collectivity of archaeologists, mainly from Britain and the Atlantic seaboard countries of the European Union, with an interest in the Neolithic period. It was formed in the Spring of 1984, the first meeting being held in Cheltenham, Gloucestershire, UK. Since then, the Group has met at least twice a year: Spring and Autumn. The Autumn meetings are held in London and address a topical theme. Spring meetings are held outside London to examine at first hand the Neolithic remains of a specific area and consider recent research relevant to the region. Spring field meetings have included: Western Ireland, Southeast Scotland, Eastern Scotland, North Wales, North Yorkshire, Northumberland, Wessex, and the Channel Islands.

All the meetings depend for their success upon the efforts and enthusiasm of local organizers. The occasion of publishing this first volume of papers provides an appropriate opportunity to thank most sincerely all those who have helped organize and host the Group's meetings over the last 11 years.

Membership of the Neolithic Studies Group is open to anyone active in studying any aspect of the Neolithic period in Europe. The present membership list, which stands at about 250 individuals, includes: academic staff, researchers and students from universities and colleges in several European countries; museum curators and museum-based research and field staff; and field archaeologists from national and local government institutions, and from archaeological trusts and units. There is no application procedure or subscription to join the Group; members are simply those currently on the mailing list. Anyone can ask to be added to the mailing list at any time, the only rule of the Group is that names are deleted from the list if the individual concerned misses four meetings in a row (ie. two years) and has not contacted the Group Co-ordinators asking to be kept on the list during that time.

As already mentioned, the Group relies on its members to organize meetings so that this responsibility is shared round. There are two co-ordinators who look after the mailing list and finances, and who juggle offers to arrange meetings so that there is a fair spread of venues and themes.

We hope that you will find this first volume of papers published by the Neolithic Studies Group useful, and we look forward to seeing you at one of our future meeting.

Timothy Darvill and Gordon Barclay
(Neolithic Studies Group Co-ordinators)

Contents

Foreword by the Co-ordinators of the Neolithic Studies Group
Abbreviations
Preface and acknowledgements
List of Contributors

Abbreviations

AMS	Accelerator Mass Spectrometry (for radiocarbon dating)
ASL	Above Sea Level
BAR	British Archaeological Reports
BC	calibrated radiocarbon dates before Christ
bc	uncalibrated radiocarbon dates before Christ
BP	uncalibrated radiocarbon dates before present (AD 1950)
CBA	Council for British Archaeology
EN	Early Neolithic
GGK	*Großgartach*
HMSO	Her Majesty's Stationery Office
HnK	Hinkelstein
KGA	*Kreisgrabenanlagen*
NM	Middle Neolithic
NS	New series
LBK	*Linearbandkeramic*
LN	Late Neolithic
RCAHMS	Royal Commission on the Ancient and Historical Monuments of Scotland
SBK	*Stichbandkeramik*
TRB	*Trichterbeckerkultur*

This volume of papers relating to Neolithic houses in northwest Europe and beyond represents the proceedings of a meeting of the Neolithic Studies Group held in the British Museum on 16 November 1992. The seminar was entitled "Neolithic Houses: Fact or Fiction?" and was organized by the present editors. Not all of the eleven papers presented on that occasion are included here, nor is there any attempt to summarize the discussion that took place. Four additional papers have been introduced to provide a more wide-ranging review of the evidence.

Following introductory papers on the study of Neolithic houses in Britain (Chapter 1) and Europe (Chapter 2), the contributions in this volume fall into three main groups. The first, Chapters 3–6, are regional reviews of the archaeological evidence for Neolithic houses in different parts of northwestern Europe. The second, Chapters 7–10, comprises discussions of a selection of specific houses in various parts of Europe. Finally, the third section, Chapters 11–13, take a sideways look at some of the issues covered in the two previous sections with a general review of interpretation and two papers which present anthropological perspectives on the use of houses in farming communities.

The term "house", and the concepts to which it is linked, are here interpreted fairly liberally. In general, attention focuses on those structures in which people live either permanently or on a semi-permanent basis. It is acknowledged, however, that the interpretation of some structures which might fall into this definition is fraught with difficulties and that there is a rather grey area covering structures which might or might not have been houses. This matter is explored further in Chapter 1. No attempt has been made to standardize terminology between papers, individual authors variously preferring to use more neutral terms such as "structures" or "buildings" in some instances.

In preparing this volume for the printers it has been editorial policy to tamper as little as possible with the papers as presented. All the references have been gathered together in a single list at the end of the volume because of the repetitious use of many sources and the enhanced value of a consolidated bibliography.

For a variety of reasons the preparation of this volume has taken longer than initially expected with the result that some of the early papers received for inclusion will have been completed about two years ago at the time of publication. Although one or two items have been added by authors during the editorial work, in general there has been little or no updating carried out.

The editors would like to thank the British Museum, and in particular Ian Longworth, Ian Kinnes, and Gill Varndell from the Department of Prehistoric and Roman Antiquities, for allowing and facilitating the smooth running of the seminar at which the papers in this volume were given. Thanks are also extended to Liz McCrimmon for assistance with assembling and checking the texts and references, Miles Russell for tracking down publications of Neolithic houses in Britain, and various staff in the School of Conservation Sciences at Bournemouth University and the Department of Archaeology at Southampton University for translating computer files from one format to another and answering endless queries and questions.

Timothy Darvill and Julian Thomas
July 1995

List of contributors

DOUGLASS W BAILEY
School of History and Archaeology
University of Wales
PO Box 909
Cardiff CF1 3XU
United Kingdom

GORDON J BARCLAY
Principal Inspector of Ancient Monuments
Co-ordinator of the Neolithic
  Studies Group Historic Scotland
Longmore House
Salisbury Place
Edinburgh, Lothian EH9 1SH
United Kingdom

TIMOTHY DARVILL
Professor of Archaeology and
  Property Development
Co-ordinator of the Neolithic Studies Group
School of Conservation Sciences
Bournemouth University
Fern Barrow
Poole, Dorset BH12 5BB
United Kingdom

ALEX GIBSON
Projects Manager
Clwyd-Powys Archaeological Trust
7a Church Street
Welshpool, Powys SY21 7DL
United Kingdom

FRANCIS J GREEN
Field Director
Test Valley Archaeological Trust
Orchard House
Orchard Lane
Station Road
Romsey, Hampshire SO51 8DP
United Kingdom

EOIN GROGAN
Director of the North Munster Project
The Discovery Programme
13–15 Lower Hatch Street
Dublin 2
Ireland

CHRISTINE HUGH-JONES
General Practitioner
41 Pretoria Road
Cambridge CB4 1HD
United Kingdom

JONATHAN LAST
Department of Archaeology
University of Cambridge
Downing Street
Cambridge. CB2 3DZ
United Kingdom

COLIN RICHARDS
Department of Archaeology
University of Glasgow
10 The Square
Glasgow G12 8QQ
United Kingdom

DEREK SIMPSON
Professor of Archaeology
Department of Archaeology
The Queen's University
Belfast BT7 1NN
Northern Ireland

JULIAN THOMAS
Lecturer in Archaeology
Department of Archaeology
University of Southampton
Highfield
Southampton, Hampshire SO9 5NH
United Kingdom

PETER TOPPING
Royal Commission on the Historical
  Monuments of England
Quern House Mill
Mill Court
Hinton Way
Great Shelford, Cambridge CB2 5LD
United Kingdom

ALASDAIR WHITTLE
Lecturer in Archaeology
School of History and Archaeology
University of Wales
PO Box 909, Cardiff CF1 3XU
United Kingdom

Chapter 1

Neolithic houses in mainland Britain and Ireland – A sceptical view

Julian Thomas

"The lack of positive evidence for house structures in lowland Britain, in areas of known settlement, is a problem which is likely to remain with us." (McInnes 1971, 124)

INTRODUCTION

The intention of this contribution is to draw attention to the problematic nature of our present understanding of domestic architecture in Neolithic Britain and Ireland. Elsewhere (Thomas 1991; 1993), I have suggested that the way in which we "read" the evidence for this period is conditioned to a great extent by a series of expectations and prejudices. These in turn are both created and reproduced through the mechanisms of archaeological discourse. Consequently, before we look at field monuments, or carbonized seeds, or animal bone assemblages, we already have a conceptual framework into which to fit our observations. This framework, I have argued, involves (amongst other things) a series of perceived connections between social evolution, changes in subsistence practice (between hunting and gathering and mixed farming), sedentism, population growth, and an increasing sophistication of material culture. Lodged within this set of ideas is a reliance upon the model of economic base and cultural superstructure, such that (visible) changes in cultural expression must reflect more profound changes in economic practice. In the particular case of domestic architecture, I have suggested that because Neolithic people are presumed to be mixed agriculturalists, it is argued that they should also be sedentary. Whereas foraging Mesolithic groups might not be expected to leave behind them traces of substantial domestic structures; Neolithic communities are assumed to have lived in houses. In a sense, then, the writing of British prehistory depends upon a conceptual division between hunter-gatherers as "others", and later populations who are rather like ourselves: farming people gradually developing towards urban society. From their earliest manifestation, these people should display all of the fundamental traits of a domesticated way of life, including that of living in houses.

Evidence for the existence of permanent domestic structures in Neolithic Britain is scanty, but not non-existent (see other papers in this volume). The argument which I will pursue here is *not* that Neolithic people were incapable of building substantial timber dwellings, if they were to consider them appropriate. Nor do I wish to suggest that such buildings were never constructed, or even that in particular localities at particular times people did not live in these structures. Instead, I will hope to show that the apparent scarcity of this kind of building is not merely an accident of preservation, but that in some regions, for a number of reasons the majority of the population lived for most of the time in rather flimsy and temporary dwellings. Those "houses" which have been excavated to date are generally in one way or another atypical, and archaeologists have tended to interpret the atypical as the norm. The existence of these timber buildings at all invites us to contemplate the complexity and heterogeneity of Neolithic settlement patterns. The notion that all right-thinking people should automatically desire to live in houses if circumstances permit seems to dominate the thinking of archaeologists as much as it does that of a present British government beset by a growing population of New Age travellers.

In Scandinavia, a rather similar concern with the interpretation of timber structures has recently become apparent. While large, timber-framed houses are rather rare in the TRB, the comparative proximity of sites of *Bandkeramik* tradition to the south seems to have conditioned the interpretation of a range of different features as longhouses. These include the long barrows of Barkaer and Stengade (Madsen and Jensen 1982, 63), and various structural elements of causewayed enclosures at As Vig, Knardrup Galgbakke and Sigersted (Eriksen and Madsen 1984). In Britain, it has long been the expectation that rectangular timber huts or houses should represent the standard form of Neolithic dwelling. Thus Childe (1949, 77) was to explain the stone cellular buildings of Orkney not as the outcome of unusual residential arrangements, but as a response to a lack of wood for use as building material. The Orcadians were merely doing in stone what everyone else in Neolithic Britain was doing in timber.

In this way, the norm for Neolithic settlement has been presented as being composed of "small social units based upon an isolated farmstead" (Megaw and Simpson 1979, 86). The result of this outlook has been that since so little evidence for houses exists, that which has come to light has often been considered uncritically. Pits with associated postholes have been seen as sunken dwellings (Stone 1934), while scatters of stakeholes have been described as houses (Webley 1958). Equally, rather than revise the conception of Neolithic society as sedentary and agricultural, reasons for the lack of evidence have been sought in depositional and post-deposition factors.

> "It is not surprising that few domestic sites have been recovered in view of the enormous accumulation of hill wash and other material that would have built up over the last 5000 years in the valley bottoms over such settlement sites." (Megaw and Simpson 1979, 86)

However, since the search for buried prehistoric settlements emerged as a research objective in the 1970s, the great amount of effort which has been expended in trying to find them has had largely negative results. Indeed, rather than correcting a perceived imbalance toward monuments in Neolithic landscape evidence, this work has often resulted in the discovery of yet more monuments. Thus, for instance, the Raunds Project in Northamptonshire has succeeded in uncovering buried concentrations of barrows and other monumental structures at West Cotton and Irthlingborough (Halpin 1987; Windell 1989).

Another significant argument against the possibility that large numbers of Neolithic farmsteads remain to be discovered in the British landscape lies in the contrast with slightly later periods. From the middle Bronze Age onwards, there are comparatively large numbers of enclosed settlements known. The emergence of sites like Itford Hill, Black Patch and South Lodge marks a change to a qualitatively different landscape from that of the Neolithic (Barrett 1994, 149–51). If similar settlements represented the norm throughout the Neolithic, it is difficult to imagine why those of the Bronze Age should survive in much greater numbers. Certainly, one cannot argue that some abrupt change in preservational circumstances took place at the end of the early Bronze Age. Recent work on alluviation and colluviation does not support a picture of any sudden and synchronized initiation of erosion and run-off across Britain and Ireland (Shotton 1978; Bell 1982). On the contrary, the interpretations proposed generally involve a complex and localized combination of climatic and anthropogenic factors. It follows that the sudden establishment of enclosed farms in the middle Bronze Age marks a genuine change in the way in which people made use of landscape, and we should not expect Neolithic land-use to be simply a less intensive version of the same pattern.

For a number of reasons, the cluster of presuppositions which lies behind the received wisdom on Neolithic domesticity is not innocent, and needs to be resisted. In the first place, there is an implied unilinear evolutionism in the understanding that all societies should be expected to progress gradually from being "simple" to a state of "complexity". The emergence of sedentary domestic communities appears to be seen as a marker along this route. This in turn suggests that the household is a unit which has a cross-cultural currency, and which can be equated with the family (Lane 1986, 183). As Strathern (1988, 94) indicates, the implication of this line of thought is that the domestic comes to be taken as a sphere of activity which is biologically-based, and somehow precedes the social. As the space of food preparation and consumption, of sexuality and of childbirth and child rearing, the "private" world of the house is often portrayed as both "natural" and female. This is then opposed with the "public" and cultural world of men (Strathern 1988, 74). However, in practice the composition of those who are co-resident within a given structure is highly culturally variable (C Hugh-Jones 1979, 45; Moore 1986, 30; Rosman and Rubel 1971, 86). Moreover, while one of the principal effects of the construction of buildings is to introduce discontinuity into social space, it does not necessarily follow that secluded spaces will be private, in the sense of being the exclusive prerogative of a small group of close kin. Indeed, the development of a separation between work-space and home-space, and between living quarters and sleeping quarters, appears to have been a relatively recent historical process (Deetz 1977). This suggests that "privacy" is a cultural construct which is specific to modern Westernized society, and hardly appropriate to the Neolithic.

All of the above indicates that it is unhelpful to begin from a position where the existence of family farmsteads in the British or Irish Neolithic is accepted as a point of faith, and to proceed to attempt to identify them within the available evidence. Instead, we should attempt to make this evidence work harder for us, by asking whether residence was permanent or transient, what kinds of co-residence were practised, how variable living structures may have been both within and between regions, and how Neolithic space may have been divided up or "domained". In this way, it may be possible to distinguish what kinds of relationships existed between people and built structures, rather than presume a kind of prehistoric suburbia.

NEOLITHIC WAYS OF LIFE

The scarcity of Neolithic houses is best considered alongside the more general dearth of indicators of an agricultural landscape (Thomas 1991, Chapter 2). Of the two most celebrated examples of Neolithic field systems, Céide Fields in Co. Mayo (Caulfield 1978) and Fengate near Peterborough (Pryor 1978), the dating of the former is somewhat equivocal, while both suggest large-scale cattle management rather than arable enclosure. Even if both were conclusively demonstrated to be of Neolithic date, it would be difficult to generalize from these isolated instances to a universal model of Neolithic agriculture. Clearly, interpretations which propose a homogeneous pattern on the basis of unique finds take no account of regional variability. Further, it is to be expected that repeated episodes of experimentation with any innovation will precede its more general adoption. "Farmyards", in any sense that we would recognize, are entirely absent from Neolithic Britain and Ireland. Samples of carbonized plant remains suggest only a sporadic use of domesticated cereals alongside a range of wild resources (Moffet *et al.* 1989; Entwistle and Grant 1989). Hence the kind of infield/outfield system which is implied by the use of a term like "farmstead" is hardly justified.

The comparatively large quantities of bovid remains which have been recovered from Neolithic sites in Britain and Ireland do appear to suggest that cattle were of considerable importance to some Neolithic communities. However, since the great majority of the bone samples concerned came from funerary or ceremonial monuments of one kind or another, it is difficult to argue that this is representative of the everyday diet (Thomas 1991, 21–5). It may have been that herds represented a form of corporate wealth, providing some nutrition through secondary products, but only slaughtered in connection with seasonal gatherings. If we consider the Neolithic use of resources to have involved a variable combination of domesticates and wild species, it is highly likely that a number of different seasonal cycles will have imposed themselves upon these communities. In the absence of buildings suitable for over-wintering, cattle would probably have been grazed on different pastures at different times of year. These might conceivably have been spatially distant from each other. Small plots of cereals and legumes may have been tended by persons who were less mobile than those following the herds, while the gathering of wild plants would have required yet another pattern of movement from place to place. In addition, we might mention the acquisition of flint and stone from distant sources, and the gathering of shed antler from woodlands as examples of activities which would have been fitted into a complex seasonal round. The significance of these different patterns of seasonal mobility is that the evidence which we have for Neolithic resource use does not accord particularly well with a picture of continuously co-resident kin-based social units. That is to say, family farmsteads. Instead, the material suggests a seasonal pattern of fission and fusion, dispersal and aggregation, in which particular segments of communities, perhaps defined on age or gender criteria, were engaged in particular tasks at particular times of year.

To be clear about what is being suggested here, the interpretation being put forward is in no sense environmentally determinist. It is not suggested that a particular pattern of seasonal availability of resources dictated a specific set of social behaviours. This is only one of a number of social patterns which might have emerged, and a system of dispersed farmsteads is equally conceivable, although it might be argued that this would have generated an entirely different set of archaeological traces. Nor, however, is what is proposed a form of Vidalian possibilism, where the environment affords the wherewithal for a range of different possible ways of life: a kind of blank cheque. Both environmental determinism and environmental possibilism preserve the notion of the environment as an externality, something "out there" producing stimuli to which human communities respond. Such a way of thinking seems to propose that societies, and social relationships, somehow exist outside of the material world, and are later impacted upon by natural phenomena. In place of such a culture/nature division, it is suggested that social relationships are thoroughly bound up with the "natural" world. There is no society without a world for it to live through, and this living through implies a deep embedding of the social in what Westerners refer to as "Nature". Human communities *dwell* in a material world, and in the course of this dwelling an accommodation is made between the rhythms of social reproduction and the seasonal rhythms by which the organic world renews itself.

It is suggested, then, that Neolithic communities in Britain and Ireland fitted into their world in such a way that their social units may have been fluid and shifting from season to season. Elsewhere (Thomas 1996) I have suggested that by the later Neolithic a range of quite distinct contexts existed for social interaction, such that social identities and forms of authority may have been specific to particular settings, gatherings, or locations. For the purposes of the present argument it is sufficient to note that concepts like "family" or "household" may be redundant in dealing with Neolithic Britain and Ireland. This presents certain problems, since as Tringham (1991a) rightly suggests, one of the central problems facing prehistoric archaeology at present lies in the conceptual leap required in thinking about the people we study as human beings. If we cannot rely upon the household units which Tringham seems to propose as something like a cultural universal, thinking about the everyday lives of Neolithic people becomes all the more difficult. The co-resident units which we might imagine at particular times of year might have taken forms like "young men", "old people", "unmarried women", "all those descended from a certain ancestor", and so on. Such a pattern of flux and high mobility might easily be responsible for a settlement pattern involving recurrent transient camps at specific locations, seemingly documented by lithic scatters (Bradley 1987), and a portable, multi-purpose lithic technology (Edmonds 1987).

A BROADER CONTEXT

While the lack of Neolithic houses in Britain (and to a lesser extent in Ireland) has often occasioned the kind of perplexity suggested by the quotation from McInnes at the start of this piece, this scarcity has seldom been considered in the context of the European Neolithic as a whole (an honourable exception being Kinnes 1985). While the illusive structures which so many field projects have hoped to uncover were doubtless the equivalents of the central European *Bandkeramik* longhouses, there is a strong case that the Neolithic of both Britain and Ireland is very distinct from that tradition. One might suggest that while the post-*Bandkeramik* traditions of Cerny, Rössen and Lengyel maintained some aspects of an inherited way of life (including the use of large timber houses), the Chasséen / Michelsberg / Funnel Beaker horizon marked a fundamental change in terms of the character of Neolithic communities in northern Europe. In both chronological and cultural terms, the earliest Neolithic of Britain and Ireland is most closely connected with these latter groups (Kinnes 1988). If we can think of the European Neolithic less as a unified and homogeneous entity and more as a series of historical developments which were only loosely connected with each other (Thomas 1993), the undoubted variation in the form and content of Neolithic settlement across the continent is more comprehensible (Chapman 1989, 33). There is consequently little reason to expect that the same features should characterize residential practices in Britain and Ireland at 4000 BC as had existed in central Europe one and a half millennia earlier.

When the comparison is made between Neolithic Britain and Ireland and the *contemporary* continental material, the contrast is none too great. There are a few rectangular buildings attributable to the Michelsberg, for instance, such as those at Ehrenstein and Aichbühl, but in an area like the Aldenhoven Platte which had dozens of *Bandkeramik* houses, there are no Michelsberg buildings at all (Whittle 1985, 210). The same can be said of the Aisne Valley (Kinnes 1985, 25). Thus even in areas where house structures had been common in the earliest Neolithic of northern Europe, they are scarce later on. In areas which were "Neolithicized" at the same time as Britain and Ireland, the pattern is similar. Within the TRB, houses few and far between over a huge cultural area, and are also extremely heterogeneous (Midgeley 1992, 317). These range from the Muldbjerg 6m x 3m hut of hazel stakes to the 21m Dölauer Heide post-built longhouse (Midgeley 1992, 333). In Scania, Larsson notes 23 early Neolithic settlements with only one house structure, Bellemegarden in Malmö (Larsson 1985, 13). It appears that across a large area of northwest Europe from around 4500 BC onwards, timber houses represented only a minor (if recurring) element of Neolithic material culture.

Recently, Ian Hodder (1990) has drawn attention to the importance of the house as a symbolic resource within the Neolithic of the Old World, suggesting a generalized structuring opposition between the domestic and the wild. It is not necessary to concur with the whole of this argument in order to acknowledge the basic point that houses held a cultural significance which went well beyond the provision of shelter. This need not indicate that the meaning of the house structure remained stable across time and space. On the contrary, I would suggest that a number of cultural phenomena which emerged within the central European Neolithic were appropriated and recontextualized by those societies which emerged from the encounter between colonizing agriculturalists and indigenous foragers around the northwest fringe of the continent. These would include not merely houses, but also causewayed enclosures, pottery vessels, polished stone tools, and earthen long mounds. These innovations should not be seen as elements in a fixed structure of meaning, but meaning*less* symbols which were given localized significance by communities engaged in reordering their cultural worlds. Thus a causewayed enclosure in Denmark and a similar enclosure in Ireland will have drawn upon the same set of resources in establishing a constructional form, but the uses to which the two monuments will have been put, and their importance to the communities which used them may have been utterly different. In a similar way, the timber structures which we refer to as "houses" may have been deployed in a number of different ways in different parts of

Neolithic northwest Europe. Our next task is to consider the meanings and functions which may have attended these structures in Britain and Ireland.

THE EVIDENCE FOR NEOLITHIC HOUSES IN BRITAIN AND IRELAND

Earlier in this essay I suggested that those British and Irish structures which have been claimed as dwellings are for the most part atypical of the contemporary pattern of settlement as a whole. We can begin to evaluate this claim by considering the issue of site location. In discussing the house at Haldon, Devon, Willock acknowledged that "the position is very exposed and commands magnificent views" (1936, 246), on the end of a major escarpment. Sites like Ballynagilly (ApSimon 1969; 1976) and Trelystan (Britnell 1982), too, were located in prominent yet windswept positions. This is not entirely in keeping with what is known of Neolithic settlement from lithic scatters (Gardiner 1984; Holgate 1988). Similarly, the unparalleled concentration of structures in the Lough Gur area may not be representative of a distribution which at one time extended out across the whole of Ireland. The Knockadoon sites are situated on a promontory which would have represented an island surrounded by marshes in the Neolithic (Ó Ríordáin 1954; Grogan and Eogan 1987, 487). This eminence forms the focus for a major concentration of monuments: chambered tombs, alignments of standing stones, and the Grange stone circle. If the Lough Gur houses were domestic structures, it is interesting to speculate as to what social circumstances would be involved in their location amongst these monuments.

At Lismore Fields, Buxton, Derbyshire, circumstances again indicate something more than a straightforward settlement. Here, a group of archetypal rectangular structures were located on a plateau between two rivers at the junction between the carboniferous limestone and the millstone grit (Garton 1991). Such a position might easily represent a significant focus in the landscape, a meeting point of routes and pathways. By all accounts, the site was subject to long-lived activity extending back into the Mesolithic, and involving ring-slots, small circles of pits, and alignments of large posts. Two timber buildings were present, Building I seemingly comprising two modules each similar to the single unit of Building II. Yet these two structures may have been separated by as much as three radiocarbon centuries, and the two parts of Building I may not have been in use (or even existence) simultaneously (Garton 1991, 13). At a number of sites it may be that "house" structures form one element in complex sequences of activity which were not purely domestic in character. At Haldon, for instance, Willock suggested that several of the hearths were constructed and used after the occupation in the house had ceased (1936, 263). At Trelystan, the two supposed houses are located on either side of a grave structure. If one accepts the excavator's suggestion that the older dates for the houses are the most secure, they would be roughly contemporary with the funerary activity on the site (Britnell 1982, 136 and 184). Given that the same site was later to provide the location for two round barrows, it is likely to have maintained an association with the dead, such that the flimsy sub-rectangular structures with central hearths may have had a role in mortuary practice rather than domestic activities. There were certainly very few stone tools on site, and the outward pitch of the stakes in the walls of Structure B might lead one to question whether it represented a roofed building at all.

In a particularly important article, Paul Lane (1986) discussed the arbitrary distinction between "domestic" and "ritual" structures in relation to the site of Mount Pleasant, Nottage, Mid Glamorgan, stressing that there could be no such thing as a "ritual structure". Instead, ritual is a form of human action which may involve a range of forms of material culture, from the most mundane to the most explicitly symbolic. Reviewing Savory's (1952) evidence from Mount Pleasant, Lane questioned the straightforward transformation of the site from dwelling to funerary site implied by the superimposition of a round barrow over a rectangular house. As he pointed out, the interpretation of the earlier structure as a dwelling is by no means unproblematic, since one wall was entirely absent and pottery of both earlier and later Neolithic tradition was present within the building. There was no hearth or ash inside the building, and most of the pottery actually came from outside (McInnes 1971, 113). Extrapolating from Lane's argument, we might question the numerous cases in which houses have fortuitously survived beneath later tumuli. Because these are sites of different functions (domestic and ritual) it has been possible to see their presence in the same location as coincidental. As an alternative, we might choose to see these various acts of construction as parts of the continuous reinterpretation of place, whereby physical intervention results in a transformation of existing meanings. Such transformations, however, always draw upon the existing meaning of a place. In the case of a site like Ballyglass, it seems most unlikely that the builders of the later court tomb were unaware that a large timber building had previously stood there (Ó Nualláin 1972a; 1972b). More probably, the tomb was located precisely because the building had rendered this a "special" place. Significantly, the southwest wall of the house is virtually contiguous with the line of the tomb's kerb. Elsewhere, rather less substantial structures of postholes have been isolated beneath tombs and rather wishfully identified as houses, as at Sale's Lot and Hazleton North in Gloucestershire (O'Neil 1966; Saville 1990). With Hazleton in particular it seems perverse to separate the small hearth and group of thirteen postholes from the other activities documented beneath the cairn, given the presence of human bone fragments and the conjoining of finds with others from the large midden nearby (Saville 1990, 20). Here we are clearly dealing with a sequence of events involving feasting and the processing of the remains of the dead, and which culminated in the construction of the chambered long cairn. The linear, screen-like character of the posthole structure may have played a significant role in the orchestration of these activities. A similar desire to find evidence of domestic activities perhaps lies behind the interpretation of the postholes at Gwernvale, Powys, as a building (Lynch 1989; Britnell and Savory 1984). Similar alignments of posts converging upon the forecourts of long mounds are known from Street House, (Vyner 1984) and Kemp Howe (Brewster 1969), where their role as a focusing device is clear.

TIMBER HALLS

Of the sites discussed so far, those at Ballyglass and Lismore Fields stand out as unequivocally representing substantial wooden buildings. A number of authors have separately pointed to the similarities between various structures of this kind (eg. ApSimon 1976; Lynch 1989, 2), and it may be realistic to isolate a group of a dozen or fewer British and Irish buildings on the grounds of layout, construction and size. This would include Ballynagilly, Fengate, Llandegai, Ballygalley, Newtown, Tankardstown South, and Gorhambury, most of which have evidence for a combination of upright posts and plank slots, some form of internal division, and dimensions of 7m to 15m by 5.5m to 7.5m (ApSimon 1976; Pryor 1976; Lynch 1989; Simpson 1993; Gowen and Halpin 1992; Gowen 1988a; Neal *et al.* 1990, 60). The "modular" character of the three constructional units at Lismore Fields adds to the impression that these structures were built according to a somewhat standardized pattern. Although built on a considerably larger scale, the building at Balbridie (Ralston 1982) has clear affinities with this group. It would also be this set of sites which would be easiest to find contemporary parallels for on the continent, for example Flögeln, near Cuxhaven (Zimmerman 1979).

The construction of these "timber halls" gives only a few clues as to their possible use. At both Ballyglass and Ballynagilly the entrances are set in one corner of the rectangle, and take the form of a screened passage, effectively rendering the interior of the building invisible from outside (Ó Nualláin 1972, 54; ApSimon 1976, 19). At Ballygalley, the structure appears to have been very deliberately "decommissioned", with the timbers removed from their slots and a cobbled surface laid over the remaining floor (Simpson 1993, 60). This recalls similar practices involved in the destruction or closing of some chambered tombs, as with the stone paving laid over the flattened remains of the monument at Pierowall Quarry in Orkney (Sharples 1984). Ballynagilly and Balbridie had both burnt down (Ralston 1982, 240), which may suggest similarities with the burning of timber structures beneath earthen long barrows. The possibility that "houses" may be to some degree interchangeable with monuments is also suggested by the building at Fengate, which shares an axis of orientation with an early Neolithic multiple burial 120m to the west (Pryor 1976; Pryor pers. comm.). This seems to echo the sequences of mutual referencing between monuments found, for example, within the Dorchester on Thames cursus complex (Bradley and Chambers 1988). More strikingly, a group of presumed timber structures in Perthshire, known from air photographs, appear to enjoy the same kinds of spatial relationships with the Cleaven Dyke cursus as do the long barrows surrounding the Dorset Cursus (Barclay 1993, 32; Barrett *et al.* 1991). The ambiguity of the archaeological evidence has implicitly been recognized before. In certain circumstances, rectangular timber structures have been interpreted as having a "ritual" character: at Balfarg Riding School, or in the case of the Danish "cult houses" at Herrup, Engedal, Tustrup and Ferslev (Barclay 1993, 12; Midgeley 1992, 441). It is worth speculating whether, had they not been found in association with a henge monument or groups of megalithic tombs and stone-packing graves, these buildings would have been given a "domestic" interpretation.

When we turn to the contents of this group of timber structures, a straightforward domestic interpretation is again thrown into question. In several cases, very large quantities of carbonized plant remains have been recovered: a circumstance very much out of keeping with other Neolithic sites. At Lismore Fields, a wide range of plants were represented, together with chaff fragments (Garton 1991, 13). However, at Balbridie the plentiful cereal remains suggested storage rather than processing (Fairweather and Ralston 1993, 317–20). At Ballygalley, crop processing evince was again present, but only outside of the building, while clear grain was found inside (Simpson 1993, 60–2). This site also produced a startlingly rich assemblage of artefacts, including over 800 flint cores, 2000 flint tools and an even greater number of flakes, roughout axes of porcellanite and fragments from axes of Langdale tuff, Arran pitchstone, and thousands of pottery sherds (Simpson 1993). At Fengate, another high-quality material assemblage was recovered, involving goods more appropriate to a funerary context. This included a fine flint sickle, a Group VI axe fragment, and a jet bead (Pryor 1974, 12). The same site produced sherds of very fine carinated bowls, which some authors have identified as having a particular social importance in the earliest Neolithic of both Britain and Ireland (Herne 1988, 16; Kinnes 1985, 26). Similar pottery was found at Ballynagilly, where a small pit at the eastern end of the building (facing the entrance) contained numerous sherds (ApSimon 1976, 20). This calls to mind the pit containing a very similar assemblage at the foot of the portal stone of the earlier chamber at the megalithic tomb of Dyffryn Ardudwy, Gwynedd (Powell 1973). Whatever interpretation we choose to place upon these timber buildings, it is clear that they we judged appropriate locations for particular depositional practices which might elsewhere be associated with the dead.

In his review of carinated fine wares in Britain and Ireland, Herne (1988) suggested that these vessels might have played an instrumental role in the cultural transformation generally referred to as the Mesolithic-Neolithic transition. Their association with several of the rectangular post-and-trench structures discussed above indicates that the dating of the latter may be of significance. Indeed, the radiocarbon dates for timber buildings in Britain and Ireland tend to cluster within the first two centuries of the Neolithic: Fengate, Ballyglass, Ballynagilly, Llandegai, Ballygalley and Balbridie have all produced dates in the range 3200–3000 bc uncalibrated. Like other forms of monumental architecture, these structures may thus have had a role in the transformation of landscape and social relations. Like other forms of Neolithic material culture, these buildings were drawn from a very widely-held repertoire of material forms, and were put to use in locally significant ways. To a largely mobile society, "houses" may have been significant locations for meeting and gathering, within which particular activities may have been undertaken in seclusion. Given the presence of fine material items, large quantities of plant remains, and depositional activities which might have evoked death and ancestry, it is likely that these activities involved exchange or redistribution, or at least the transfer of resources between different segments of disaggregated communities, and the processing of the remains of the dead. As Kinnes (1975) points out, Neolithic mortuary practices in Britain appear to have involved a number of different kinds of sites. What this may mean is that the circulation of the dead, or representative parts of their anatomies, served to draw places together in spatial narrative, much as the seasonal movements of the living did. The connection of timber buildings with the dead is further emphasized by the incorporation of elements of their architecture into that of the long mound tradition. The clearest example of this lies in the series of timber structures beneath the long barrow at Nutbane in Hampshire (Morgan 1959). It may be this incorporation which lies behind the decline of free-standing timber buildings as a monumental form in the middle to late Neolithic.

STRUCTURES IN ENCLOSURES

If one group of buildings seems to be concentrated in the earliest part of the Neolithic, it is notable that several others are contextually clustered. I have attempted to stress the heterogeneity of Neolithic settlement patterns, and one aspect of this variability is undoubtedly social differentiation. While most causewayed enclosures seem to have originated as temporary structures subject to sporadic use, some appear to have eventually become fortified settlements (Thomas 1991, 32–8; Edmonds 1993). The best example is perhaps Crickley Hill, Gloucestershire, where a post-built rectangular structure lay parallel to a metalled pathway into the interior of the enclosure in the final phase of its use (Dixon 1988). If some part of society were dwelling inside these enclosures it must surely have been a minority, and perhaps a minority whose position was resented, to judge from the evidence of armed attack on Crickley, Hambledon Hill and Carn Brea. However, at Hambledon the evidence of settlement within the Steepleton enclosure provides little in the way of house plans, while at Carn Brea the clearest structure is a lean-to set against the enclosure wall (Mercer 1981, 19).

The excavations of Carn Brea and Helman Tor have demonstrated the existence of fortified hilltop sites in western Britain during the Neolithic. The recognition of this phenomenon allows us to reconsider another of the better-known house sites of the period, Clegyr Boia, Dyfed. Here, two structures were located, the rectangular Hut 1 and the sub-circular Hut 2. Hut 2 was overlain by the rampart of the Iron Age or later enclosure, and this appeared to demonstrate that the two buildings belonged to an unenclosed Neolithic settlement (Williams 1953, 24). However, for a number of reasons this interpretation is not entirely secure. To the northeast of the enclosure lay a rock-cut ditch. This contained sherds of Neolithic pottery, but since it had no bank, Williams argued that it must have been a quarry for the enclosure bank (1953, 34). However, if the enclosure had multiple phases of construction, any bank may have been removed as a source of building material. The possibility of multiple builds is also suggested by the different forms of construction of the rampart in the east (where it has an internal face, or perhaps two builds), and to the north, overlying Hut 2 (Williams 1953, 31). Neolithic pottery from the rampart material on the eastern side of the enclosure was interpreted as having been redeposited. Indeed, with the exception of a few fragments of iron waste, all of the material culture from the excavation was of Neolithic date. While much of the Iron Age and Dark Ages of Wales are aceramic, there is a strong argument to be made that Clegyr Boia was at some point a Neolithic enclosed site. Other known "houses" may also have formed elements of more complex sites. Ballygalley, for instance, may be enclosed by a ditch (Simpson 1993, 62)

CONCLUSION

Recent studies of the British and Irish Neolithic have begun to uncover an alien cultural world, very much removed from our own everyday experience. None the less, the tendency has been to treat "houses" as a category of evidence which is relatively self-evident. While monuments, prestige goods and burials are accepted as the outpourings of a florid cultural superstructure, the expectation appears to be that beneath this will have lain a relatively stable economic base. As the context of a range of activities which are perceived as biological universals (food production and consumption, biological reproduction), the house is itself presumed to be a stable element of social life from later prehistory onwards. For this reason, the evaluation of archaeological traces which may represent domestic structures has sometimes lacked a critical edge. Much of the British evidence may represent structures which were both flimsy and temporary: the tiny horseshoe shaped structure from Little Paxton, Cambridgeshire, for example (Rudd 1968). Where scatters of numerous postholes and stakeholes cannot easily be resolved into coherent structures, it seems likely that they constitute traces of sporadic or cyclical occupations (eg. Spong Hill (Healey 1988); Willington (Wheeler 1979)). The repeated re-use of particular locations, possibly on a seasonal basis, might involve dwellings in which particular structural elements might be re-used, and moved from place to place – flexible wooden members or hide coverings, for example. It this connection it is worth considering that even in the case of the supposedly substantial building at Ronaldsway on the Isle of Man (Bruce *et al.* 1947), it is difficult to imagine the postholes supporting a coherent timber frame, as opposed to a tent-like structure. Here too, the sunken floor was cut into gravel which would have slumped had the occupation lasted for any great while (McInnes 1971, 115), while the assemblage of numerous polished axes, stone plaques and cattle long bones suggests a deliberate deposit rather than carelessness.

Both in Britain and in much of continental northwest Europe, Neolithic settlement is likely to have been highly variable in form, but often ephemeral in character. Scandinavian sites like Mosegården and Lindbjerg, giving no more than a vague indication of the structure of buildings, are probably relatively characteristic (Madsen and Jensen 1982, 66; Midgeley 1992, 328). Where more substantial buildings have come to light, they can be argued to be in one way or another atypical. Major timber framed buildings were a potential element of British and Irish Neolithic material culture, and the timber structures associated with the earthen long mound tradition clearly demonstrate the existence of sophisticated carpentry techniques. However, it seems that where such buildings were constructed they represented specialized structures of some kind or several kinds, connected with the activities of an extended community rather than a domestic group.

Chapter 2

Houses in context: Buildings as process

Alasdair Whittle

> "Old at once was the house,
> And I was old" (Edward Thomas, *The New House*)

PERSPECTIVES AND PROBLEMS

Changing interpretations

Recent years have seen firmer foundations being laid for a fruitful study of Neolithic houses. The house is no longer just treated as a machine for living, or as the shell for one or other social unit inhabiting it. Efforts have been made, for example, to visualize the nature of households within sixth-fifth millennium BC Vinča culture settlements of varying sizes, as at Selevać and Opovo in Serbia (Tringham and Krstic 1990; Tringham 1991a; McPherron and Srejović 1988). With reference to northeast Bulgaria in the Copper Age in the fifth millennium BC, it has been suggested that the house can be regarded as a "living" entity, encapsulating social memory and a strong sense of communal continuity (Bailey 1990; Bailey, this volume). The large-scale rescue excavations of sites like Ovcharovo and Golyamo Delchevo have made it possible to relate material inventories to houses in detail, and to explore notions of possession and individuality within the collectivity of tell settlement (Bailey 1991). At a wider scale, mirroring the attention given to the cosmology represented by northern Scottish late Neolithic houses of the fourth-third millennium BC (Richards 1990a; Richards 1991), the concept of the "domus" has been applied to the European Neolithic as a whole (Hodder 1990; Hodder 1992). This model proposes that there were a set of ideas centred on the house, which were both a metaphor for and the mechanism for social and conceptual domestication.

Buildings and contexts: some recent discoveries

At the same time, there have been further stunning excavations of various buildings, improving the data base as broader interpretive approaches are more widely adopted. The Bulgarian and Serbian examples noted above deserve to be cited again. At Opovo, careful excavation has revealed superimposed house floors and their contents which can only have come from a two-storey building. Other evidence (including the generally flimsy nature of constructions) indicates that the site, in the flat wetlands of the Danube-Tisa basin north of Belgrade, may have been only seasonally occupied (Tringham 1991a;

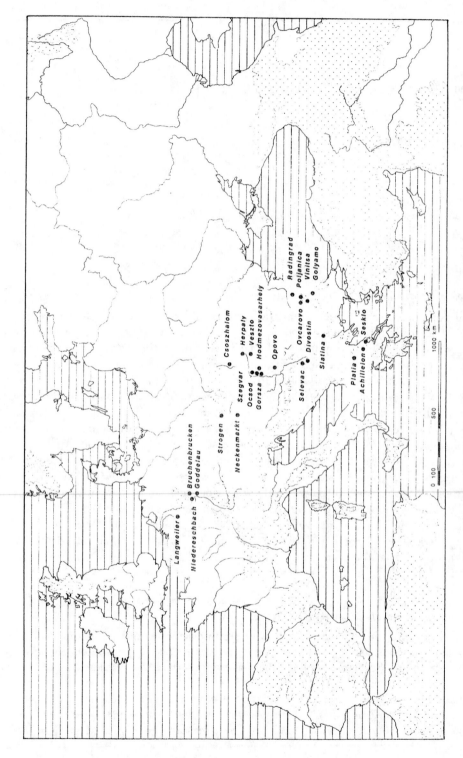

Figure 2.1: Simplified location map of the main sites mentioned in the text

Tringham *et al.* 1992). In what circumstances do people invest in buildings of this kind which may only have been used for part of the year?

Other elaborate and complex buildings, including two-storeyed examples, have been excavated on the Hungarian plain, belonging to the Late Neolithic Tisza-Herpály-Csőszhalom complex of the first half of the fifth millennium BC (Kalicz and Raczky 1987a). For example, at the tell at Vésztő-Mágor, a house 13m by 5.5m had two rooms with plastered floors (Hegedűs and Makkay 1987). In one room, there were a sitting female figurine, clay tables and anthropomorphic pots in a group on the floor. The context for such cult equipment appears domestic, since in this and the other room there were pots, clay bins, stone and bone tools, and loom weights. Many fish scales were found here. This was probably therefore the sort of context in which other notable figurines were found, especially in southern parts of the plain, including the seated male figure from Szegvár-Tűzköves or the so-called Venuses (seated female figures) of Kökénydomb, from the tell at Hódmezővásárhely-Kökénydomb (Korek 1987; Banner 1959). Szegvár-Tűzköves has both a tell and an adjacent horizontal, single-layer occupation (Korek 1987). Substantial buildings also occur in low tells (and perhaps also in single-layer occupations). At Öcsöd-Kováshalom houses ranged in length from 7m to 18m (Raczky 1987). Up to half a dozen were set in small fenced compounds, several of which were scattered over a broad area. At Gorsza a low tell formed, beginning with occupation defined only by pits and a ditch. In the second phase there were substantial buildings, including the exceptional House 2 (Horváth 1987). This had six rooms and an end annexe, laid out in the form of a U, with a narrow central passage. There were also upper floors or lofts. Each room had an oven, and there were looms and clay bins, and many pots on the floors. The internal walls were decorated with incision and red paint. The innermost room had two decorated rectangular clay bins, which have been suggested as cultic equipment, but the context again appears firmly to be domestic.

In this area, the settlement pattern was complex. It has been proposed that tells were the defining characteristic of this phase, and that these were both dispersed and perhaps defensive in nature, central places for the control of valuables like cattle (Sherratt 1982). Recent research has shown a more varied scene, which I discuss further below. But houses belonged to varied settings, and there was much coming and going.

The theme of renewal is emphasized also in the recently excavated house at Slatina, within Sofia, Bulgaria. That belonged to the early Neolithic, probably around 6000 BC, and was part of a tell settlement of several phases of occupation (Nikolov 1989; Nikolov 1992). Among many details very well preserved by the burning of the house, it was possible to see that the floor had been re-plastered at least 50 times. Most commentators assume that this was an annual event. Was this just domestic pride bursting out once a year, or part of a celebration of renewal and re-occupation?

Houses as monuments

A rather unusual combination is therefore emerging of fruitful theory and rich data. Houses are beginning to take their place alongside monuments such as megaliths and enclosures in a wider archaeology of the Neolithic which emphasizes values, beliefs, and senses of identity, place and time. This kind of approach has been rewarding in northwest Europe in particular. By paying close attention to the nature of monuments, for example, it has been possible to suggest that the start of the Neolithic was more to do with creating new attitudes to nature, place and time than with the technicalities of subsistence or technology (Bradley 1993; Thomas 1991).

A similar set of ideas underlines the "domus" model (Hodder 1990), but there is a tendency, as discussion moves from the northwest to central and southeast Europe, to take buildings themselves for granted. *The Domestication of Europe* has little to say about the first buildings of southeast Europe, and in passing to central Europe engages with the longhouses of the LBK with virtually no initial acknowledgement of their extraordinary character, especially in the context of what had preceded them on the Hungarian plain. I believe that this taking for granted of the house is based on other implicit assumptions about the Neolithic of southeast and central Europe: that there was an absolute difference between foragers and farmers; that farmers were sedentary; and that sedentary farmers automatically and inevitably build permanent houses which they live in all the time.

There has been another significant generalizing account of long-term social development, *The Domestication of the Human Species* (Wilson 1988). This has many useful things to say about settled existence and life in houses, including the play between the individualization encouraged by the privacy of houses and the ethics of hospitality and generosity. But it too assumes too readily that houses reflect sedentary settlement and fixed households.

This paper therefore argues that there is beginning to be sufficient evidence to examine the context of early houses in more detail, as the Hungarian and other data already presented begin to hint. My argument runs in part parallel to that of Bradley's *Altering the Earth* (1993). In many parts of southeast Europe, early houses – like monuments in northwest Europe – can be seen as statements or claims, part of the process of creating a new sense of identity, place and time. In central Europe, the process of change may have been more rapid, and house construction may have been one means of consolidating trends already operating among the indigenous population.

I shall very briefly indicate the kind of evidence available and the results of the kind of approach advocated here, and argue the case at greater length elsewhere. I shall refer to southeast Europe, including northern Greece, northeast Bulgaria and the Hungarian plain, and then to the LBK of central and western Europe, especially in its earliest recognized phase. In both areas, I start from the point of view, which again must be argued at much greater length elsewhere, that the beginning of the Neolithic was more to do with the transformation of indigenous population than with the arrival and spread of colonizers. I believe that in both areas the early Neolithic lifestyle was still characterized by a degree of mobility. In Lieberman's terms (1993; *cf.* Kelly 1992), the lifestyle may have been one of "radiating mobility" rather than of "circulating mobility". In southeast Europe the indigenous population may have shifted from circulating to radiating mobility at the start of the Neolithic; in central and western Europe, foragers of the inland woodlands may already have shifted to radiating mobility (*cf.* Jochim 1990). Farmers did not fully settle down for a long time, perhaps long after the Neolithic, and it might be more profitable to abandon the term altogether and adopt terms like "cultivators" and "herders". For what it is worth, there is an abundant ethnography suggesting both that foragers could easily and rapidly adopt (and as easily abandon again) new subsistence techniques (eg. Bird-David 1992; Kent 1992) and that cultivation could be incorporated into mobile annual cycles, as practised for example by the Penobscot of Maine (Speck 1940; *cf.* Thomas 1991).

SOUTHEAST EUROPE

Early settlement in Thessaly

Areas like Thessaly in northeast Greece have abundant tell settlements. Many grew to impressive size, and survey has shown close spacing (Demoule and Perlès 1993). A carefully argued model suggests that cultivation of rain-fed plots on terraces or in foothill locations was more important than animal husbandry in a still very wooded environment (Halstead 1989). There is evidence, however, which suggests that the situation may have been rather more varied, in the early stages at least, from the seventh millennium BC onwards. At Platia Magoula Zarkou, a tell in the Peneios valley in the northern part of the west Thessalian basin, deep excavation of limited extent was combined with local sediment coring and wider re-evaluation of valley history (van Andel *et al.* 1995). The results are surprising. The tell is now on a terrace above the river, but it appears that the major episode of downcutting did not take place till at least the middle of the Neolithic. The early settlement was on a creek at the edge of a very active floodplain which was annually flooded. It seems very unlikely that occupation could have been continuous. Many other sites may have been engaged in exploiting floodwater deposits (Sherratt 1980), perhaps as part of annual cycles of radiating mobility.

Unfortunately, at Platia Magoula Zarkou the *sondage* did not reveal a large area (and is still unpublished in detail). More information is available from a number of other early sites, of the seventh and earlier sixth millennia BC (Wijnen 1982). Whether or not there was an aceramic phase, most early levels of tells are characterized by thin occupations and recurrent abandonments. This may reflect a timescale to be measured in generations. It clearly took time for preferred places to be established. Early valley sites like Argissa may also, like Platia, have had a year-to-year cycle of seasonal occupation and abandonment. Because most excavations of early levels have been limited in extent, we know rather little about buildings. The initial picture seems to be one of ill-defined scoops and pits, as at Argissa (Milojcić *et al.* 1962), succeeded gradually by various stone-footed or timber-framed rectangular buildings. In general terms, Theocharis (1973) referred to the more structured look of sixth millennium BC settlements compared to those of the seventh. One important example is Sesklo in southeast Thessaly (Theocharis 1973; Kotzakis 1995). Occupation levels in the tell gradually become thicker through the sequence, and the building evidence more substantial. The first definite architectural evidence from the "acropolis" of the site comes in EN III, where there are signs of walled and roofed mudbrick and *pisé* (compacted mud) structures. Excavation has also shown much occupation outside the tell. This was of similar date to that on the tell, but the variously defined buildings were frequently abandoned, and renewal did not lead to mound formation. This suggests that houses were part of the creation of special places. They encouraged repetition and routine, and perhaps a kind of formalized behaviour based on the sharing of closely ordered space and hospitality, that may not have been so central in other, non-tell contexts.

The building sequence and context of Achilleion, Thessaly

Although excavations there were of limited extent, the sequence from Achilleion in southern Thessaly (Gimbutas *et al.* 1989) helps to amplify this perspective. It is not an ideal example, since it is situated in low foothills above the plain (a location shared with many other early sites). It lies above the southeast part of the west basin proper, above the valley of a tributary of the Enipeios, in rolling country rising to a range of low hills. This is dissected by small streams and Achilleion lies close to one of them. It is between 200m and 300m above sea level. Clearly this site cannot be linked to floodwater cultivation, and anyway recovery of carbonized remains was limited. But the site could be integrated into a general model, if it were seen, at least in its earlier stages, as a seasonal occupation connected with grazing; as at most other early sites, sheep/goats were the most numerous domesticated species. The development of buildings and their contexts, however, despite the other drawbacks, is of the greatest interest (Figure 2.2).

At Achilleion, the bottom level Ia was only 0.2m thick and not present in all the test squares (of an admittedly small excavation). Extrapolation from the radiocarbon dates has suggested a maximum duration of 100–150 years. The discernible structures were "pit-dwellings". By contrast, layer IVa later in the sequence was estimated to have lasted only 75–150 years, but was characterized now by substantial buildings and was well over 1m thick in some places.

In phase Ia, there was a possible pit-dwelling ("pit house" in the report), followed in Ib by reuse of the pit and the appearance of plaster floors with artefacts of assorted kinds, including food preparation equipment. The earliest structure dated to late phase Ib, lying immediately above the features just described. The structure had a rectangular end, formed of compact *pisé* above a stone footing set in a bedding trench. It had a plaster floor, with a food preparation area and a work area, with artefacts of various kinds and two clay figurines. In phase II the layout of the area was further elaborated. There was a small post-framed house (little more than 4m by 2m). Inside at its east end there was a pebble-lined firepit, with a horseshoe-shaped superstructure around one side. It contained many bones. There were two figurines and a fragment of an anthropomorphic vessel nearby, as well as various tools and animal bones. Just outside the northwest corner of the structure there was a hearth, with around it a quern, a grinding stone, a ladle, a scraper and blades, an axe and two figurines, as well as pots. Next to that was a bigger pit, with discarded bone. Further to the east, there was a probable yard, belonging to the post-built structure just described or another. Its plastered surface was bordered by small clusters of stones. On it lay a wide variety of artefacts, including blades, antler tools, pottery and figurines. It had a domed clay oven next to an area with food processing equipment and animal bones; a figurine lay on the bench or front platform of the oven. There was a pit next to the oven.

This phase might only have lasted as little as 25 years. In the succeeding phase IIb, there is information from a bigger area. Continuity of style of layout was maintained, but another small post-framed house was built to the south of the former structure. This too

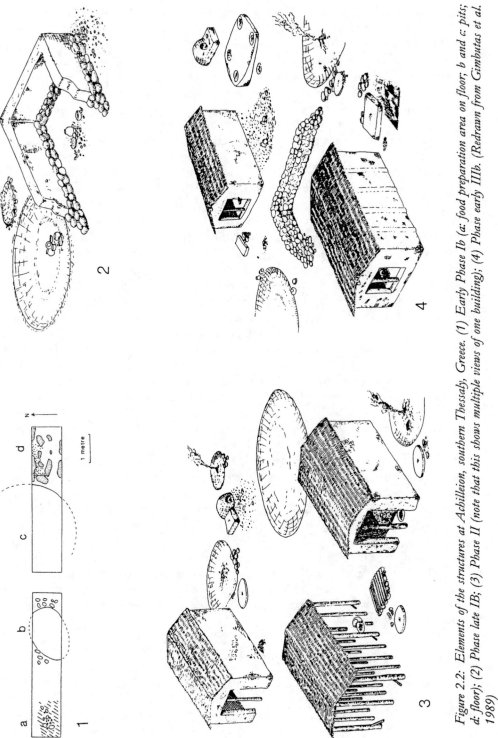

Figure 2.2: Elements of the structures at Achilleion, southern Thessaly, Greece. (1) Early Phase Ib (a: food preparation area on floor; b and c: pits; d: floor); (2) Phase late IB; (3) Phase II (note that this shows multiple views of one building); (4) Phase early IIIb. (Redrawn from Gimbutas et al. 1989)

had hearths outside it (including another clay domed oven) and work and food preparation areas beyond, with various artefacts. The work areas were littered with stone, antler and bone tools Where the former house had stood there was now a large circular hearth with a hardened surface adjacent, with food preparation equipment on it.

In phase IIIa, there were no structures in the excavated area, but deposits continued to accumulate. There were large burning areas, pits and few artefacts. In phase IIIb there was a resumption of the style of layout seen in phase II, with post-built house, external hearths and pits, and a yard area with domed clay oven, "fire platform" or raised rectangular hearth, plastered floor and pit. There were many artefacts and several figurines in the latter area.

After re-arrangements in phase IIIb (showing among other things a longer post-built house), two-roomed houses appeared in phase IV, with stone footings set again in bedding or foundation trenches. Inside, these had plaster floors, hearths and probable raised benches. Outside, other features continued, including hearths, pits and work areas. In this phase, a ditch was dug around the excavated settlement area, perhaps more to demarcate than to enclose it. In phase IVb, stone-footed (perhaps stone-walled) buildings continued, but were now set on a different alignment.

This detail is unusual and important. It shows that one cannot simply assume a given, universal model of settlement from the mere existence of a tell mound, which may have changed much during a long history. There was considerable continuity through the sequence, but there were also disruptions and changes. Again, the eventual accumulation of a mound is compatible with shorter or longer abandonments, and with relocations within the total area of the mound. The distribution of artefacts and other residues around the settlement is also suggestive of abandonments. Tools, vessels and figurines in work areas and by ovens and hearths may indicate an intention to return. There is no specific evidence from Achilleion for the seasonality of occupation. The artefactual evidence would be compatible with periodic, perhaps seasonal leavings of the site, perhaps not even by the whole community, and the impression from the architectural sequence is of a trend to larger and more solid buildings. Combined with a more intensive rate of mound accumulation, this too could suggest that permanent occupation became gradually more established.

It is conventional to date the appearance of sedentary settlement from the appearance of well-built structures. Those from phase II onwards at Achilleion would probably qualify, though those from phase II itself were of modest size. The evidence for activity outside and between the structures is at least as striking as the structures themselves. Activity could be characterized as formalized and ordered, in that there were set areas for certain tasks, and most tasks including tool use and food preparation took place in the open, rather than within the structures themselves. This use of space need not entail permanent occupation.

The Hungarian plain and northeast Bulgaria

There may still have been much radiating mobility on the Hungarian plain by the Tisza phase of the earlier fifth millennium BC (Kalicz and Raczky 1987a). There were still smaller sites with generally single occupation layers dispersed through the wetlands, as in the preceding Körös and LBK phases, but larger sites also now appeared. Some were "flat" or very low tells, with build up rarely exceeding 2m, but of considerable size, up to several hectares, like Gorsza near the Tisza-Máros confluence in southern Hungary or Öcsöd-Kováshalom in the Körös valley near Kunszentmárton a little further north (Figure 2.3). The latter covered 21ha in all, with two main occupation levels. It actually consisted of at least five foci of habitation, none of which need have been permanent. There were also low tells, with deposits up to 4m deep. These are found especially in the southern and eastern parts of the plain, but occur as far north as Csőszhalom near Tiszaújváros in the northern part of the plain. Recent excavations have shown how the tenure of a particular location could change through time, dispersed, short-lived nuclei of occupation gradually coalescing to form larger tells, as at Berettyóújfalu-Herpály in the Berettyó valley of the eastern plain (Kalicz and Raczky 1987b; Figure 2.3). Nearly all sites were close to water, on terrace edges above larger and smaller floodplains and wetlands. The largest sites appear to have been spaced at intervals of several kilometres, but it is clear from recent survey and excavation that they were not isolated.

There was movement throughout this unstable context. The elaboration and decoration of houses finds direct parallels in the elaboration of decorated pottery and figurines. If the "living" house could be equated with social identity, pots too may have been linked to particular persons, ancestors and spirits (*cf.* David *et al.* 1988). The house need not be separated from the material inventory which fills it. Together this material frame and its constituents could have served to create a sense of identity through shared, repeated behaviour, a sense of place through multiple re-occupations, and a sense of time through alignment with the behaviour of one's predecessors. The house was the specific focus for the reinforcement of novel social relations. And not the least interesting feature of the Hungarian sequence is that on the plain these new arrangements did not in the end endure. In the succeeding Tiszapolgár phase of the early Copper Age, settlement again dispersed, and there was only a little continued occupation of tells (Kalicz and Raczky 1987a).

In northeast Bulgaria, the sequence was in some ways different from both Thessaly and the Hungarian plain. In the Neolithic period from the seventh to the sixth millennia BC, only scattered, small sites are known in this area (Todorova 1986). As in the wider Starčevo-Körös-Criş complex, there are very few identified buildings, and most excavators have recognized only "pit-dwellings".[1] Sustained occupation began in the Copper Age of the fifth millennium BC, for example inland in the upper Vrana valley around Târgoviste. But the sites which now appeared, like Ovcharovo, Poljanica and Radingrad and others like Vinitsa and Golyamo Delchevo (Todorova 1982; Todorova 1986; Todorova *et al.* 1975; Todorova *et al.* 1983), by and large seem to have been occupied for long periods, without major stratigraphic hiatuses. The sites had highly organized lay outs from the beginning, with perimeters defined by palisades and ditches and houses more or less tightly packed within the interiors. Poljanica had four entrances aligned on the cardinal points of the compass. These were successful foundations, since they went on in use for centuries, and most show growth, for example again Poljanica over its first few phases.

In this rather different sequence, the house was actively used as an element of social cohesion and identity. As far as we can tell, each fresh phase of one of these settlements saw a more or less simultaneous renewal of all the houses. The house "lived" from

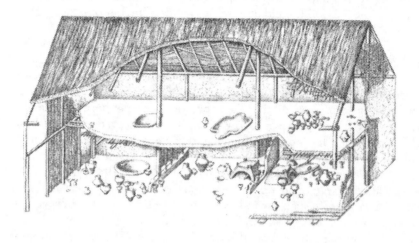

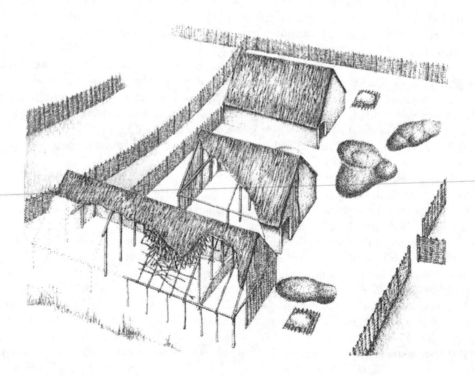

Figure 2.3: Reconstruction drawings of houses on the Hungarian plain. Top: Berettyóújfalu-Herpály (Herpály culture); Below: Öcsöd-Kováshalom (early Tisza culture). (From Kalicz and Raczky 1987b; and Raczky 1987)

generation to generation (Bailey 1990; Bailey, this volume). This collective continuity seems more important than the slight variations in house size and layout, which have been claimed as evidence for intense inter-lineage competition (Chapman 1990), though the material inventories of the houses, including figurines, and burial practice in the adjacent cemeteries may reflect a certain amount of individualization (Bailey 1991; Bailey 1994). The house was part of a wider material frame. The perimeters of these sites do not really seem defensive. They were most firmly defined in initial phases. When sites expanded, such as Poljanica, the perimeters tended to become less formal and pronounced, an odd development if increase in human numbers had produced inter-site competition and conflict. Perimeters, like houses, were part of the means by which claim was laid to place. This may have been all the more important if these sites were not occupied continuously all year round (Bailey 1991).

CENTRAL AND WESTERN EUROPE

Even the proponents of indigenous transformation have usually accepted the hypothesis that the appearance of the *Linienbandkeramische Kultur* (LBK) in central and western Europe was due to colonization, connected in some way to population growth around the fringes of the late Starčevo-Körös-Criş complex. I now believe that much more attention needs to be given to the possibility that this was a transformation of indigenous woodland populations (*cf.* Modderman 1988). I will argue the case at greater length elsewhere, but among other aspects we can note the increased evidence for indigenous valley occupations (eg. Mordant and Mordant 1992), the evidence for restricted mobility in certain inland situations (eg. Jochim 1990), the more gradual spread of the LBK shown by new German-Austrian and other research into the *älteste* or earliest/first phase (eg. Kreuz 1990; Lenneis 1989; Lüning *et al.* 1989; Pavlů 1990; Figure 2.4), and the possibilities of less importance for intensive plot cultivation than often supposed, and of greater mobility of settlement, both within annual cycles and from generation to generation. If we follow Bogucki's view (1988) of the risks and uncertainties involved in forest farming on the loess, and compare what had preceded the LBK in the Danube-Tisza/Tisa basin, it would be very odd to expect an immediate and wholesale shift to fixed settlement.

The details of LBK house plans are very well known (Modderman 1970; Modderman 1988). They have been perhaps most intensively studied in the northwest area of the LBK, on the Aldenhoven plateau and on the Graetheide in Dutch Limburg. Modderman's model of three units, variously combined - middle or basic unit on its own, middle part plus northwest end, and middle part plus northwest end plus southeast end - has been applied rather successfully to the Aldenhoven evidence, for example to over 100 house plans from Langweiler 8 (Boelicke *et al.* 1988). It is less clear that the model need apply to other areas to the east (Coudart 1989); it may be less helpful, for example, in southern Poland (Milisauskas 1986; Milisauskas and Kruk 1993) and Bohemia (Pavlů *et al.* 1986). Although there is thus a danger of misreading the degree of inter-regional uniformity, I nonetheless want to use studies from the northwest briefly to examine general aspects of the use of dispersed longhouses. Then I shall turn to the very beginning and very end of the LBK sequence to look again at houses in relation to context.

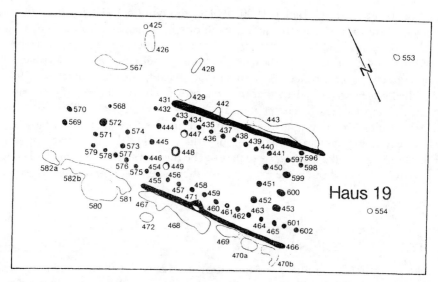

Figure 2.4: Ground plan of one of the älteste LBK houses (no. 19) at Niedereschbach, near Frankfurt, Germany. (From Bernhardt and Hampel 1992)

Detailed study of flint utilization makes it clear that each dispersed longhouse was engaged in its own production (de Grooth 1987). Stone adzes, imported from distant sources, were circulated through larger and smaller settlements, without being accumulated by the inhabitants of the larger settlement foci or of the longest and largest houses (Bakels 1987). The Aldenhoven evidence suggests (Boelicke *et al.* 1988; disputed by Modderman 1989) that around the longhouse there was a formalized pattern of activity, with pottery used in the southern half, flint in the northern half and heavy stone artefacts in a northwest zone. Shared space between longhouses was also important; in this zone there were often many pits which do not appear to "belong" to any particular building (*cf.* Milisauskas and Kruk 1993). There is not space here to discuss the issues of longhouse household composition. Suffice it to claim that van de Velde's Elsloo-derived model (1990, with earlier references) of lineage-based wards of two or three houses within settlements does not convince me. Among many other difficulties, the model assumes a continuity of household composition, and the existence of lineal descent; more open, non-lineal descent is at least as likely (Bogucki 1988, 180). House size tended to vary from generation to generation in any one part of a LBK settlement. It is hard to see house length alone as an expression of intra-group status variation. Much may have depended on particular circumstances of labour mobilization at the moment of house renewal, particularly if, as argued, there was much mobility in the settlement pattern.

This brief discussion serves to suggest both a formalization in the use of longhouses and of longhouse settlement space, and a likely fluidity of the composition of households and settlement foci. I believe that the two aspects are connected, and shall briefly discuss them in relation to the *älteste* LBK. The weakness of this procedure at this stage is that I am using models derived mainly from the established northwestern LBK, whereas the earliest LBK is distributed from western Hungary, through Slovakia, the Czech Lands and eastern/northern Austria, into Germany as far west as parts of the Rhine and as far north as Magdeburg. It remains uncertain when the earliest phase began or how long it lasted, but presumably it belongs to the mid sixth millennium BC.

Earliest LBK sites had varied locations (Kreuz 1990). They correlate with *loess* and other fertile soils, although as Bogucki has pointed out (1988, 73), it would have been hard to avoid them, once well-watered valley locations had been chosen. Not all earliest sites were in fact either close to water or in "ideal" valley locations (Kreuz 1990; Lenneis 1989). Cereal cultivation has been well documented, but the species used were rather varied from area to area. Few animal bone assemblages have been published yet, but studies of sites from the Burgenland (eastern Austria) like Strögen, Bez. Horn, and from Lower Austria (north of the Rhine) like Neckenmarkt, Bez. Oberpullendorf, show some variation, cattle predominating at some sites but pigs at others, and woodland game are well represented (Kreuz 1990; Pucher 1987).

The density of earliest sites appears to vary from region to region, generally declining to the west and north (Lenneis 1989; Pavlů 1990). Houses have been found on many earliest sites by the current German-Austrian research project. They do not appear to be as formalized as houses from the established LBK, but the familiar elements of side daub pits, five post rows with the three internal posts carrying the roof weight, and impressive length (up to at least 20m), were all present. Houses were dispersed, and excavation suggests rather small groups of a few houses, as at Goddelau, Kr. Gross-Gerau or Bruchenbrücken, Kr. Friedberg. The biggest *älteste* site so far appears to be Nieder-Eschbach, Kr. Friedberg. Here over 20 houses in all have been uncovered, but some belong to the succeeding Flomborn phase (Kreuz 1990; Lenneis 1989).

Such constructions could have had an important role in a lifestyle of radiating mobility. Pooled labour necessary for construction would have created a shared investment in place. From the beginning – although analyses of earliest situations have yet to be published – the longhouse may have encouraged formalized patterns of behaviour, emphasizing repetition, routine and conformity. The house may be an expression of open descent systems and the flexible composition of social groups. The longhouse, set in a flux of punctuated mobility, facilitated integration, interchange and cohesion. I have not avoided the tendency to treat the longhouse as a social agent in its own right. We do not know the circumstances in which people first decided to create such large structures: a remarkable development whether colonizers or natives were involved. If the latter were involved, as I have suggested, we could consider the possible connotations of the materials used. The LBK longhouse interior was busy with wood, in a way that has always seemed curious. Is there a conscious link here with the animistic concerns of forager beliefs, which seem to have been focused on the natural world? The longhouse "enculturates" the surrounding forest of trees.

The link between longhouses and megaliths has often been made. The detailed sequences suggested for the Aldenhoven plateau (eg. Boelicke *et al.* 1988; Stehli 1989) make it possible to look at, for the first time in detail, a moment of transition to a different kind of monument. This is also informative about the character of longhouse space. At the very end of the Aldenhoven sequence, in phase XIII of Stehli's version 2, a single-ditched enclosure appeared at Langweiler 9, in the space previously occupied by pits *between* longhouses or longhouse wards. This was short-lived. In phase XIV, the dwindling number of houses at the adjacent, larger site of Langweiler 8, were accompanied by a triple-ringed enclosure. This too was short-lived, and more or less devoid of internal features. There were few finds in the quickly silted ditches. This was not the end of the longhouse tradition in the area, since there are Grossgartach and Rössen successors, but most of those appear to have been grouped in more nucleated clusters, often bounded by palisades (eg. Dohrn-Ihmig 1983). This is not the place to go into the possible reasons for this shift, but it is as though these enclosures were an attempt to inscribe the memory of the important communal space to which the longhouses had belonged. The context of the house was as important as the structure of walls and roof.

SUMMARY: HOUSE, SPACE AND PLACE

I have been concerned to investigate the contexts in which the first houses were built as much as the structures themselves. The house provided much more than shelter. It encouraged the formalization of behaviour. In relation to other buildings it created a shared space, and the evidence of Achilleion in Thessaly was examined in detail to show the importance of communal space between houses. In most regional sequences, houses become gradually more solid and larger, though this was not the case in northeast Bulgaria and in the LBK area. Houses by and large belonged to lifestyles characterized by "radiating mobility", seen particularly clearly on the Hungarian plain. Building and using houses in formalized, repetitive ways was one of the means by which people created for themselves new attachments to place, and through this new senses of identity and time.

Acknowledgements

I should like to thank Douglass Bailey and Richard Bradley for discussion and criticism, and Joan Taylor for help with the Penobscot. Without implicating them in any of the views expressed here, I am grateful to Kostas Kotsakis, Nandor Kalicz, Eszter Bánffy, Ferenc Horváth and Eva Lenneis, for information and discussion.

Notes

1. At Divostin in Serbia there were both pit-dwellings and insubstantial timber-framed, above-ground buildings (McPherron and Srejović 1988), and above-ground buildings have been recognized at Ovcharovo-gorata in northeast Bulgaria (Angelova 1992).

Chapter 3

Neolithic Houses – A central European perspective

Jonathan Last

INTRODUCTION

In their introduction to the Neolithic Studies Group meeting on Neolithic houses in Britain, Tim Darvill and Julian Thomas problematized the relative lack of domestic structures in terms of the decline of monumental timber architecture associated with the "Neolithicization" of Britain and southern Scandinavia, and the question of why the Continental Neolithic heritage was found inappropriate. But what is this "heritage" exactly, and how are we to read the architectural evidence in terms of social and economic structures?

One problem with our understanding of the Continental background is the emphasis that is usually laid on the early Neolithic Linearbandkeramik (LBK) cultures at the expense of the admittedly less well understood middle Neolithic (MN). This dates back to the (pre-radiocarbon) 1930s when the excavations at Köln-Lindenthal (Buttler and Haberey 1936) captured the imaginations of the readership of *Antiquity* and British archaeologists:

> "Our knowledge of the houses lived in by the Windmill Hill (Neolithic A) people is almost negligible ... It is not to be supposed that our Neolithic forbears dispensed with regular dwelling-houses, field barns and granaries, nor yet that they were markedly inferior to those of the Rhineland or of Swabia at the same period." (Clark 1937, 469)

> "But there is no reason to suppose that the southern English Neolithic was so immeasurably inferior to those economically comparable, if culturally distinct, civilisations of the Continent, where ... the Danubian village of Köln-Lindenthal with its timber houses, barns and granaries stands as an objective witness to the high degree of organized village life reached by the North European Neolithic cultures." (Piggott 1954, 26)

Since then, the tendency to seek models for the absent British Neolithic settlements in the LBK has continued despite the realization that radiocarbon methods date the end of the LBK the best part of a millennium before the British Neolithic begins. Vestiges of this were apparent in the ethnographic papers given at the Neolithic Studies Group – why should accounts of Amazonian or Scottish longhouses be thought particularly instructive?

Clearly there is still a need to reinforce the point that the Continental heritage at the end of the fifth millennium BC is not one of longhouses at all. Even if Whittle (1977) is right to see the British early Neolithic pottery as deriving ultimately from Rössen, and similarities with Michelsberg as parallelizms, the final Rössen cultures *c.*4500 BC are very different from their LBK inheritance and the changes we can see in the Rhineland sequence Rössen – Bischheim – Michelsberg are instructive for understanding the contemporary British early Neolithic and its lack of visible houses. The argument I wish to put forward here is that the general trend to smaller houses in the later fifth millennium BC, deriving ultimately from southeast Europe, reflects important changes in economic and social organization, changes which may in fact have been necessary before a Neolithic way of life could be introduced to Britain and Scandinavia.

THE LBK BACKGROUND

It is nonetheless necessary to begin with the LBK in order to understand the origin of the cultural sequence discussed here and the logic of its development (Figure 3.1). Here is not the place to go into detail about LBK houses and settlements, which have been adequately dealt with elsewhere in both site reports (eg. Boelicke *et al.* 1988) and syntheses (eg. Coudart 1989). Although the LBK is broadly similar in material culture and architecture from Moravia and Poland to the lower Rhine and Paris Basin, an increasing regionalization in ceramics is apparent over time, and the unity of the LBK breaks up before 5000 BC. We may summarize the salient points about houses and settlements up to this time thus:

E. SLOVAKIA	S.W. SLOVAKIA	MORAVIA	BOHEMIA	BAVARIA	ELBE-SAALE	RHINE-MAIN
Bodrogkeresztúr	Ludanice	Jordanów	Jordanów	Wallerfing	Jordansmühl	Michelsberg
	Brodzany Nitra		Lengyel	Münchshöfen	Gatersleben	Bischheim
Tiszapolgar						
	Pečeňady	MBK II	V	Oberlauterbach	Rössen	Rössen
Tisza / Lengyel	Svodín	IV I	SBK IV		later SBK	Planig-Friedberg
			III			Großgartach
Bükk	Proto-Lengyel	SBK	II I	SBK	earlier	Hinkelstein
		Šárka				
Tiszadob	Železovce		LBK	LBK	LBK	LBK
Alföld LBK	LBK	LBK				

Figure 3.1: Simplified outline chronology of the central European Neolithic

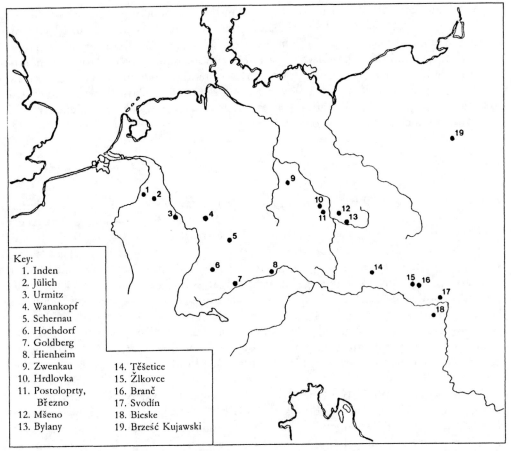

Key:
1. Inden
2. Jülich
3. Urmitz
4. Wannkopf
5. Schernau
6. Hochdorf
7. Goldberg
8. Hienheim
9. Zwenkau
10. Hrdlovka
11. Postoloprty,
    Březno
12. Mšeno
13. Bylany
14. Těšetice
15. Žlkovce
16. Braně
17. Svodín
18. Bicske
19. Brześć Kujawski

Figure 3.2: Location map of major sites mentioned in Chapter 3

(a) Longhouses of tripartite modular form with a possible functional basis to the division (Figure 3.3a), although the general absence of preserved living floors leaves this idea as provisional.

(b) A consistent construction method (several rows of three roof-bearing posts producing a four-aisled structure) and orientation (from roughly north-south in Bohemia to west-east in the Paris Basin), implying a strong element of tradition and important symbolic meanings in house construction and use.

(c) Borrow pits by the long sides of the houses subsequently used for domestic refuse and thereby allowing dating or phasing of structures.

(d) Organization in terms of individual farmsteads or hamlets rather than true villages. The Rhineland *Hofplätze* were identified by the occurrence of pits in a consistent spatial relationship to houses (Boelicke 1982).

(e) The appearance, nevertheless, from the earliest LBK onwards (Lüning 1988), of communal works in the form of enclosures of unknown function, some of which are not directly related to settlements (eg. Langweiler 8, Langweiler 9) while others enclose contemporary houses (eg. Darion, Köln-Lindenthal (van Berg 1989)).

Although, therefore, the LBK house proclaims the economic and social self-sufficiency of the household (Hodder 1990, 122), co-operative labour is not excluded and may indeed be implied by the size of the house as well. The power of conservative tradition in architecture and other practices must imply an integration not only of communities but of whole regions. The LBK house was constantly experienced as a "structuring structure" by the inhabitants who moved and interacted through the linear, graded space that the house presented. Tradition was experienced as a series of movements and thus became grounded in practical consciousness.

AFTER THE LBK

Certain changes in late LBK communities led to the emergence of more clearly defined regional groups in its final stages, for example Šárka in Bohemia and Želiezovce in Slovakia. The latter group shows southeast European influences in the human and animal representations, which are more frequent than in the west (Pavúk 1981); it is also characterized by the presence of large storage pits and the absence of the southern (granary) part of the longhouse. This removal of storage functions from the house structure shows Bükk influences, although it was not a communal project as each house probably had its own pit (Pavúk 1986). Only later in the Neolithic was grain storage detached from the control of individual households, implying changes in socio-economic structures. Storage pits are found also at LBK sites to the west, such as Bylany and Langweiler, but they are fewer and less clearly related to particular houses.

In the Rhineland, the LBK is followed by the related cultures of Hinkelstein (HnK) and Großgartach (GGK). No HnK houses are known, but a late GGK settlement has been excavated at Jülich-Welldorf (Dohrn-Ihmig 1983). The houses here show transitional forms recalling LBK, Stichbandkeramik (SBK) and Rössen, but are characteristically naviform in shape (Hampel 1989). There are fewer pits than on LBK settlements and most are empty, indicating changing work and discard practices. In southern and central Germany and Bohemia, early SBK houses are similar to the LBK to the extent that they are still fairly rectangular and may have associated borrow pits, as at Straubing-Lerchenhaid and Zwenkau-Harth (Quitta 1958). Mšeno in Bohemia, which dates to the end of the early SBK, also shows transitional features: one published house is nearly rectangular and post-built, another more trapezoidal with postholes and a trench (Lička 1990a). An early SBK house at Hrdlovka-Liptice is slightly trapezoidal and shows a characteristic doubling of the perimeter post-rows (Beneš 1991), although this is also found in a Šárka house at the same site (Beneš 1991; Figure 3.3b) and on other LBK sites, for example Hienheim (Modderman 1977). Therefore the immediately post-LBK structures are not so different from what went before, although the shifts away from a rectangular shape and towards a greater load-bearing function of the wall-posts are already noticeable. Variability and perhaps also experimentation are evidenced. Site structure is not apparently developed, although Welldorf may be partly enclosed.

The later SBK differs far more from its LBK origins in aspects of ceramic forms, polished stone industry and structural features, all reflecting influences of the emergent Lengyel culture in Slovakia and Hungary (Zápotocká 1986). In the west, Rössen shows a more direct development out of GGK, while Oberlauterbach in Bavaria is an SBK group related to Rössen. Rössen houses continue the tendencies seen at Welldorf to convex walls and a reduction in internal postholes as the outer wall, now usually marked by a continuous trench, takes more of the load from the roof. Most apparent is a big increase in the length of houses. The best-studied site is that of Inden 1 (Lüning 1982), where the following changes from the LBK pattern are apparent:

(a) Large dwelling-houses are accompanied by smaller *Nebenbauten* which may have served as stores or work areas (Figure 3.3c).

(b) Houses have fewer internal divisions, although in some cases trenches partly divide off the northwestern or southeastern sections.

(c) There are fewer and larger pits than in the LBK, no longer associated with specific houses. This may reflect both changes in wall construction (perhaps less daub was required with a trench-founded wall) and greater communal co-operation in activities like pit-digging and clay extraction.

(d) A proper village structure is seen in the provision of enclosure fences and the organization of the individual farmsteads, grouped in a more regular fashion around a large, central house.

Whether the architectural changes reflect changes in the use of space is unclear in the absence of preserved living floors, but altered traditions in house construction ought to indicate alterations in symbolic meanings bound up in the houses. In particular, an emphasis on the façade and entrance may be indicated by the frequent presence of an open "porch" area, as well as the greater width of the front part of the house. The changes in architecture and organization of space indicate, as Lüning (1982) has pointed out, social and economic changes. He argues that we see a shift from single-family households in the LBK to multi-family households in the big Rössen structures. A higher average number of people per house would explain the smaller number of houses overall in this period, as well as the greater social cohesion implied by the village structure.

The later SBK seems rather different. Many sites are known, often with earlier LBK material as well, including Bylany, Hrdlovka and Hienheim (Figure 3.3d). Houses are smaller than in Rössen, may have convex walls, as at Hienheim, but are often trapezoidal, as at Bylany. Hampel (1989) calculates that 56% of SBK houses are trapeziform while 53% of Rössen houses are "trapezoid-naviform". The developed site structure seen at Inden is so far lacking on SBK sites, although *Nebenbauten* are apparently found at Mšeno (Lička 1990b), but the latter culture along with Oberlauterbach includes the phenomenon of the rondels or *Kreisgrabenanlagen* (KGA). Although these may have been used for some time, they were a short-lived phenomenon in that all were built in a restricted period corresponding to SBK IV or MBK 1a. Within the SBK they are seen as a cultural borrowing from Lengyel. In general they consist of concentric circular ditches with four entrances, implying a communal area and a complex grading of space. They have no obvious defensive function and some central-place or ritual role is likely (Petrasch 1990). The KGA at Těšetice-Kyjovice in Moravia, for instance, produced a large number of broken female figurines from the enclosure ditch. This site is particularly interesting because earlier SBK settlement features were succeeded by features of the Moravian Painted Ware culture (MBK), a variant of Lengyel, perhaps implying an incoming population (Kazdová 1990). Unlike many of the other rondels, houses are associated with Těšetice but they are small and semi-subterranean, quite unlike LBK or MN structures and clearly of south eastern derivation. The presence of large borrow pits is, however, within the MN tradition although there is no evidence of the sort of complex spatial organization in the arrangement of features found, for instance, at Svodín (E. Kazdová, pers. comm.).

There is no space here to discuss the nature of the KGA phenomenon, but it does appear that these central places fulfil a similar integrative role to the large houses and developed site structure of the Rössen settlements. If we can draw any general conclusions about post-LBK social change beyond that of cultural variability there is a case for suggesting we see greater intra-site integration and cohesion, perhaps at the expense of the broader regional networks implied for the LBK. This fits with Hodder's (1982b) argument that greater emphasis on ceramic decoration in the MN reflects a concern with group identity and social boundaries. The rondels could have had the role of bringing people together within a complex spatial organization which would allow differential access to knowledge or resources and the consequent reinforcement and reproduction of social hierarchies and networks. The increasing organization of space seen in different fashions in different areas implies more social control by certain individuals or groups. Thomas (1987, 408) quotes Sahlins' argument that the higher level entities of hierarchy within segmentary lineage societies operate only under conditions of social stress, although possible causes of "stress" at this time elude us, unless we may argue for adverse effects on agricultural productivity from climatic change and soil erosion. The LBK pattern is replaced by a more integrated and hierarchical society that nevertheless maintains the sanction of tradition implied by aspects of house form, construction and orientation.

This picture can be elucidated further if we look at contemporary Lengyel settlements which represent a fusion of elements of southeastern European culture and the LBK tradition. After the Želiezovce phase of the LBK there is a pre-Lengyel phase represented by the post-built houses reported from Bicske (Makkay 1978; 1986). In early Lengyel we see phenomena related to the SBK and MBK rondels. At Svodín in Slovakia, a series of large post-built houses was arranged in radial fashion along the outer perimeter of an enclosure (Němejcová-Pavúková 1986), combining the concentric spatial order of the rondels with the developed settlement structure of the Rössen culture. The houses of the earlier phases are generally post-built and three-roomed while the latest phase has two-roomed, trench-built structures less like the LBK tradition (Figures 3.3e and 3f). Slightly later, in Lengyel II, the site of Žlkovce gives us the clearest picture yet of a developed spatial structure involving a large enclosed settlement arranged round a central circular enclosure (Pavúk 1991). The houses here are fairly large (on average *c*.16m by 6m), rectangular, post-built, two-roomed structures, with a dividing wall and megaron-type open southern part without a front wall, similar to the Rössen porches (Pavúk 1982). Hence a comparable pattern of reduced internal posts and changing internal divisions of space is evidenced, but the elongated Rössen structures and trapezoidal SBK houses are not found.

What the MN changes represent in terms of social structure is not so clear; there is no direct evidence for Lüning's multi-family Rössen houses within SBK or Lengyel although available internal space may well have been greater than in longer LBK houses with more internal posts. At Žlkovce the longest houses (up to 36m) are found within the central

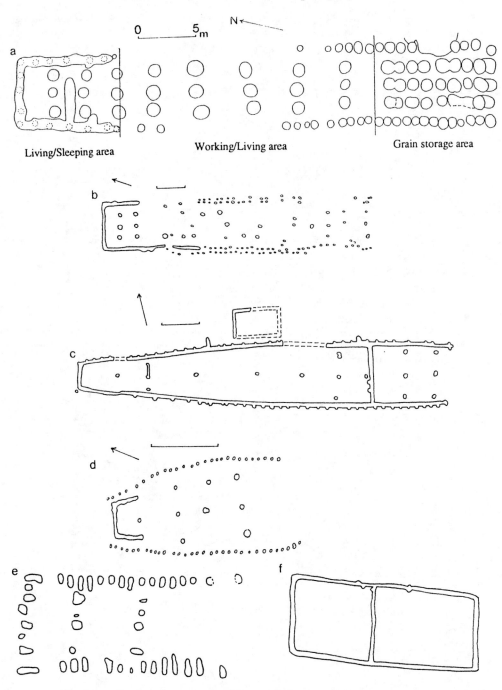

Living/Sleeping area   Working/Living area   Grain storage area

Figure 3.3: Ground plans of LBK and MN house structures. (a) Bylany (after Pavlů and Zápotocká 1983); (b) Hrdlovka (after Beneš 1991); (c) Inden (after Lüning 1982); (d) Hienheim (after Modderman 1977); (e) and (f) Svodín (after Němejcová-Pavúková 1986)

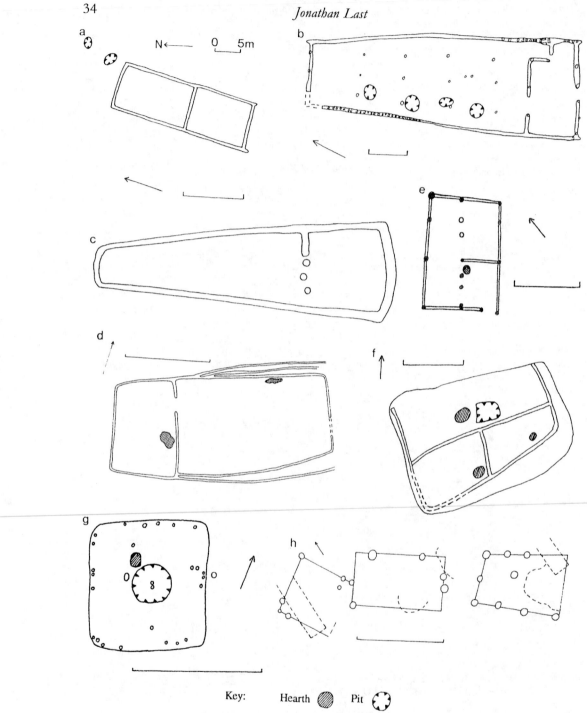

Figure 3.4: Ground plans of LN house structures. (a) Branč (after Vladar and Lichardus 1968); (b) Postoloprty (after Pleinerová 1984); c. Brześć Kujawski (after Grygiel 1986); (d) Schernau (after Lüning 1981); (e) Goldberg (Michelsberg) (after Bersu 1936); (f) Wannkopf (after Höhn 1991); (g) Goldberg (Altheim) (after Bersu 1937); (h) Hochdorf (after Keefer 1988)

enclosure (Pavúk 1984), suggesting status or functional differences rather than increased numbers of inhabitants. But the Lengyel evidence supports the general impression that the key change is in the investment of labour in communal enclosures which, whatever their function, make statements about the unity and internal focus of the community. This represents a significant change from LBK settlement patterns but is still quite different from the later fifth millennium pattern.

THE END OF THE MIDDLE NEOLITHIC

The further changes that take place at the end of Rössen, SBK and early Lengyel are crucial for our understanding of the nature of British Neolithic settlements. The alteration is almost total – ceramic assemblages change from decorated to plain, and from regionally bounded groups to more diffuse entities, settlement patterns change and large enclosed sites develop, economies are more locally specialized and houses become smaller and less visible archaeologically. We cannot understand the last of these and how it relates to the nature of British EN domestic architecture without addressing the broader socio-economic shifts implied by the other changes at this time.

In the east of the region late Lengyel structures show a variety of forms. The best known site in Slovakia is Branč, which has settlement features of Lengyel III (Brodzany-Nitra group) and IV (Ludanice) (Vladar and Lichardus 1968). Houses of several types were found, including the large, rectangular two-roomed structures known from the earlier Lengyel phases, as well as small structures of three types: trench-built, post-built and semi-subterranean. The larger houses are frequently accompanied by pairs of ritual pits or *Opfergruben* lying behind the structures (Figure 3.4a).

Although the expansive late Lengyel succeeds the SBK in Bohemia, trapezoidal houses continue here. The apparently regular arrangement of paired structures at Březno (Pleinerová 1984), with the eastern houses more carefully built, recalls the Rössen *Nebenbauten*. The large house from Postoloprty (Soudsky 1969; Figure 3.4b) includes a small front room and a large back room with three pits. Soudsky argued these were hearths and reflected a multi-family occupation, but they may be ritual features (Lüning 1982). The house also had a foundation deposit near the southeast corner. Such features may be more common in late Lengyel and have a clear southeastern focus, but they are found from the LBK onwards and throughout our region (see below).

Of a similar date, contemporary with Lengyel IV and Michelsberg, is the Brześć Kujawski group in southern Poland. A precursor may be the similar structure from Niedźwiedź, provisionally dated to the Malice phase (contemporary with SBK IV) (Burchard 1973). The Brześć Kujawski structures are interpreted not in terms of complex villages like the earlier Lengyel sites in Slovakia, but as "household clusters", more akin to the LBK *Hofplätze* (Grygiel 1986; Figure 3.4c). They seem also to serve as models for the form of the subsequent TRB long mounds; the idea that the British and northern European long barrows derive from earlier longhouse models is quite common (eg. Hodder 1990, 142–156) and implies a shift in the focus of labour and symbolism from the domestic to the funerary sphere.

In southern Germany the picture is rather different and the end of Rössen sees a further fragmentation into related regional groups of mixed Rössen and Lengyel derivation before the broader Michelsberg horizon. These include Bischheim, Aichbühl, Goldberg, Schwieberdingen and Münchshof. The first three of these have provided house-plans which indicate a broad shift to smaller, rectangular two-roomed structures recalling, though not exactly mirroring, earlier and contemporary Lengyel houses in Slovakia. Lengyel influence in the west is not a one-way process: choices are being made among the post-Rössen and post-SBK groups as to which elements of southeastern culture are adopted.

Change may have taken place within a generation if the evidence from Schernau may be taken as representative. This site consists of two Bischheim houses of semi-subterranean construction which has allowed the preservation of old living surfaces within the house-pits (Lüning 1981). One house is roughly rectangular and consists of two rooms, only the rear one being fully preserved. A row of posts down the central axis of the house indicates a gable roof. From the distribution of finds there seems to be some consistency over time in the location of specific activity areas, but cooking/eating and working debris occur within the same room. The distribution of finds within the second house (Figure 3.4d) is slightly different but there is further evidence that the rooms are differentiated according to personnel rather than function. This structure is more trapezoidal in shape and at some point in its life was extended in length. The first, smaller house had older Rössen pottery only in the back room but Bischheim sherds throughout, suggesting the former were used only in the cooking area. In the later house there is no longer Bischheim material in the back room, but more in the front by a new hearth. In the upper part of the house-fill the amount of activity evidenced in the back room declines and eventually the hearth there goes out of use. Lüning interprets this sequence in terms of a family using Rössen and Bischheim pottery initially for different functions. When the younger generation matures the house is extended and the front room gains a hearth; the older generation in the back now uses the older pottery exclusively, while Bischheim vessels alone occur in the front. As the older generation ages there is less activity in the rear of the house. Finally the hearth in the back room is put out: the younger generation is alone.

This Bischheim house also marks the end of the long sequence of trapezoidal structures in west-central Europe. Rectangular two-roomed houses are found also on the contemporary Goldberg site, already very different from the Rössen/SBK tradition, although they have a central row of roof-bearing posts (Bersu 1936; Figure 3.4e). The building technique, with the outer trench-built wall taking most of the weight from the roof, is clearly of Late Rössen derivation, but while House 1 at Schernau, like the structures at Inden, has at least in its earlier phase a row of internal posts along the central axis, in House 2, as at Brześć Kujawski, even this is absent and the wall alone acts as a roof support. Other settlements like Creglingen-Frauental (Lückerath 1986) and Nördlingen-Baldingen (Zeeb 1990) are similar in terms of size, shape and method of construction of houses, although the fill of the house-pits on each site is secondary, so information on the use of space is less forthcoming. The Bischheim houses at Creglingen have posts on the long axis, the Goldberg facies structures at Nördlingen do not. At the latter site there is some regularity in the position of hearths towards the front of the house and on the east side; the houses are also laid out in a regular fashion with a number of east-west rows. This shows a similar site structure to contemporary lake-villages such as Aichbühl.

Similar houses have been found at another Bischheim site near Sindelfingen, where the two-room layout, as found at Schernau, is clearer (Ade-Rademacher *et al.* 1987).

In the succeeding Michelsberg and Schussenried cultures all remnants of the old MN tradition have gone, except for the exceptional longhouses at the rather extraordinary site of Mairy in France (Marolle 1989). The small, rectangular two-roomed structure is predominant, whether pile-built as on the lake sites, or post- or pit-built as on the dry land sites. While the Bischheim houses are middling in size (House 2 at Schernau is at least 14m long) the later structures tend to be smaller and more lightly-built; hence they are less frequently preserved. The lack of Michelsberg houses is a phenomenon similar to the lack of contemporary British Neolithic houses, implying a similar cause. One that is known from Wannkopf in the Wetterau is quite large (14m by 6–9m), trapezoidal and with three rooms, though not in a linear arrangement (Höhn 1991; Figure 3.4f). It is semi-subterranean and has an internal pit like some Bischheim houses. Other Michelsberg houses include the five huts from Urmitz, which are small (up to 6m by 4.6m) rectangular pit-houses with postholes in the corners and a central hearth and posthole (Boelicke 1977). Round houses are occasionally reported, such as those from the Glauberg (Hermann and Jockenhövel 1990, 158). Subsequently, in the Altheim culture, contemporary with late Michelsberg, small pit dwellings are the rule. The small sub-rectangular Altheim pit-houses from the Goldberg, with a surface area of 12 to 28 square metres may be contrasted with the earlier rectilinear post-Rössen houses, which had an area of between 20 and 88 square metres (Bersu 1936; 1937; Figure 3.4g). Altheim huts of similar type are known also from more recent excavations at Piesenkofen (Uenze 1992) and Landshut (Engelhardt 1983).

The Schussenried houses at Hochdorf, on the other hand, are post-built, but without a central post-row and may be two-roomed (Keefer 1988; Figure 3.4h). They are small, measuring on average approximately 5m by 3.5m. In size and construction they are similar to the smaller post-built structures from Branč. Keefer (1988) sees the reduction in internal space that occurs from Rössen through Bischheim and Aichbühl to Schussenried and Michelsberg as related to an extension of activities away from the dwelling so they are held in common by the whole settlement. Alterations in the character of settlement are seen also in new forms (enclosures, high settlements), specialized economies (sites where the faunal assemblages are predominantly of wild game), and agricultural intensification (a clear increase in grain storage pits, removed from the vicinity of individual households – although this may be an earlier post-LBK phenomenon) and the colonization of new areas such as the Alpine wetlands. Some one-third of Michelsberg settlements lie outside the old core areas of Neolithic settlement. A reduced emphasis on the domestic structure may reflect a higher degree of physical and social mobility.

We see at this time, therefore, the culmination of a suite of gradual and more sudden changes producing a transformation in settlement patterns, economies, site structure and house construction, as well as ceramics, burial rite and other aspects of material culture. This new late Neolithic adaptation was similar to that of the post-Rössen groups which initiated the Neolithic in Britain and southern Scandinavia, whether by cultural influence or direct colonization. Possibly these changes were necessary before the Neolithic as a way of life (a cultural package rather than just an economic mode) could be introduced to new regions (Thomas 1988), and the expansive nature of the LN may relate to the idea of increased mobility. Some differences are also evident: the developed settlement structure of the lake villages is not found in northern Europe. Perhaps the focus of the community in the latter area was not the settlement but the new range of monuments which may be, at least in part, a Mesolithic contribution.

NEOLITHIC HOUSES – AN OVERVIEW

We still lack a real interpretive framework for understanding prehistoric houses. To make interpretive sense of the sequence discussed here, for instance, it is necessary to consider how domestic architecture as an aspect of material culture may be related to social structure and socio-economic practice. The approach of Coudart (1992), which relates the relative number of variable and uniform elements of the domestic structure to the social cohesion and cultural durability of the group should prove a valuable one. For instance, the greater variability seen in houses of the MN cultures compared to the LBK might be a factor in the longer duration of the latter. But we should beware of programmatic statements – something else is needed to explain the extent and duration of the Michelsberg cultural horizon other than uniformity of houses.

In the late Neolithic, the smaller, structurally variable and less archaeologically visible houses witness a declining emphasis – in terms of the investment of labour and symbolic meaning – in the domestic structure. This may be related to a higher degree of community integration seen less in terms of site structure than in economic intensification and specialization. The LBK tradition in which the house was the focus of meaning and action was transformed in the MN, but essentially this same ideology was preserved until the end of Rössen and early Lengyel. The symbolic character of the domestic structure may be shown by the foundation deposits which occur, albeit only occasionally, in houses from the earliest LBK right through to Bischheim and late Lengyel. In the LBK they usually involve human burials, particularly of children and females (Veit 1993). The young woman buried in the southeast corner of an early LBK longhouse at Stary Zamek (Kulczycka-Leciejwiczowa 1988) may be compared with the child burials in construction pits and inside houses of the later Rubané at Cuiry-lès-Chaudardes in the Aisne Valley (Ilett and Coudart 1983). In the east of the region, Makkay (1986) reports human bones in a posthole of a later LBK longhouse at Káloz and a goat skull in another pit, probably of the same structure. Animal deposits of this type are more typical in the MN in this area, for example, in the proto-Lengyel phase at Bicske (Makkay 1986) and in the late Lengyel structure at Postoloprty, where an arrangement of three large querns contained a pig skull and other finds (Soudsky 1969). The deposition of grinders seems to be a more western phenomenon, exemplified in an SBK structure at Hrdlovka in Bohemia (Beneš 1991) and the Rössen longhouse at Deiringsen-Ruploh in Westphalia (Günther 1976). These deposits might be interpreted as relating to fertility and reproduction, stressing the role of the house itself in such processes within locally specific symbolic codes. Such deposits seem more developed in the east and may have been formalized later in, for example, the Branč *Opfergruben* with their evidence for serial deposits not restricted to the foundation of the house.

In the British Neolithic the house as locus for material action of this type is replaced by causewayed enclosure ditches and other monuments. Comparisons might be made with the role of the MN rondels but should not be pushed too far as the kinds of structured deposition found on British and Scandinavian sites are absent from the rondel ditches, which are more likely to be marked by abnormally high quantities of specific material such as the flint cores from Svodín (Petrasch 1990, 500–501). The lack of a monumental timber architecture in Britain also refers only to domestic structures; the timber construction of monuments such as the Haddenham long barrow shows great accomplishment and indicates no lack of technical skill but rather a different focus for such practice.

The east European origin of many of the practices and styles discussed here is also of interest. From the origins of the western LBK onwards, cultural impetus seems to come from the region of Slovakia and Hungary. It is especially notable that house-building traditions are very different in the Carpathian cultures. The LBK pit-house at Bicske (Makkay 1978) and the above-ground structures from Peder (Šiška 1989) have in common their small size, comparable to the small, often sunken structures that appear in the western LN. The subsequent Bükk culture, which influenced Želiezovce practices, consists of large settlements of small houses (*c.*5m by 3m) with minimal post construction (Lichardus 1974), such as those from Šarišske Michal'any (Šiška 1986). The Tiszapolgar house at Tiszaföldvar is similar again: single-roomed and measuring 5m by 4m. It also revealed a number of ritual deposits, including a dog skeleton and obsidian blade that may have lain under the southern wall and recall a similar dog burial from Branč (Siklódi 1983). This tradition of small houses shows a number of differences from the LN structures of similar size in west-central Europe, but it is possible that the latter reflect a comparable socio-economic structure, locally reinterpreted but deriving, like other elements of culture, from the southeast. This new "southeastern" Neolithic in turn facilitates the extension of a Neolithic way of life into northwest Europe.

The picture briefly discussed here does not lend itself to easy simplification but we can summarize it as follows:

(a) LBK. Independent households. House structure conservative and traditional.
(b) MN. Greater regionalization. Structuring of communal space visible in features like enclosures, villages, location and size of pits. House form still standardized, reflecting changes in social structure.
(c) LN. End of longhouse tradition, altered socio-economic conditions seen in numerous features. Houses no longer focus of symbolic action, more mobile and fluid social networks allowing adoption of similar way of life in new regions.

Throughout the EN and MN sequence the house was in all probability a highly ritualized structure, imbued with rich symbolic meanings that were reproduced in and by people's actions and movements. Possibly LBK houses presented a spatial depth that emphasized domestic resources (grain) and work activities in the front and middle parts while secluding living areas. However, the burials indicate the role of the house in human reproduction. In the MN the structures are more open and less divided, façades are emphasized and perhaps domestic life was foregrounded and more interactive within a larger residential group. Spatial divisions mapped out social groups (families) rather than activities, yet connections to a broader notion of fertility are seen in deposits of animal parts and grindstones. In the LN the symbolism disappears and houses are smaller, flimsier and variable in shape and orientation. The locus of ritual activity alters and new spatial patterns emerge both within sites and of sites within landscapes.

Any attempt to understand the nature of British Neolithic settlement, therefore, has to emphasize the range of Neolithic adaptations that the preceding Continental sequence shows. Longhouses will not be found in the British Isles because the longhouse tradition was part of a Neolithic way of life radically different to the LN cultures of which the British Neolithic is a part.

Chapter 4

Neolithic houses in Ireland

Eoin Grogan

INTRODUCTION

In 1939, while excavating the ringforts on the nearby hill of Carraig Aille, Seán P Ó Ríordáin identified the foundations of a rectangular structure on the peninsula of Knockadoon jutting out into Lough Gur in Co. Limerick. Although he suspected that this would prove to be contemporary with the ringforts, on the basis of surface similarities to associated material, Site A turned out to be the first Neolithic house found in Ireland (Ó Ríordáin 1954, 299). Its discovery led to a campaign of excavations at Lough Gur continuing to 1954, much of it centred on the peninsula, largely dedicated to the recovery of settlement evidence. Although less than 1% of the peninsula was excavated the remains of at least 22 structures, both houses and less substantial buildings, were identified (Ó Ríordáin 1954; Grogan and Eogan 1987; Grogan 1980). The remarkable total of 14 Neolithic houses provides a unique opportunity to study building techniques and changes in architectural style over time.

To date over 50 houses associated with Neolithic material have been found in Ireland (Figure 4.1). Of these at least 14 are rectangular and over 40 circular or oval. In addition to these examples a further eight sites have produced smaller buildings which may not have been domestic dwellings even if they did have ancillary domestic functions such as storage or workshops. Only the houses at Sites A and B, Lough Gur (Ó Ríordáin 1954), the structures at Knocknarea 1 and 2, Co. Sligo (Bengtsson and Bergh 1984) and the second house at Tankardstown South, Co. Limerick (Gowen and Tarbett 1988) were discovered as a result of research excavation targeted on the identification of house structures: the remainder were chance discoveries.

At Ballygalley, Co. Antrim, Ballynagilly, Co. Tyrone and Slieve Breagh, Co. Meath, open area excavation designed to identify domestic or industrial activity produced evidence for five houses (Simpson *et al*. 1990; 1994; ApSimon 1969; 1976; Herity and Eogan 1977, 49). The innovative campaign of Ó Ríordáin's on the Knockadoon peninsula provided an exemplar of this approach. Remarkably, three houses, Tankardstown 1 (Gowen 1988, 26–42), Newtown, Co. Meath (Gowen and Halpin 1992) and Pepperhill, Co. Cork (Gowen 1988, 44–51), were found in the course of pipeline construction. Three houses, two at Knowth, Co. Meath (Eogan 1984) and that at Ballyglass 1, Co. Mayo (Ó Nualláin 1972a), were chance finds beneath megalithic tombs, while domestic dwellings have also come from beneath the tombs at Townleyhall 2, Co. Louth (Eogan 1963), Ballyglass 2, Co.

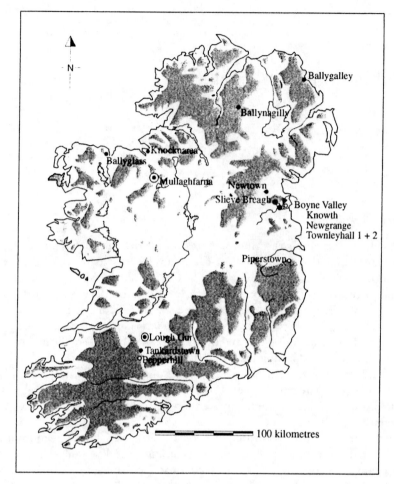

Figure 4.1: Distribution of Irish Neolithic house and other sites with occupation evidence

Mayo (Ó Nualláin 1972b) and during the course of the excavations at the passage tomb cemetery at Newgrange, Co. Meath (O'Kelly 1983).

With a record of recovery as diverse at that outlined above it is significant that there is such a degree of homogeneity in the available evidence. Apart from the distinctive domestic style at Lough Gur (see below) the set of structural cross-references for the houses is remarkable although not surprising given the degree of similarity in other aspects of Neolithic cultural assemblages.

PLAN, LAYOUT AND SIZE

Fourteen rectangular houses have been identified while the corner of another site at Pepperhill has also been excavated. While the size and floor area varies considerably

(Table 4.1; Figure 4.7) there is a considerable homogeneity amongst these buildings as a whole. Two distinct building techniques can be recognized, the first is represented by a group with vertical plank walls and is found throughout the country, and the second by post and wattle walled houses that occur only at Lough Gur. Only one of the 15 sites, Knowth 1 (Eogan 1984) which has a shallow wall trench, does not fit into these basic groups.

Plank-walled houses

There are eight plank built houses (Ballygalley 1 and 2, Ballyglass 1, Ballynagilly, Knowth 2, Newtown, Tankardstown 1 and 2; Figure 4.2) as well as smaller structures at Ballyglass 2 and possibly the house at Pepperhill. The walls were of vertical split planks set in bedding trenches supported on a framework of vertical posts and (presumably) horizontal members. Although not always clearly identified, such structures require a minimum of four corner posts. The identifiable span between posts ranges from *c.*1–2.4m. At Ballyglass and Tankardstown 1 the placements of the posts is clearly indicated and symmetrical; at most sites the posts are generally evenly spaced. The size and placement of the planks could be identified at Newtown and Tankardstown 1. The excavator suggested that the Ballynagilly walls were supported in a wall plate (ApSimon 1969; 1976).

The houses consist of single (Tankardstown 1, Ballynagilly and Lough Gur site B), double (Newtown) and triple roomed buildings (Ballygalley 1, Ballyglass 1 and Tankardstown 2). The overall length of the tripartite houses is between 12m and 15m. These sites have a length:width ratio of between 2:1 to 3:1 with an overall floor area of 42–90 square metres. In each instance the central compartment appears to form the living area and is between one and a half and twice the area of the other compartments combined. These principal rooms are 27.9–62 square metres in area. The apsidal entrance and end compartments at Ballygalley contrast with the neat rectangularity of Ballyglass and Tankardstown. However, the central compartment which occupies 70% of the interior is proportionately similar to that at Tankardstown which takes up 72%. This compares with only 50% at Ballyglass where the entrance compartment takes up one third of the house.

Only one house, Newtown, consists of two compartments and it has a length:width ratio of 1.4:1, similar to those of the single roomed structures (Table 4.1). It is possible that houses with two or three rooms were relatively common. At both Ballynagilly and Lough Gur site B2 the ground-plans appear to be incomplete and both lack convincing evidence for end walls. It is possible that both represent the central room of compartmented houses. Ballynagilly is, furthermore, one of only two plank built rectangular houses with only one room, the other being Tankardstown 1.

It has been assumed here that the central, or in the case of Newtown the larger eastern, compartment functioned as the principal living quarters of the occupants. The purpose of the other areas in uncertain but it seems reasonable to believe that they served ancillary domestic functions. At other Neolithic sites separate smaller structures may have served similar functions (see below). Although the ground-plan of Newtown had been partly disturbed the western end of the house may have been open in the form of a large porch or workshop. The entrance wall at Tankardstown 2 may also have been discontinuous representing a similar arrangement. At Ballygalley the ground-plan suggests that both the entrance and end compartments may have been roofed and partly enclosed by walls; lighter walls or screens, not requiring foundations, may have been used on occasion to completely enclose these areas. A similar arrangement probably occurred at Ballyglass where a much slighter foundation trench forms one corner of the end compartment.

The orientation of these houses may provide a further indication of the function of these partly walled areas (Table 4.1). At Ballygalley the house is orientated east-west with the unwalled side of both the entrance and end areas facing south. The open area at Newtown faces west while that at Ballyglass looks southeast. Only Tankardstown 2, where the possible porch faces northeast, was the open area not positioned to take advantage of maximum shelter and light.

Single roomed houses range in length from 6m to 9.3m with a length:width ration of as little as 1.1:1 (Figure 4.2; Table 4.1). They are, however, very similar in size to that of the principal, central, compartment of the composite structures with an area range of 26.4 to 62 square metres. In addition to the houses at Tankardstown 1, Ballynagilly and probably Knowth 2 (George Eogan and Helen Roche pers. comm.) and Pepperhill there are two smaller structures at Ballyglass 2, about 275m to the south of Ballyglass 1 from beneath another court tomb (Ó Nualláin 1972b). Ballyglass 2i is D-shaped and Ballyglass 2ii has an oval ground-plan.

Post and wattle walled houses

The second style is that which characterizes most of the buildings at Lough Gur including three of the rectangular houses (site A, site B2, circle K2; Figures 4.2 and 4.5). The principal feature of these houses is the very thick cavity wall created by widely spaced wall facings of upright timbers (Figures 4.8 and 4.9). The walls are between 1m and 1.6m thick. Between these lines of outer and inner posts was a loose stone footing of limestone, occasionally up to 0.50m in height. This appears to have functioned as a damp-proof course for the organic fill, perhaps sods, straw or rushes, which was packed between the wall facings. The paired arrangement of the posts may have been to allow them to be braced together through the thickness of the wall. Although this would have been an unnecessarily elaborate system it would have given considerable structural strength to the walls. Although no direct evidence has been recovered it is probable that the wall facings were of wattle. This building technique is found in rectangular, circular and sub-circular (oval and D-shaped) structures (see below).

Circular houses

There is a considerable diversity in the layout and building technique amongst the houses with a circulinear plan. Over 40 individual houses have been excavated although the pre-tomb passage tomb settlement at Knowth (9+), Lough Gur (6+) and the final Neolithic occupation at Newgrange (18+) account for the vast majority. Few of the houses are truly circular: among these are examples at Lough Gur site C1 and C3, and the two

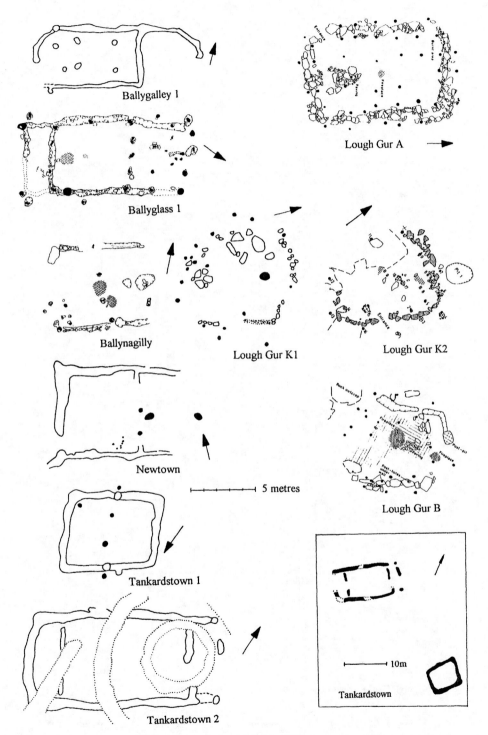

Figure 4.2: Ground plans of rectangular Irish Neolithic house plans. (Sources: various)

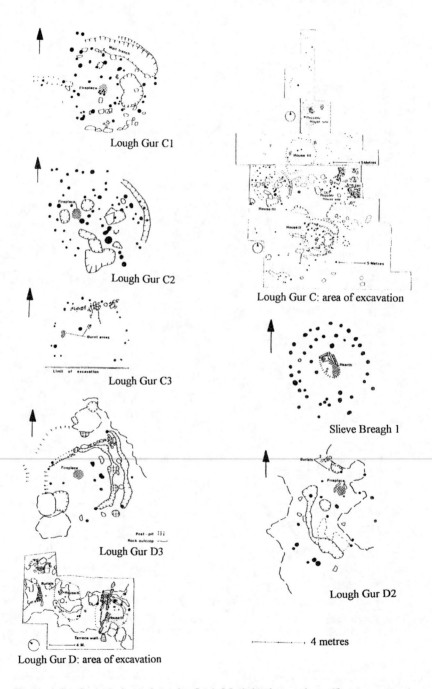

Figure 4.3: Ground plans of circular Irish Neolithic house plans. (Sources: various)

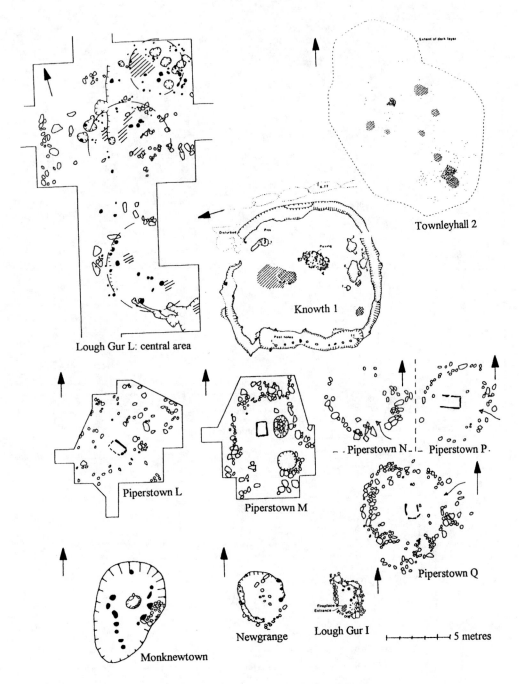

Figure 4.4: *Ground plans of Irish Neolithic houses*

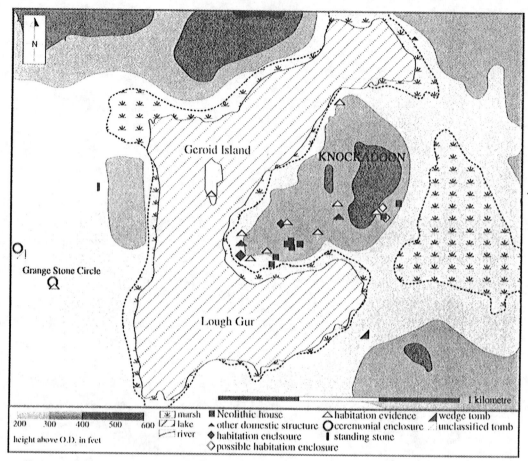

Figure 4.5: Lough Gur, Co. Limerick. Location of Neolithic houses, enclosures and other structures

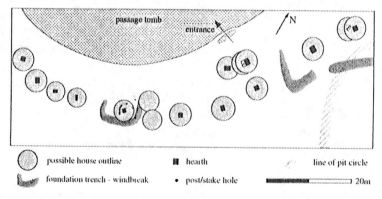

Figure 4.6: Newgrange, Co. Meath. Location of Neolithic structures. (From Cooney and Grogan 1994)

houses at Slieve Breagh (Figure 4.3). There are some clearly oval structures, for example Ballyglass 2ii, Lough Gur site C2 and D2, as well as D-shaped buildings like Lough Gur site D3 and Ballyglass 2i (Figure 4.3).

Two principal constructional styles also occur among the circular houses. The first consists of houses have walls supported by a single ring of posts as at Lough Gur site C3 and Slieve Breagh 2. They also include probable houses at Lough Gur site C and circle L, the pre-tomb houses at Knowth and the less substantial structures at Townleyhall 2, also under a passage tomb in the Boyne Valley (Figures 4.3 and 4.4). Similar structures at Newgrange associated with the final Neolithic settlement in the lee of the main mound appear not to have had post or stake holes although the evidence shows a series of 18 hearths with circular structures erected over them (Figure 4.6). One of these had postholes indicating internal roof supports; at least two of the houses appear to have wind-breaks erected on the southeastern, exposed, side (O'Kelly 1983; Cooney and Grogan 1994, 79–81). Internal supports are also indicated at Lough Gur C3, D2 and D3 but it is not possible from their positions to determine the nature of the roofing arrangement. The circular houses are generally smaller than the rectangular examples although there is some overlap (Figure 4.7; *cf.* Table 4.2). There is also a smaller size range with a concentration of houses around 20square metres in area.

ROOFING, INTERNAL ORGANIZATION AND ASSOCIATED FEATURES

Roofing

No direct evidence for roofing techniques or material has been recovered. It is probable that all of the houses had roofs of straw or rushes although the use of hides cannot be ruled out especially in the case of lighter buildings such as those at Townleyhall 2. In every instance where the charcoal from the timbers has been identified the structural members, both posts and planks, are of oak. Although no structural timbers have survived the evidence from contemporary trackways indicates a high level of carpentry skills including the making of joints and the production of cleft planks (O'Sullivan 1991).

The rectangular plank-built houses at Ballyglass, Ballynagilly, Newtown and Tankardstown 1 probably had vertical gables (Figure 4.10; Grogan 1988). There is no convincing evidence at any of the rectangular houses for substantial ridge poles although lighter timbers may have been used to facilitate the coupling of rafters. The roof supports consist of the framework provided by the main wall posts with wall plates resting on these to support the rafters. Internal joists are suggested by the arrangement of posts and slot-trenches at Ballgalley, Ballyglass, Ballynagilly, and Tankardstown as well as the Lough Gur houses A, B and K2.

The rounding of the gable ends of Lough Gur A and K2 together with the arrangements of the wall and internal posts indicate that these houses had hipped roofs (Figure 4.9). Slight rounding of the end walls at Ballygalley and Tankardstown 2 may suggest similar roofing.

It is probable that the circular houses had conical or rounded roofs. Several have evidence for rings of internal roof supports (eg. Lough Gur C1, C2; Slieve Breagh 1). In some instances, for example, Monknewtown and Piperstown, the rafters may have rested directly on the ground or on circles of loose stones; the floors of Monknewtown and the small middle Neolithic house at Newgrange, were scooped out to provide additional internal height.

Doorways

Well-defined doorways could be identified at Ballyglass 1, Slieve Breagh 1 and Lough Gur site A while the approximate location of the door was indicated at Tankardstown 1 and 2, Ballygalley 1, and Newtown. At Ballyglass 1 and Slieve Breagh 1 there appears to have been a slight porch projecting forward of the wall. There is no evidence for the nature of the doors themselves. In the case of Ballyglass there appears to have been a corresponding passage leading from the door to the main central compartment along the west wall. Some postholes to the east of this passage, in the entrance compartment, could represent supports for a spit level prompting comparisons with the layout of some LBK houses in west central Europe (Grogan 1980; Cooney and Grogan 1994, 49).

Internal partitions

Partitions occur within the compartmented plank-built houses; the form of some of the foundations for these indicate that these may have been formed of planks like the main house walls. In other instances, for example the northwest wall of the main compartment at Ballyglass 1, posts may have supported wattle walls or screens.

Hearths and fireplaces

Most houses have produced evidence for internal hearths or fireplaces, usually a single example close to the centre of the house. Formal rectangular hearths defined by stone edging occur at Newgrange, Piperstown, and Slieve Breagh. Generally, however, open fires appear to have been common. At Lough Gur site C1 a group of small stakeholes beside the fireplace suggest a spit or apparatus for hanging pots over the fire. Despite the risks posed by internal hearths, only two of these timber houses, Pepperhill and Lough Gur site A, appear to have been destroyed by fire.

Internal pits

Pits occur within several houses and in most instances these appear to have been used for refuse. In some cases the size of the pits, for example Lough Gur sites C1 and C2, indicates the probability that they were covered as they would otherwise constitute a considerable hazard.

Floors

Floors generally appear to have been of beaten earth although paving occurs in some of the Lough Gur examples, for example sites A and B; in the former the paving was laid down over a layer of habitation debris that filled a hollow in the southern area of the floor beside the entrance. It is possible that posts that seem not to form part of the structural component of the house may have supported timber partitions, or furniture, such as beds, shelves or cupboards, of the type that have been found in stone in the Orkney houses (Clarke and Sharples 1990).

OTHER STRUCTURAL EVIDENCE

In addition to the sites with clear evidence for houses a large number of other sites have produced evidence for Neolithic structures. Some of these, such as the small building beside Knowth 1 (Eogan 1984, 233, fig. 78, pl. 72b), appear to be ancillary buildings directly associated with houses. Both substantial and light weight structures are represented. Among theses are sites with evidence for specialist activity such as the flint extraction site at Goodland (Case 1973) and two shelters associated with working pebble flint from the beach at Dundrum Bay, Co. Down (Collins 1952). Buildings that appear too small to have served a domestic function are represented at several sites including Site I at Lough Gur (Ó Ríordáin 1954; Figure 4.4) and the small structure outside the entrance to the main tomb at Newgrange (O'Kelly 1982, 76–7; Figure 4.6). At Dalkey Island, Co. Dublin, Liversage (1968) excavated a large area and Neolithic material, heavily disturbed by later intensive activity, came from through the area. All of these appear to have been seasonal and/or specialist sites. Habitation evidence without surviving evidence for structures is even more common such as beneath the passage tomb at Baltinglass, Co. Wicklow (Walshe 1941), and the court tomb at Ballybriest (Carnanbane), Co. Antrim (Evans 1939). Occupation material has also come from a number of sites which indicate permanent, long-term settlement. Extensive enclosed hilltop settlement at Donegore and Lyles Hill have not, however, produced evidence for houses (Mallory and Hartwell 1984; Evans 1953; Gibson and Simpson 1987; 1989). Considerable disturbance had also occurred at Feltrim Hill, Co. Dublin (Hartnett and Eogan 1964) where the permanence of the occupation is shown by the large quantity of material including saddle querns.

NO FIXED ABODE?

The evidence from the largely middle – final Neolithic sites at Knowth, Newgrange, Townleyhall 1 and 2, Knocknarea, Monknewtown and Piperstown raises the question of how, or indeed why, we should differentiate between a "house", with all the connotations of permanency, and "hut" implying an ephemeral, temporary structure. In trying to understand the nature of the underlying settlement pattern it is important to consider a number of factors of which the sturdiness of the buildings themselves, their size and location may only be a minor and archaeologically subjective part. Clearly, at a wider level it is not the domestic dwellings alone that provide us with evidence for settlement organization. In the overall context of the Irish Neolithic it is evident that both permanent and temporary elements occur within the same settlement pattern (Cooney and Grogan 1994, 42–7; in press).

Eoin Grogan

Table 4.1: Details of rectangular Irish houses

Site	Orientation	Entrance	Length (metres)	Width (metres)	L:W	Area (square metres)	Entrance area	Central compartment	End compartment	Possible number of occupants
Ballygalley 1*	W-E	W	13.0	4.2	3.1:1	42.0	29.4	3.2	9.5	7
Ballygalley 2*	W-E	?	?	5.0	?	?				
Ballyglass 1*	NW-SE	NW	12.0	4.8	2.5:1	57.6	27.9	17.9	9.3	7
Ballynagilly*	E-W	?	6.5	5.5	1.2:1	35.8	–	35.8	–	9
Knowth 1	N-S	NE	10.8	8.9	1:1.2	96.0	–	96.0	–	24
Knowth 2*										
Lough Gur A	N-S	SW	9.3	4.5–5.3	1.3:1	c.45.6	–	c.45.6	–	11
Lough Gur B	NE-SW	?NE	c.6.0	4.4	1.4:1	26.4+	–	26.4+	–	7
Lough Gur E			7.0	6.2	1.1:1	45.3	–	45.3	–	11
Lough Gur K1	E-W	?	7.2	6.6	1.1:1	c.48.2	–	c.48.2	–	12
Lough Gur K2	NE-SW	SE	6.5	4.5	1.4:1	29.3	–	32.0	–	8
Newtown*	SE-NW	?W+E	9.5+	6.6	1.4:1	62.7+		33.7	24.7+	8
Tankardstown 1*	NE-SW	NE	6.6	5.2	1.2:1	34.3	–	34.3	–	9
Tankardstown 2*	NE-SW	NE	13.9	6.3	2:1	87.6	58.4	11.6	11.3	16

* Plank-built houses

Table 4.2: Details of circular/oval Irish Neolithic houses

Site	Entrance	Diameter (metres)	Area (square metres)	Possible number of occupants
Knowth (9+ sites)	?	6–8	28.3–50.3	7–12
Lough Gur C1	?SW	5.0	19.6	5
Lough Gur C2	SE	6 × 4.7	22.5	6
Lough Gur C3	?	5.4	22.9	6
Lough Gur Site C (possible)1	?	c.5	c.19.6	5
Lough Gur D2	?SE	6.7 × 5.0	26.9	7
Lough Gur D3	?SE	5.0 × 4.4	c.17.4	5
Lough Gur L central	?	c.5.0 × 3.5	c.14.2	4
Lough Gur L A	?	c.4.5	c.15.9	4
Newgrange	?N	4.2 × 3.2	13.4	3
Newgrange final Neolithic (18 sites)	?	5–6	19.6–28.3	5–7
Slieve Breagh 1	SE	4.6	c.16.6	4
Slieve Breagh 2	?	4.9	c.19.0	5

Table 4.3: Details of other Irish Neolithic structures

Site	Entrance	Length (metres)	Width (metres)	Area (square metres)	Possible number of occupants
Ballyglass 2i*	?	5.0	4.0	16.0	4
Ballyglass 2ii*	?	5.7	2.7	c.10.0	3
Dundrum Bay 1	?	diameter 2.4 × 2.0		4.8	1
Knocknarea 1	SE	7.5	4.5	28.3	7
Knocknarea 2	NE	6.5	4.7	24.6	6
Lough Gur I	?	2.3	1.5	3.5	1
Monknewtown	?SW	7.4	4.7	28.8	7
Piperstown L	?	diameter 4.8		18.1	5
Piperstown M	?	6.0 × 4.5		21.7	5
Piperstown N, P, Q	S, SE, NE	diamter c.4.5		c.15.9	4
Piperstown A	?SE	5.5 × 4.5		24.8	6
Piperstown B	?	2.3 × 2.0		4.6	1

* Plank-built house

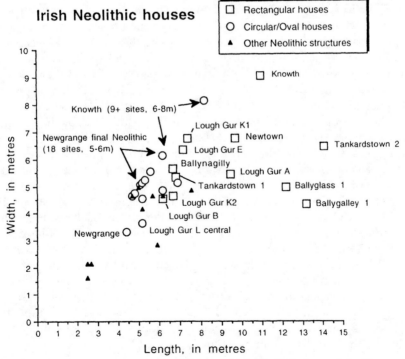

Figure 4.7: Scatter diagram showing the distribution of Irish Neolithic house sizes. (Prepared by Aidan O'Sullivan)

Many of the houses, among them most of the rectangular examples and several circular houses, seem without question to indicate the permanent residence of individual families. At the other end of the scale are the remains beneath the passage tomb at Townleyhall 2, to the west of the main Boyne Valley passage tomb cemetery complex. Nine hearths or fireplaces and 142 stakeholes represented at least nine structures and two stages of occupation. The very light timbers together with the apparent overlap of several ground-plans within a relatively limited area have been interpreted as representing temporary and probably seasonal occupation in tent-like structures (Eogan 1963). A similar situation may occur at Townleyhall 1, Co. Louth, enclosed by a low earthen bank and internal ditch, which produced 150 stakeholes and a single fireplace (Liversage 1960). Although more substantial, the oval houses at Knocknarea produced evidence for the intensive production of flint tools and indicate specialist activity perhaps of a seasonal nature (Bengtsson and Bergh 1984). Seven circular or oval houses at Piperstown, Co. Dublin appear to have had their walls or roof supports bedded in rings of loose stone (Rynne and Ó hÉailidhe 1965; Figure 4.4). Two of these were excavated: the central feature of each, as well as of two unexcavated examples, was a rectangular hearth identical to those at Slieve Breagh and Newgrange. The evidence, in the form of largely undiagnostic flint working, indicates an earlier prehistoric if not definitely Neolithic date for these structures. Apart from the apparently insubstantial nature of the buildings, the very high altitude, over 365m ASL, may suggest short term, if periodic, occupation.

At a superficial level the houses at Newgrange appear to be no more substantial than those at Townleyhall or Piperstown. However, the hearths seem to be the focal points for discrete, regularly spaced circular structures. The quantity of material from the area of occupation, which covers an area of at least 1,500 square metres, in addition to evidence for smaller post built structures without hearths or fireplaces (see for example O'Kelly 1983, fig. 8), are suggestive of an intensive phase of habitation rather than intermittent or seasonal activity. The spatial arrangement of the houses suggests four clusters each consisting of four houses, possibly representing different kin groups within the settlement (Figure 4.6; Cooney and Grogan 1994, 79–81).

Large scale agglomerated settlement also seems to be indicated by the second, middle Neolithic, settlement stage at Knowth. Here at least nine large circular houses with diameters of *c.*6m-8m (average floor area: *c.*39 square metres) appear to have been defined by circles of stakeholes (Roche 1989; Eogan 1991, 108, fig. 2). These occurred within a habitation area of *c.*2100 square metres on the northeastern side of the main mound and sealed beneath both it and four satellite tombs. In one area at least six successive stages of re-building were identified. Another feature of settlement permanence are the habitation enclosures of the type emerging at Lough Gur during the middle Neolithic (Grogan and Eogan 1987; Figure 4.5) and encircling both rectangular (K2) and circular houses (L central, site 10; Figure 4.4). On the limestone plateau of Mullaghfarna, Co. Sligo, beneath Cairn O of the extensive passage tomb cemetery at Carrowkeel a cluster of over 60 such enclosures have been identified (Macalister 1912 *et al.*, 331–2, pl. 23; Grogan 1980; Figure 4.11). Some of these (eg. Nos. 1, 3, 6, 41, 44, 54) are large enough to have contained houses, others may represent the foundations of the houses themselves and some may have had ancillary domestic functions.

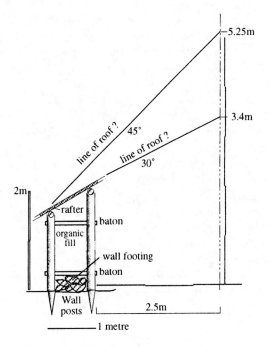

line of roof ?
45°

line of roof ?
30°

5.25m

3.4m

2m

rafter

baton

organic
fill

wall footing

baton

Wall
posts

2.5m

——— 1 metre

*Figure 4.8: Lough Gur, Co. Limerick.
Reconstructed cross-sections of wall and
house structure*

*Figure 4.9: Reconstruction of
Neolithic house at Lough Gur
Site A house, Co. Limerick.
(Drawing by Ursula Matten-
berger)*

SITE CONTEXT

The nature of the evidence varies very considerably: some houses have been subjected to limited excavation (eg. Pepperhill where only one corner of the house was exposed) while others occur within large-scale area excavation. Some houses may, however, represent "isolated" farmsteads. Although a large area was excavated at Ballynagilly there does not appear to be any indication of buildings other than the house itself.

Where substantial excavation has occurred the houses do not usually form isolated features and are associated with indications of associated domestic activity such as ancillary buildings, hearths, pits, work areas, shelters or huts, paved or cobbled yards and, infrequently, evidence for some element of enclosure. In several instances more than one house has been identified within the occupation area. This includes at least two houses at Ballygalley, Knowth (primary phase), Slieve Breagh and Tankardstown, groups of three or more houses at Knowth (passage tomb phase), Lough Gur (early, middle and final Neolithic phases; Figure 4.5), Newgrange (final Neolithic phase) and Townleyhall 2. Extensive areas of occupation with evidence for smaller domestic buildings, hearths, pits, shelters and paving have come from Lough Gur, Knowth (both the primary western Neolithic and the passage tomb phases) and Newgrange, while extensive settlement without surviving evidence for structures has been found at Feltrim Hill, Lyles Hill, and Doonegore. It seems probable, therefore, that settlement agglomeration with clusters of

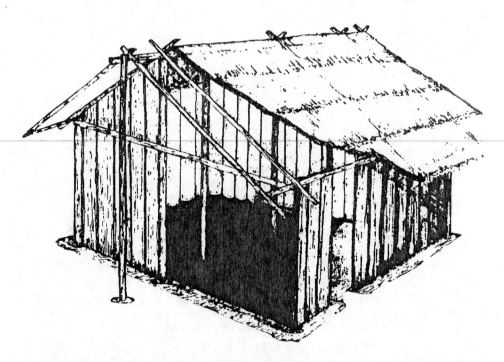

Figure 4.10: Reconstruction drawing of Tankardstown South 1 Neolithic house, Co. Limerick

two or more houses in contemporary use were a feature of the Neolithic in Ireland.

Another feature of houses, and other habitation evidence, is the frequency with which they have been located beneath, or on the site of, megalithic tombs (Grogan 1980). This is the case at Ballyglass 1 and 2, Knowth, Newgrange and Townleyhall 2 among the houses while habitation material came from beneath tombs at Baltinglass, Ballybriest, Ballintoy (Mogey 1941), Ballymarlagh (Davies 1949) and Dún Rúadh (Davies 1936), Co. Antrim and beneath two satellite tombs (site L and Z) at Newgrange (O'Kelly *et al.* 1978). At Ballyglass 1 the excavator suggested that the house had been deliberately demolished to facilitate the construction of the house (Ó Nualláin 1972a). The association of sacred and secular activity may reflect both a conscious intent to incorporate one within the other as well as indicating Neolithic perceptions of centrality within the familiar landscape of the community. At a more basic level, the superimposition of these elements indicates a similarity in the siting preferences for both homes and tombs.

There is a marked preference in the location of house sites on sheltered south to west facing slopes in close proximity to, and frequently overlooking, significant bodies of water. This is shown, for example, by the lake-side positions at Ballynagilly and Lough Gur, and river terraces at Knowth, Newgrange, Tankardstown and Townleyhall 2.

In several instances houses were rebuilt on the site of an earlier structure. Among these are examples at Ballygalley site 2 (Simpson *et al.* 1994), Lough Gur site B (Figure 4.2) and circle L, Knowth and Newgrange. This replacement of one domestic structure by another is an indication of the longevity of some habitations but also perhaps of the concept of a family "site" within an agglomerated settlement.

FUNCTIONS

The houses themselves formed the focal point for everyday domestic activity. None of the houses seem larger than that required to house a single family. Indeed, the size of some structures could only have accommodated a group of 4–6 people. Tables 4.1–4.3 show an indication of the number of individuals who could be comfortably accommodated within the house based on a requirement of 4 square metres per person. This is provided as a rough guide only since it is clear that there is no simple relationship between size and occupancy (eg. Whittle 1988, 70–3). This clearly has important social implications and suggests that the nuclear family formed the basic unit of society. Moreover, the evidence hints that larger kinship groups were significant at a sub-community level. The agglomerated sites have produced evidence for internal spatial organization suggesting that close relatives may have lived in clusters within the overall settlement. Examples include the grouping of houses at Newgrange (Figure 4.6; see above), Lough Gur sites C, D and circle L (Figures 4.3–4.5).

While there is some variation the houses seem to have been primarily domestic in function, that is there is little evidence for other, for example industrial, activity within the building. Exceptions include the houses at Knocknarea which appear to be specialist, and perhaps seasonal, sites. The material assemblages are generally small, although in several cases no differentiation was made in the excavation reports between finds from, and those in the vicinity of, the house. The overall impression is of general domestic

Eoin Grogan

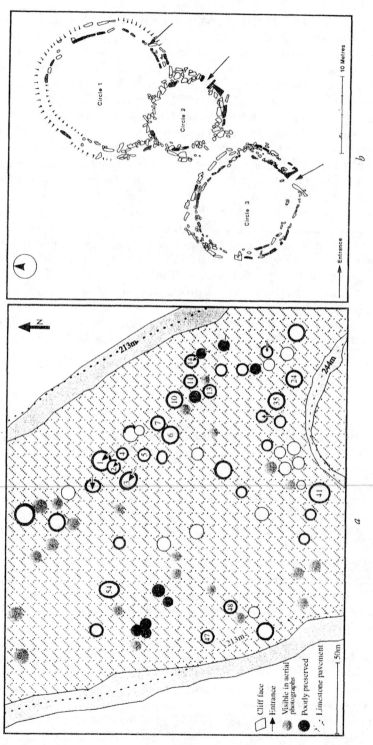

Figure 4.11: a, Mullaghfarna, Co. Sligo: General plan of the habitation enclosures. b, Mullaghfarna, Co. Sligo: Detailed plan of enclosures 1–3

rubbish including pottery and stone artefacts, personal items and food remains but not, significantly, debris from butchering or crop processing or evidence for artefact manufacture. The range of evidence from many sites suggests that these latter activities were carried out on other parts of the habitation area, whether in the open, as with the flint knapping floors identified at Knowth (Eogan 1984, 232–3, fig. 78), or in small structures or shelters. While it is tempting to believe that the tripartite rectangular houses accommodated separate functions under the same roof there is no direct evidence to support such a theory.

CHRONOLOGY AND CHANGING ARCHITECTURE

Only at Lough Gur can the process of change in architectural styles be glimpsed in any detail. However, it is possible to indicate a gradual trend towards circularity in house plans during the Neolithic. Most of the early Neolithic houses appear to be rectangular. The sites of Ballyglass 1, Ballynagilly, Tankardstown and Pepperhill have produced dates ranging from *c*.3900–3600 BC. By the middle Neolithic some circular dwellings were being built including substantial structures at Lough Gur and Slieve Breagh as well as more lightweight houses as at Knowth (Roche 1989) and Townleyhall 2 (Figure 4.4). Similar, but undated houses occur at Piperstown. Although the houses were temporary or seasonal in use the evidence at Townleyhall 2, Co. Louth (Eogan 1963) suggests circular huts about 6m in diameter.

At Lough Gur some continuity in building techniques is indicated into this period. The circular houses at Circle L and Site C are associated with assemblages containing a high proportion of decorated middle Neolithic pottery. Sub-circular and oval houses at Site D and Circle L produced Beaker pottery of the final Neolithic. However, all of these houses were constructed using the same basic principle of wall construction, a stone footing supporting an organic wall fill and retained by opposed pairs of wall posts (see Figures 4.8 and 4.9). This continuation of the Lough Gur house style can be attested over a period of several hundred years, from *c*.3500–2500 BC.

CONCLUSIONS

The evidence from the Irish Neolithic indicates the importance of the house as a focal point for everyday, domestic and social activity. Indeed the weight of the data is leading to an increasing convincing picture of permanency in the settlement pattern. A degree of mobility, perhaps of segments of the social group rather than the whole community, seems nevertheless to form part of settlement organization and specialist, seasonal and temporary sites have been identified. This diversity in the settlement pattern occurs throughout the Neolithic (Cooney and Grogan 1994, 50–2). While isolated farmsteads occupied by one family may have been part of the overall pattern there is also increasing evidence for settlement agglomeration with groups of between two and twenty or more houses represented at several sites. Within these larger habitations there is also some evidence for the spatial organization of the settlement around kin groups. Towards the end of the Neolithic there are indications of social differentiation within settlement sites with the enclosure of some houses (Grogan and Eogan 1987, 468–71; Cooney and Grogan 1994, 49–50). The overall settlement pattern is not static during the Neolithic and changes in the dispersal and organization of settlement within the landscape, as well as developments in the spatial arrangement of domestic sites, are evident (Cooney and Grogan in press). Nevertheless it is clear that throughout the period the house was perceived as one of the key elements in social and settlement organization.

Acknowledgements
This research began as a masters degree in University College, Dublin (completed in 1980) and I am grateful to my supervisors, the late Ruaidhrí de Valera and Seamas Caulfield, and to George Eogan and Gabriel Cooney for their invaluable help and support. My thanks also to George Eogan, Mags Gowen, Eoin Halpin, Helen Roche and Derek Simpson for access to information on unpublished material. Sarah Cross and Aidan O'Sullivan have offered helpful comment about the paper. I am grateful to Aidan O'Sullivan and Aoife Daly for assistance in preparing the illustrations. The reconstruction drawing of the house at Lough Gur Site A (Figure 4.10) by Ursula Mattenberger has graced many a lecture.

Chapter 5

Neolithic buildings in Scotland

Gordon J Barclay

INTRODUCTION

The buildings described in this paper belong to a number of different regional "Neolithics", not to a unitary "Scottish Neolithic". As Kinnes has stated: "Scotland ... is a country of great geographical variability, remarkably diverse in landscape and climate..." whose unity "...rests upon its separation from the south rather than in its own uniformity. There is no reason, other than that of modern political expediency, why the "Scottish Neolithic" should exist as an entity..." (Kinnes 1985)

As elsewhere, the shortage of data for Neolithic settlement and economy throughout most of Scotland is striking, in contrast to the quantity (if not quality) of data on burial and ceremonial sites gathered since the last century. Problems arise from concentration on this relatively well-known aspect of the Neolithic. As Richards (1991) has noted "...studies concerned with social organization and its transformation have focused on chambered tombs and henge monuments...", which have been used to erect "frail [interpretative] structures". In addition, for historical reasons, the interpretation of the Neolithic has been based on data predominantly gathered from the north and west, and/or from monuments largely constructed of stone. In most of Scotland, Neolithic activity is as yet attested only by burial and ceremonial monuments and by artefact discoveries. In the arable areas of Scotland the density of site types classifiable as Neolithic is growing rapidly as a result of aerial photography; however, the types of Neolithic site which can as yet be recognized easily from the air are ceremonial and funerary. The majority of the buildings of the Neolithic (and mainly of the late Neolithic) have been identified in Orkney and Shetland. Indeed, it is only in these areas that we have any balanced picture of the Neolithic, as there are burial, ceremonial and domestic sites in close proximity and in substantial numbers. But care must be exercised in using sites and interpretations from these areas to interpret the Neolithics of the rest of Scotland.

In this paper I will look at the roofed buildings which have been excavated in Scotland, together with other structures which might be interpreted in this way. Throughout I use the term "building" rather than "house" because of the difficulties of drawing a distinction between some domestic structures and buildings which may have had different functions. Space prevents any consideration of buildings associated with Beaker material or of early Bronze Age date.

There are few comprehensive surveys of the buildings of the Neolithic. McInnes (1971) summarized the later Neolithic material; at that time only four sites were described: Skara Brae, Rinyo, Northton and Eilean an Tighe. Of these the last two had no coherent buildings of the period. Since then a surprisingly large number of individual buildings have been investigated. Consideration is hampered by a dearth of published data; many of the most important excavations are so recent that there are only interim reports (eg. Barnhouse (Richards 1990b), Loch Olabhat (Armit 1988; 1992)). Others, although undertaken in the 1970s, are not yet fully published (eg. Noltland and Balbridie). Fortunately, we have the promptly published excavations of Shetland sites by Calder (1950; 1956; 1961), Scord of Brouster (Whittle *et al.* 1986), and Knap of Howar (Ritchie 1983).

The data available tell us very little about the possible range of Neolithic domestic structures: the few tens of known buildings, from the hundreds or even thousands which must have existed over the 1500 or more years of the Neolithic, provide too small a sample for reliable general conclusions yet to be drawn. Even the relatively well understood domestic architecture of Orkney and Shetland is not as well known as we would wish. And from that large area of Scotland which contains the most easily cultivated and the most productive agricultural land – the eastern coastal plain and the south west – there is only a handful of excavated settlement sites, Balbridie being the only substantial, coherent building.

Because of the regional nature of the Neolithic in Scotland the description and much of the discussion is arranged in discrete sections, starting in the north. Space does not allow any significant discussion of domestic sites where there is no coherent building, or where buildings are too fragmentary to add much to the discussion, and the same constraint prevents the rehearsal of detail of recently published and easily available discussions about the nature of the use of domestic space (eg. Richards 1990b; 1991; this volume).

SHETLAND

Shetland has perhaps the highest concentration of visible Neolithic domestic structures, together with their field systems, in mainland Britain. Yet they rarely appear in syntheses of the British Neolithic. Perhaps it is the difficulty of distinguishing Neolithic from later buildings that has resulted in the relative lack of attention paid to them. We owe our considerable knowledge of these sites largely to the efforts of one man, C S T Calder, who undertook an impressive programme of research through field survey and excavation in the decades after the second world war (Calder 1950; 1956; 1961; summarized effectively by Henshall 1963, 151). He wholly excavated six buildings and surveyed many others, with their associated field systems, and recovered ample evidence of an agricultural way of life. He identified 60 other buildings as being of the same type as those he investigated, although the "typical" sort of building he identified remained in use through to the end of the Bronze Age.

Whittle's work at Scord of Brouster (Whittle *et al.* 1986) has built very effectively on this early work, providing a greater range of information on the buildings, their field systems and their contemporary environment. Some of the buildings and the local Zetland group of chambered tombs share a number of characteristics. First, there is the heel-shape most clearly visible at the so-called Stanydale "temple" (Figure 5.1), but also visible in the possible first phase of the "Benie Hoose" (Figure 5.2). The construction techniques used in the tombs and buildings are also similar, in their use of massive and irregular blocks, laid carefully, with the portals and divisions between recesses marked by upright stones.

The "typical" buildings vary considerably in plan but are characteristically oval and the main chamber, entered from one end, generally has a number of recesses. The type was in use for a long time; for example at Scord of Brouster elements of Building 2 were dated to 3340–2879 BC (CAR-252) and of Building 3 to 1737–1434 BC (CAR-477).

The chronology of many of the Shetland houses is unclear. The pottery assemblages (Henshall in Calder 1956; Whittle *et al.* 1986, 59) have parallels in Hebridean styles and Beaker. The few available radiocarbon dates show that basic building forms had a long life and the artefact assemblages are not clearly understood. The typical oval building at Ness of Gruting, excavated by Calder and interpreted by him as Neolithic (1956), produced a radiocarbon date for material within the wall of 2270–1890 BC (GrN-6168) (Barcham 1980). Amongst the finds within the building and in and under its walls were polished stone axes a carved stone ball, and large quantities of Neolithic pottery. The precise date of the building is still in doubt. Whittle (Whittle *et al.* 1986, 139), in discussing the nature of the irregular Building 2 at Scord of Brouster, has pointed to the dangers of assuming that "typical" structures are indeed so. While such "typical" buildings exist in significant numbers little attention has been paid to the very large numbers of small, irregular buildings, similar to Scord of Brouster Building 2, recognized in field survey in northern Scotland in recent years (eg. Mercer 1980). It may be that many of these structures are Neolithic.

Structurally, the houses are simple. The walls, generally very thick, were built of mixed material faced internally (surviving up to over 1m in height) and often externally; they surround areas within which there is often little evidence of roof support structures. The "temple" at Stanydale has only two internal postholes (each holding two posts) on its axis; the house at Gruting School (Figure 5.1) has a scatter of small postholes, but there is no evidence to show how large structures like Ness of Gruting were roofed. The source of timber for relatively large roofing spans is also difficult to determine. The posts at the Stanydale "temple" were identified as spruce and the charcoal in the floor deposits also showed Scots Pine to be present; timber of both species must have arrived either as driftwood (from Scandinavia in the case of the spruce), or as directly imported timber; neither species grew locally. Calder preferred direct import (1950) as he believed it unlikely that the 700+ linear metres of timber probably necessary for the "temple" could have been obtained as driftwood. Reconstructions and descriptions of the buildings assume low pitches, but how adequate rain shedding was arranged is a matter for further study. There is ample evidence, from the buildings, for part of the economy of these farming communities, in the form of cereal grains, querns and ard points.

The two complex buildings excavated by Calder at Whalsay, the "Benie Hoose" (Figure 5.2) and the Standing Stones of Yoxie (Figure 5.1) (Calder 1961) lie close to each other within a field system. The Benie Hoose seems to have at least three main phases of construction. The first is a heel-shaped building, the wall face of which is visible within

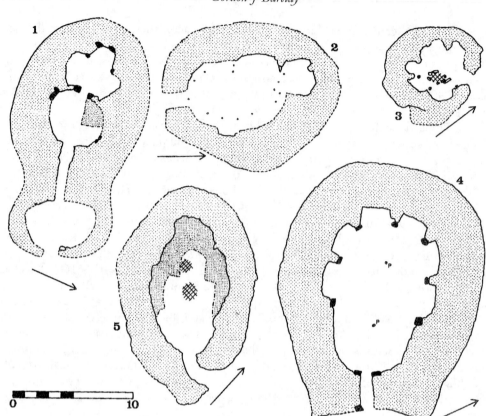

Figure 5.1: Ground plans of Neolithic buildings in Shetland. (1) Standing Stones of Yoxie, Shetland (the darker-toned area is a later alteration); (2) Gruting School; (3) Scord of Brouster Building 3; (4) Stanydale "Temple"; (5) Ness of Gruting (the darker-toned area is a later alteration). In numbers 1 and 4 the black marks are upright stones (except where marked "p" in 4); in 2 and 3 the black spots are postholes, post-settings or post-supports. The cross-hatched areas are hearths. (Sources: various)

the later structure. The second phase seems to involve the addition of a further chamber or forecourt. Both chambers have hearths and drains. Finally, the inner chamber was reconstructed in such a way that two recesses were lost and the outer chamber was divided differently. The plan reproduced here is a simplification of Calder's original.

The structure known as the Standing Stones of Yoxie has three chambers with paved access between and through them. The inner chamber has a trefoil arrangement of recesses, reminiscent of some of the local chambered tombs.

The oval building at Gruting School (Calder 1956) has a chamber 7.6m by 5.6m with a smaller chamber of 2.75m diameter off. The post setting in the main chamber might represent more than one phase of roof support. The wall has shallow recesses. The building has no hearth, and accordingly Whittle argues (Whittle *et al.* 1986, 139) that this building did not have a straightforward domestic function.

At Scord of Brouster, excavations revealed three buildings (in the sequence Building

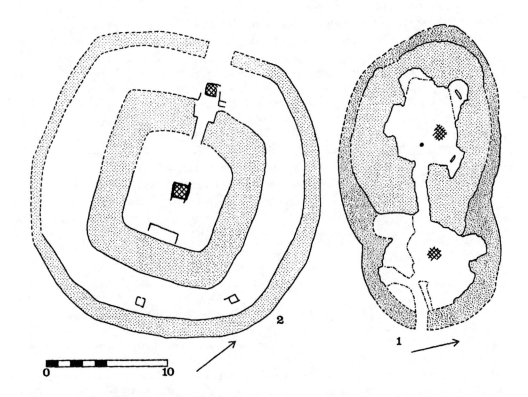

Figure 5.2: Ground plans of Neolithic buildings in Shetland and Orkney. (1) The "Benie Hoose", Shetland. The house has three main phases – a: the light-toned area; b: the dark-toned area, and finally c: the additions marked by the dot and dashed lines in the inner and outer chambers. (2) Building 8 at Barnhouse. The cross-hatched areas are hearths. (Sources: various)

2, Building 1, Building 3) spanning the Neolithic to the Bronze Age. The excavator has suggested that the buildings were used sequentially rather than concurrently (Whittle *et al.* 1986). The buildings are scattered through an extensive agricultural system of field banks, lynchets and clearance cairns.

Building 2 has an irregularly kidney-shaped plan with one or two recesses measuring 5.2m by 3.8m internally. Phase 2 is radiocarbon dated to 3341–2671 BC (CAR-252).[1] It has no convincing hearth feature nor any obvious entrance. Whittle (Whittle *et al.* 1986, 137) suggests that it may be a "specialized or seasonal structure". Building 1 is an oval building measuring 7m by 5.4m internally with hearth features and six recesses, which underwent reconstruction over a considerable period. Phase 2a is dated to 2890–2480 BC (CAR-246).[2] Phase 2b produced dates of 2890–2470 BC (CAR-247), 2910–2480 BC (HAR-2413) and 2270–1780 BC (CAR-248) (recess 6).

At Stanydale, Calder excavated a remarkable building, the Stanydale "temple" (Calder

1950) and a house (Calder 1956), lying close to other buildings within a field system. The "temple" is a very large structure which may be interpreted as a roofed building, with the roof ridge held up by four posts, set in two double postholes, or as an open court with free-standing posts. It has a single large chamber (maximum 11.9m by 6.7m), entered via a paved passage through the centre of the concave façade. In the western half are six contiguous, apsidal recesses measuring *c.*2.4m by 1.2m. The walls are an average of 3.8m thick. There are six standing stones arranged in an arc to the south of the building (Calder 1950, fig 8). Calder interpreted the structure, as is clear from its name, as a religious building, and drew on parallels in the Mediterranean area, particularly Maltese structures. The building does not seem to be purely domestic and an interpretation as a communal focus for religious or ritual activity seems likely.

The Stanydale house has two chambers, the outer 6.4m by 4.7m, entered via a complex passage through walls 1.8m to 2.7m thick; the inner, a small circular chamber measures 2.1m in diameter. There is a central hearth and the larger chamber has two small recesses. At the south end is a poorly preserved small rectangular enclosure.

ORKNEY

The only two buildings known in Orkney which may be from the earlier part of the Neolithic are from Knap of Howar. They measured 7.5m by 3m and 10m by 4.5m internally (Ritchie 1983, fig 2), and have superficial parallels in rectilinear structures of the period elsewhere in Scotland (eg. Eilean Domhnuill, Western Isles (Armit 1992) – see below). However, there are problems with the relationship between the buildings at Knap and the midden material into which they were dug (and to which the radiocarbon dates may relate) which should be borne in mind (Kinnes 1985, 27); the primary midden dates vary considerably, from early to late Neolithic, and the date of the visible structures is not absolutely certain.

Building 1 had a wall of drystone facing on both sides containing a core of midden material. The area enclosed was rectilinear with rounded corners, totalling approximately 10m by 4.5m. It was divided into two rooms by a stone partition. Room 1a was furnished with a low bench. Room 1b had a trough quern, hearth and a wall recess.

Building 2 was of similar construction and shape to Building 1, with three compartments measuring in total 7.5m by 2.6m – 3.6m. The innermost room was "intensively furnished" with wall-recesses. The middle room had a hearth. Immediately to the east of the northern partition was a low stone kerbed area. In a second phase the door of Building 2 was blocked and the interior remodelled. It is not clear how these houses were roofed. The middens provided evidence of an economy based on arable agriculture in the form of cereal grains and querns and on a wide range of wild resources.

Five settlements of the later Neolithic have been investigated in Orkney: at Rinyo (Childe and Grant 1939; 1947), Skara Brae (Childe 1931; Clarke 1976a; 1976b), Links of Noltland (Clarke *et al.* 1978; Clarke and Sharples 1990), Barnhouse (Richards 1990a; 1992) and Pool (Hunter *et al.* in press). As yet only interim accounts are available for the excavations undertaken in Orkney in the last 25 years (apart from Knap of Howar). Skara Brae is the best known Neolithic settlement in Britain and has been the focus of discussion of house construction and the organization and development of settlements. The settlement's remarkable preservation offers unrivalled opportunity to analyze the organization of space, but, as Richards laments (1991), much of the rich artefact assemblage, which would have added considerably to this area of study, was discarded by the excavator when the site was cleared out.

The resemblance of the architecture and internal arrangement of the Orkney late Neolithic buildings to that of the Orkney tombs has been the subject of much discussion (eg. Hodder 1982a). The buildings and most of the tombs share an entrance oriented southeast to northwest.

Although there is an interim account of the excavations undertaken 20 years ago at Skara Brae (Clarke 1976a), the most useful analysis of the buildings at Skara Brae is provided by Richards (1991) who describes the settlement and the individual buildings and attempts an analysis of "socially constructed space" (Richards 1990b). There are ten buildings in the settlement, with clear signs of refurbishment and rebuilding of individual buildings over an unspecified period. Clarke has identified (1976a, 11) differences between earlier and later buildings (exemplified by Buildings 9 and 7) – the former smaller with recessed "beds" and "dresser", the latter larger but with "beds" and "dresser" set out into the greater floor space. However, the pattern of central hearth, right and left hand "beds" and a rear "dresser", with a central hearth is maintained through time, as is the difference between the size of the left- and right-handed "beds" (the right is larger). The use of space in the buildings is determined by the positioning of the entrance, the central hearth and the furniture. In Building 7 the paving slabs of the entrance curve around to the right and furniture to the left would prevent access in that direction. Richards (1991) notes that if access is gained in this way in all buildings of this pattern, then the left hand bed area is that furthest from the entrance. The large central Building 2 at Barnhouse makes this arrangement even clearer, in that access is directly into the right chamber and access to the left chamber can only be obtained from the right side of the first chamber. Richards (1990b) has written compellingly of the cosmology of the late Neolithic people of Orkney, as it is given concrete shape in the architecture of their houses and tombs.

Richards suggests that the settlement was not buried deliberately in midden material, but that the buildings were given a turf "jacket". Building 8 is sufficiently different to merit comment. It is separate from the rest of the buildings, has two means of access (one through an elaborate porch), and an atypical arrangement of features in which the general pattern of internal arrangements is maintained but different elements are substituted. It is clear that it would be unwise to assume that all buildings, even if superficially shaped and equipped in the same way as houses, are ordinary houses.

Richards' own excavation at Barnhouse (1990a) has shed further light on the complexity of later Neolithic Orcadian settlements and on the variability of structures within them. The excavation revealed a hierarchically organized group of six small "early type" Skara Brae/Rinyo buildings adjacent to a larger building (Building 2). The small buildings share the same internal arrangements as those at Skara Brae; Building 2 by contrast has two chambers although in other respects it is an unusual "early type" Skara Brae building, while the architecture of the larger is of similar nature and layout to the passage graves of Quoyness and Quanterness. Similarly, the sophistication of its construction is only matched at Maes Howe.

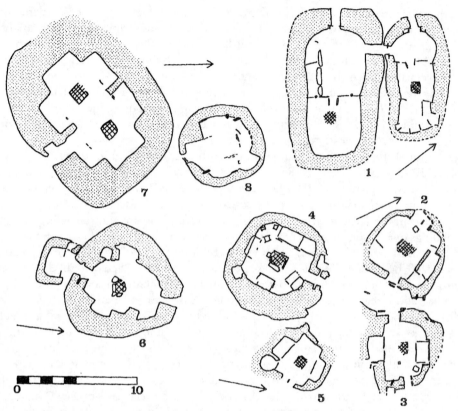

Figure 5.3: Ground plans of Neolithic buildings in Orkney. (1) Knap of Howar Buildings 1 and 2; (2) Rinyo Building A; (3) Rinyo Building G; (4) Skara Brae Building 7; (5) Skara Brae Building 9; (6) Skara Brae Building 8; (7) Barnhouse Building 2; (8) Barnhouse Building 3. The cross-hatched areas are hearths. (Sources: various)

It is ironic that the damage caused to Barnhouse by ploughing, in reducing it to bare wall footings, made it possible (in a way it has not been possible at deeper stratified sites) to examine a large area and the relationship between many buildings. While Building 2, which has already been mentioned, is a large enough structure, it is dwarfed by Structure 8. This is a roughly square building centrally positioned on a sub-circular clay platform enclosed by a stone wall. Richards (1990a) points to the similarity of this arrangement to that at Maes Howe and the Stones of Stenness henge. The building has internal arrangements clearly related to, but different from, those in an ordinary building; for example, it has an enlarged central hearth and a "dresser" on the wall facing the entrance.

The importance of the hearth, touched on in the description of Skara Brae, is also reflected at Barnhouse. The central hearths and the fire kindled upon them seem to have had considerable significance, both for basic family needs and the orientation of the house (Richards 1990b). The complex Building 2 at Barnhouse (Figures 5.3 and 5.4) has two large hearths, one in the right hand chamber, associated with features and furniture for cooking; the second lies in the left chamber, assuming a more restricted position in the "inner" area of the structure. Access to this area can only be gained by crossing a cist slab. The symbolic significance of hearths is clearly demonstrated by the covering of the first hearth in this building and, even more strikingly, by the position of the hearth in the middle of the entrance of Structure 8 (where it was probably slabbed over and invisible) and in the similarity of the square features in the middle of the Stenness henge (Ritchie 1976) and the Balbirnie Stone circle (Ritchie 1974). Richards (pers. comm.) suggests that the parallel with Stenness may be very close indeed, with the possible remains of an "entrance hearth" 5–6m north of the central setting.

In the absence of the excavation report for Links of Noltland we must rely on two brief interim reports (Clarke and Sharples 1990; Clarke *et al.* 1978); the former contains the only published plan. Only one building was investigated and this was not bottomed. The excavator noted broad parallels between Skara Brae Building 8 and this large two-chambered building at Noltland, in its location outside the midden area and its apparently specialized function, although the shape and size are not comparable. The incompleteness of the excavation prevents further discussion of the function of the building. Its fill is interpreted as deliberate.

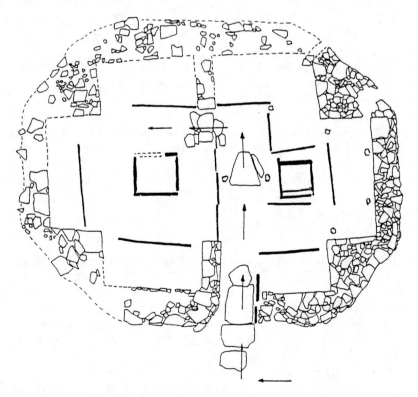

Figure 5.4: Ground plan of Building 2 at Barnhouse, Orkney, showing access routes. (Reproduced by permission of Colin Richards)

At Pool a range of sub-circular buildings was excavated (Hunter *et al.* in press); later disturbance and the limited areas which could opened at the bottom of a deep site has restricted the number of complete plans available. Some, for example Structure 8 (the most complete), conform to the Skara Brae. There are also hints that there is a broadly similar development from early (smaller) to later (larger) houses.

The site at Rinyo (Childe and Grant 1939; 1947) revealed possibly seven buildings, of more than one phase. The overall internal arrangement of the houses parallel the other Orcadian sites. The paving in House A suggests access directed along the right hand side of the hearth, as Richards (1990b) would suggest was the norm.

THE WESTERN ISLES

Modern excavation in the Western Isles has discovered an extraordinary potential for the preservation of Neolithic settlement evidence, but as yet only a limited number of sites has been investigated.

Armit (1992) recovered the remains of two repeatedly reconstructed rectilinear buildings at Eilean Domhnuill, superficially similar, in their relationship one to the other, to the Knap of Howar buildings. The structures measure 6.5m by 4.5m and 4m by 3m internally (Armit 1988; 1992). The walls of the buildings were built of a mixture of soil and stone, up to 2m thick. The buildings have not yet been radiocarbon dated, but examination of the pottery suggests a date of *c.*3500 BC. They lack the furnishings and built-in "dressers" of the buildings in Orkney. There is no evidence for internal subdivision in the published plans. The simplified plan presented here is of the Phase 1 buildings; in later phases both buildings had a hearth.

Other sites, such as Bharpa Carinish (Crone 1993), Northton (Simpson 1976), and Eilean an Tighe (Scott 1951) may have had structural features but not enough survived to allow reconstruction. This should be mentioned as a distinctive if unfortunate regional characteristic.

THE MAINLAND OF SCOTLAND

The North

There are no known Neolithic buildings in the northern part of Scotland (from Inverness to the north coast of Caithness and Sutherland). As has already been mentioned Whittle has noted (Whittle *et al.* 1986, 138) that there are many small irregular structures in northern Scotland (eg. Mercer 1980) which seem superficially similar to Building 2 at Scord of Brouster. It seems unlikely that the northern part of the Scottish mainland, so rich in chambered tombs, does not contain settlement evidence comparable that from Skara Brae and Noltland.

During the excavation of a possible Clava cairn at Raigmore, Inverness, Simpson discovered the remains of a timber structure containing a hearth, associated with Grooved Ware. Publication is well advanced; in the meantime a generalized plan is presented here (Figure 5.5; Simpson pers. comm.). The building (perhaps of two phases or with double walls) appears to consist of post-built walls enclosing an area *c*.7.5 to 9m long by 5m broad.

The North East

The coastal plain from Inverness round to the Tay contains much of the best agricultural land, and some of the most easily cultivated, in Scotland, with clear evidence of Neolithic settlement represented by artefact discoveries, by earthen monuments of a type familiar in eastern Britain (long barrows, cursus monuments, henges) and by the recumbent stone circles. Yet in this area only Balbridie represents the domestic architecture of the period, and there is doubt that the structure is a normal house.

The massive building at Balbridie, Kincardineshire (Ralston 1982; Fairweather and Ralston 1993), has to date no excavated parallel, either for internal scale (24m long and 10m broad) or construction (the Benie Hoose in Shetland is comparable in external size, but far smaller inside). A number of broadly comparable cropmark sites is now known (including one across the River Dee at Crathes) but some may well be of later date or different function. A series of 14 radiocarbon dates puts the building in the early – mid fourth millennium BC; perhaps the most reliable dates are the accelerator dates for seeds (eg. 5770–5490 BC (OxA-1767), 5930–5600 BC (OxA-1768); 5973–5600 BC (OxA-1769)). Fairweather and Ralston (1993) comment that "...the farmers of Balbridie were – in terms of their building and, it would seem, of their strategy with cereals – closer to continental European practice than has normally been identified in the British Isles."

The building differs from those of the Western and Northern Isles in more than scale. Because the site is on arable land no floor surfaces survived and there is nothing to compare with the information on furniture and fittings recovered elsewhere. We have only the main structural elements to guide us.

The building is defined by a wall slot containing substantial posts and possibly the remains of plank walling. Within the enclosed area are several arrangements of posts, some of the elements of these lines set in transversely arranged slots. There are two longitudinal lines of seven posts *c*.1m in from both side walls which could have served to support two longitudinal roof beams; some of the posts of this line are incorporated into the ends of transverse slots. The roof could not have been supported on the walls and these posts alone and it is possible that posts, both free-standing and within the transverse slots, nearer the axis, supported two further longitudinal beams. I have marked the possible positions of such beams as toned lines on Figure 5.5.

There are as yet no published plans which show the precise location of postpipes but it can be suggested that the internal slots fulfilled the same function as the wall slots – that is holding both structural timbers supporting longitudinal roof beams and continuous walling. If this interpretation is correct, all the internal slots would support screens and where there were no slots or where posts were set in separate holes this would indicate a deliberate arrangement where access was not to be restricted by a screen. If this interpretation is correct then some interesting observations can be made about the interior architecture. A screen runs transversely across the building, immediately inside the entrance. This would not only force people to entering to turn either left or right but, significantly, would prohibit visual access into the interior.

The way in which the slots and posts are arranged implies that different parts of the roofed space had different functions. The central transverse slot has a gap, implying a break in the screen not paralleled in the other four transverse slots. The arrangement of four posts immediately to the west of the central slot contrasts with the less encumbered space to the east. Finally, the central post occupying part of the space between the western transverse slot and the next slot to the east, is not paralleled at the entrance end.

The West

Marshall (1978) undertook excavation at Auchategan where she identified settlement of a number of phases, including fragmentary remains of two phases of Neolithic buildings. Rennie has also undertaken extensive excavation in the area, on hillside platforms interpreted as for charcoal burning (eg. Rennie 1986); she located the remains of further timber structures. Charcoal from a hearth associated with a round timber structure 9.5m in diameter on platform 9 at Dunloskin has been radiocarbon dated to 3794–3037 BC (GU-2063) and 3650–2997 BC (GU-2064). Rennie (1984) has also located at Ardnadam three roughly rectangular structures between 7.5m by 5.5m and 3.5m by 3m, with indications of axial postholes, associated with Neolithic pottery around a working area with hearths and worked stones. Charcoal from the hearth of the most southerly structure has been dated to 3699–3342 BC (GU-1549).

The South

At Beckton, in Dumfriesshire, excavation revealed patterns of hearths, floors, pits and postholes, and what may have been an oven or kiln, some associated with Grooved Ware (Pollard 1992). Some of the postholes fall into patterns (two possible four-posters) and lines, but their association with the Grooved Ware is uncertain. While the nature of the post-built structures is as yet uncertain, the location of the site on a small knoll overlooking a stream, would seem a likely situation for settlement, wither temporary or permanent.

OTHER SETTLEMENTS

It is worth mentioning, in passing, the evidence for settlement sites of the Neolithic where buildings have not been found. There are as yet no known large-scale Neolithic enclosures to compare with the causewayed enclosures of southern Britain; Mercer's (1983) exploratory excavation of a large hilltop interrupted-ditch enclosure at Dodd in East Lothian showed that site to be Iron Age. However, there are hints of such features at Balloch Hill, Argyll and Bute (associated with Neolithic pottery: Peltenburg 1982) and at Carwinning Hill, Cunningham (Cowie 1979) where causewayed ditches were recorded under later hillforts. The excavation of a probably domestic Neolithic enclosure at Kinloch Farm, Fife (Barber 1982) and radiocarbon dates from North Mains, Strathallan (Barclay and Tolan 1990) have suggested there may also be a tradition of enclosed Neolithic and Bronze Age settlement in eastern Scotland which has yet to be explored. One of the most interesting possibilities as a major enclosure of this period is at Leadketty, Perthshire (unpublished RCAHMS aerial photograph). Likewise the enigmatic multivallate hilltop enclosures at the Brown Caterthun, Angus (Piggott 1982, 182), and the Barmekin of Echt, Aberdeenshire (Piggott 1982, 120), which have numerous gaps in their ramparts, look decidedly odd in comparison with Iron Age hillforts in the area, and a Neolithic date is being seriously considered.

OTHER STRUCTURES?

There are a number of timber structures which might be interpreted as roofed structures, or where an interpretation as a roofed building has been considered and dismissed.

Analysis of Structure 2 at Balfarg Riding School (Figure 5.5) (Barclay and Russell-White 1993) and comparison with the similar Structure 1 demonstrated that it had almost certainly not been roofed. There are others where cropmarks might be interpreted as roofed buildings. For example, at Littleour, close to the Cleaven Dyke (a cursus in Perthshire) (RCAHMS 1994, 14 and 28), and at Clash, close to the Auchenlaich long

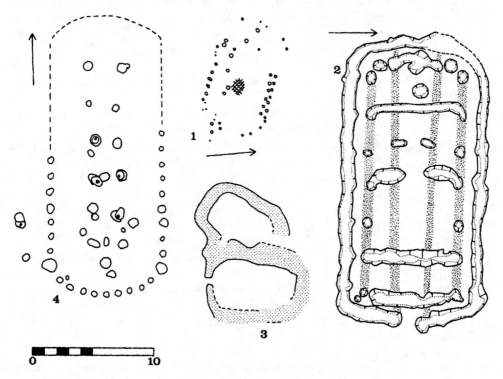

Figure 5.5: Ground plans of Neolithic buildings in Scotland. (1) Raigmore, Highland; (2) Balbridie, Grampian; (3) Eilean Domhnuill; (4) Structure 2 at Balfarg – this is almost certainly not a roofed building (the black dots show where one post can be proved to have replaced another). The open and filled spots are postholes; in 2 the defined areas are postholes and wall-slots. (Sources: various)

cairn (Foster and Stevenson in preparation), are cropmarks which might be interpreted as Neolithic buildings of domestic or funerary function or as buildings of a later period. Timber rings associated with stone circles or within henges have been interpreted as roofed buildings. However, this author believes that there is no evidence that these structures (for example the features recently published by Haggarty (1991) at Machrie) were roofed.

At Wellbrae (Shell Chemicals 1993) a rectangular structure measuring 32.8m by 14.4m (divided at 20.5 m from the western end) contained complex deposits of Neolithic pottery. Its interpretation is not yet clear.

THE BROAD VIEW

To conclude, the Northern Isles have produced abundant evidence for the houses and settlements (and in Shetland the agricultural systems) of the late Neolithic. The quality of preservation allows an almost unparalleled opportunity to examine not only the nature and arrangement of houses and settlements, but also the way in which the buildings were used, and indeed the way in which the inhabitants viewed their world. For example, Richards (1991) notes the pattern of construction of the settlement at Skara Brae as a whole, drawing parallels with the Barnhouse settlement: buildings were repeatedly refurbished and rebuilt (on much the same, but never identical, site), emphasizing the notion of continuity and prompting speculation on the role of kinship and inheritance in the allocation and use of building sites. There is more yet to be drawn from these marvellous sites.

A striking aspect of the Orkney settlements is the presence amongst "normal" houses of larger or somehow unusual buildings, separated to some extent from the others and possibly with specialized functions – Building 8 (and perhaps also Building 7) at Skara Brae (Clarke 1976; Richards 1991; Richards pers. comm.), Buildings 2 and 8 at Barnhouse (Richards 1990) and perhaps the Noltland building (Clarke and Sharples 1990, 67). All have versions of normal internal arrangements. Broad parallels with the "temples" or "halls" in Shetland can also be drawn – in the sense that they are larger structures isolated in some way from "normal" buildings. Whatever the function of these larger buildings it may be that the vast timber "hall" at Balbridie in northeast Scotland (so large that five or six Skara Brae floor plans could be fitted into it) served some comparable function within a group of smaller structures, which were not sought in the excavation and may have been obliterated by ploughing. It is too early yet to suggest that this hierarchy of buildings is a characteristic of Neolithic settlement in Scotland. It is also inappropriate to suggest that patterns of dispersed or nucleated settlement (characterized respectively by the Shetland and the Orkney sites) are certain.

A feature of many of the well preserved northern buildings is the lack of clear evidence about the ways in which they were roofed. Major structures, such as the Stanydale "temple" have limited evidence for supporting posts; many buildings appear to have none at all. Further work is needed in the interpretation of internal features that might have played some part in supporting roofing.

The Western Isles also have great, but as yet scarcely explored potential, as may other areas where later intensive agricultural activity has not removed the evidence. However, the evidence for settlement in the arable areas of Scotland is more elusive. Gibson (1992) has discussed the processes by which relatively slight timber structures will have been degraded or destroyed. In addition the detection of features over 5000 years old is complicated by the effects of natural soil processes; they have, after all, since their formation undergone more than half of the natural processes acting upon soils since the last glaciation. It is therefore hardly surprising that in general only more substantial structures survive to be found by chance (eg. Balbridie) or slight structures survive in small patches of land spared the rigours of modern agricultural ploughing (*cf.* Lismore Fields, Derbyshire (Garton 1986)).

The search for settlement is hampered by the limits to our understanding of the guises in which it will appear. As with Balbridie (which was interpreted as a Dark Age hall before excavation) elements of our Neolithic settlement evidence may already be clearly visible (for example in the cropmark record) but not yet recognized for what they are. For example, if there is a tradition of enclosed settlement of the period in eastern Scotland (as discussed above) some considerable effort will be needed to sift it out from the other enclosures of many periods appearing as cropmarks.

The importance of discovering the Neolithic settlement of lowland Scotland cannot be overstated. The mass of artefactual discoveries and the growing number of ceremonial and funerary structures show the intensity of Neolithic activity on the low-lying, well drained light agricultural land facing continental Europe. For too long the interpretation of the many regional Neolithics of Scotland has depended on the interpretation of one, relatively well studied regional Neolithic (Barclay 1992). The balance needs to be redressed. Work is needed in the cropmark record and in arable fieldwalking of the kind so successful in Orkney (Richards 1990) if progress is to be made.

Acknowledgements
I am very grateful to Colin Richards, Patrick Ashmore and Niall Sharples for their comments on drafts of this paper. My thanks to Derek Simpson for allowing me to publish a plan of the Raigmore building in advance of the excavation report.

Notes
1. Phase 1 of this structure is pre-building occupation.
2. Earlier phases represent pre-building occupation.

Chapter 6

Neolithic buildings in England, Wales and the Isle of Man

Timothy Darvill

INTRODUCTION

British Neolithic settlements in general, and their structural remains in particular, have not had a very good press over the last 60 years. Musing on the theme of prehistoric houses in 1937, Grahame Clark reiterated General Pitt Rivers' remark that because "our knowledge of prehistoric and early people is derived chiefly from their funerary deposits ... they might as well have been born dead", before moving to argue that "the discovery and excavation of prehistoric houses, particularly those of Neolithic and Bronze Age date should be a prime aim of British Archaeology in the immediate future" (Clark 1937, 469). Thirty years later, Isobel Smith was forced to conclude that since house-plans had apparently failed to be revealed either by accident or diligent searching, Neolithic people constructed their houses in such a way as to leave no permanent or recognizable traces in the ground (Smith in Field *et al.* 1964, 367). This line of explanation prompted a series of ingenious proposals for ephemeral house structures and migratory settlement patterns which would leave no archaeologically recoverable evidence (Bradley 1970a, 264; McInnes 1971, 126), while paving the way for two further arguments which supported the "no houses" position. First of these was the idea that soil erosion brought about by agriculture had erased the remains of ancient houses. Second was the proposition that where structures and buildings were found they must have served a "ritual" or "non-domestic" function. All three of these arguments can still be found deeply embedded in recent interpretations (eg. Richards and Thomas 1984; Pryor 1991, 51; Pollard 1992; Barratt 1994, 132–53).

However, in recent years, two things have come into sharp focus which rather change the picture and demand a re-appraisal of available evidence. First, is a shift in our expectations of what Neolithic houses should look like and thus what sort of evidence will be found. Traditionally, expectations of finding longhouses of the sort represented at *Linearbandkeramic* sites such as Elsloo, Stein, or Köln-Lindenthal (Modderman 1970; Buttler and Haberey 1936) have run high, fired-up perhaps by their splendour (Clark 1937, 468; Childe 1949) and the knowledge that they occur less than 200km away across the English Channel (eg. Ilet 1987). Now it is recognized that the relatively late date of early Neolithic settlement in Britain precludes this, and while memories of such structures may indeed be perpetuated in the design and symbolism of long barrows (Ashbee 1966, 46–7; 1984, 99; Hodder 1984), houses for the living will be far more modest constructions perhaps not unlike the late fifth millennium BC structures represented at Berry-au-Bac,

	Calander dates BC	Approx. C14 dates bc	Britain	Northwestern France	Northeastern France and Rhineland	Denmark
5th Millennium BC	4700	3950	Late Mesolithic	Néolithic Ancien: Late LBK and Atlantic Cardial	Epi-Bandkeramik: Hinkelstein Grossgartach	Ertebølle
	4600	3900				
	4500	3800				Early Neolithic: Early TRB
	4400	3625	Early Neolithic: Grimston-Lyles Hill Ware etc.			
	4300	3460			Late Rössen	
	4200	3350				
	4100	3350				
	4000	3250		Néolithic Moyen: Chasséen Cerny Michelsberg		
4th Millennium BC	3900	3075			Néolithic Moyen: Chasséen Michelsberg NMB	Middle Neolithic: TRB
	3800	3075				
	3700	2950	Middle Neolithic: Southern Decorated Wares etc.			
	3600	2910				
	3500	2770				Late TRB
	3400	2940				
	3300	2570		Néolithic Final: SOM		
	3200	2740				
	3100	2600			Néolithic Final: SOM CSR Corded Ware	Final TRB
	3000	2410				
3rd Millennium BC	2900	2400	Late Neolithic: Peterborough Ware Grooved Ware			
	2800	2260				
	2700	2280				Corded Ware
	2600	2175				
	2500	2070	Beakers	Beakers	Beakers	Beakers
	2400	1950				
	2300	1875				
	2200	1830				
	2100	1800				
	2000	1750				

Figure 6.1: Outline chronological framework used in Chapter 6

Aisne, France (Dubouloz *et al.* 1982), and Wittenwater, Uelzen, Denmark (Voss 1965), relating to late Rössen and TRB communities respectively.

Second, is the re-alignment of views about the nature of Neolithic society itself, based largely on the insights provided from anthropological studies of potentially comparable communities. The idea of a simple binary distinction between structures classifiable as being either domestic or ritual cannot be supported. In earlier papers in this volume both Thomas and Whittle develop the archaeological arguments for seeing houses within a broader social context in which space is structured and given meaning through architectural devices which are themselves symbolic expressions of beliefs and understandings about the world that these communities created for themselves. Something of the workings of such systems, their complexity, and the implications for the archaeological investigation of early buildings can be seen clearly in the papers by Richards and Hugh-Jones later in this volume.

With broadened expectations as to what kind of buildings might be represented, and how structural evidence might be interpreted, the remainder of this paper reviews current evidence for buildings found in England, Wales and the Isle of Man datable to the period 4500 BC to 2100 BC.[1] It is argued that not only are Neolithic buildings diverse in form and character, but also that they are more numerous and widespread than commonly believed. A trawl through available sources revealed reports on approximately 109 certain and probably buildings from 64 different sites, including the four early fifth millennium BC structures at Bowmans Farm, Hampshire, discussed by Green (this volume).

A provisional gazetteer of Neolithic buildings is appended to this paper, although sadly not all examples are fully published and there are inevitably difficulties with the dating and definition of some structures. No hard and fast rules have been applied to the selection of evidence for inclusion, although in general there must be signs of structural integrity, associations with artefacts of the period, and strong suggestions that what is represented could have been a roofed building. Specifically excluded are the free-standing timber circles often associated with henges (Gibson 1994), and timber mortuary structures forming components of long barrows, oval barrows, round barrows, and Bronze Age ring cairns (Ashbee 1960, 41–65; Ashbee 1984, 33–54; Lynch 1972).

Before turning to the evidence itself, which is reviewed below chronologically, some attention must be given to the matter of context. This is considered under three sub-headings: construction, survival, and recovery.

NEOLITHIC BUILDINGS IN CONTEXT

Context of construction

Buildings do not just happen, they were deliberately created within the context of the systems of social action in which they played a part. This is a dimension of archaeological evidence that is only just beginning to be glimpsed, but it can be proposed that different buildings occupied a range of positions in relation to systems of action, even though they may appear superficially (to the detached observer) the same. Conversely, apparently similar buildings may have been used and understood in quite different ways by their builders. Throughout, however, there are likely to be regularities in the structuration of action within buildings that reflect or perpetuate much bigger patterns in the relationship between action and the meaning of space (Carsten and Hugh-Jones 1995; Hugh Jones, this volume; Darvill in press).

Regional traditions are likely to be important here, and it cannot be assumed that the same sorts of buildings will have been constructed all over Britain. The linkages between social formation, economy, and environment, for example, are infinitely complicated to the extent that generalization is almost impossible.

During the Neolithic, buildings were constructed in a range of situations, and no doubt for a variety of purposes. Examples have been recorded within enclosures (eg. Etton, Cambridgeshire, Crickley Hill, Gloucestershire, Hembury, Devon, and Carn Brea, Cornwall), although it cannot be assumed that all buildings within an enclosure relate to the primary construction of the site. This is demonstrated by the LN sub-circular building within the central part of the Briar Hill MN causewayed enclosure, Northamptonshire. While single, apparently isolated buildings have long been recognized, and often taken as typical of the EN and MN, groups of up to six buildings are known (eg. Willington, Derbyshire). At other sites (eg. Barford, Warwickshire) stratigraphic evidence exists for the partial superimposition of successive buildings.[2] There is also a great range in the sizes of recorded buildings to the extent that it cannot be assumed that all were used for the same activities; sets or assemblages of buildings with complementary usage and meanings must be considered at some sites. Associations between buildings and between buildings and other kinds of structures, their locations, and the arrangement of material culture within them are matters that urgently require detailed consideration.

Context of survival

Five thousand years is a long time for the remains of a building to survive in the ground. As Richard Bradley and others have pointed out, circumstances for preservation must be favourable if the remains of structures are to be found (Bradley 1970a, 264; Gibson 1992). However, rather than focusing on the obvious processes of natural and accelerated attrition that has caused remains to be lost (agriculture, development etc.), a more positive approach, also hinted at by Bradley (1970a, 266), is to examine contexts which promote survival.

The largest preserved sample of early Neolithic land surfaces is under middle and later Neolithic monuments such as barrows and enclosure banks; the largest preserved sample of late Neolithic land surfaces is sealed below early Bronze Age round barrows. Although fragmented, these tiny patches of intact ancient landscapes have yielded a bewildering range of remains. Of the 109 buildings recorded in the Gazetteer, 23 (21%) were located below later monuments.[3] Good examples include Trelystan, Powys, Durrington 68, Wiltshire, Mount Pleasant, Glamorgan, and Kemp Knowe, Humberside.

Recognizing these remains is not always easy, and re-interpretation is a feature of many cases: for example Playden, East Sussex (Bradley 1978; Cleal 1982), Chippenham 5, Cambridgeshire (Gibson 1980), and Durrington 68, Wiltshire (Pollard 1995).

The argument is often advanced that burial monuments overlying buildings and structures are perpetuating the memory of an earlier tradition (see summary in Bradley 1970a, 265–6). It does not necessarily follow, however, that because the later monument is a burial structure the earlier phase has to be closely related to burial too. It is easy to understand the case where a house is demolished or covered to form the burial place of the inhabitant(s) when they die. Such explanations have been advanced for structures at Little Cheney, Dorset (Catherall 1976) and Levens Park, Lancashire (Sturdy 1972), and might well apply to others. Elsewhere, the remains of the building sealed by the later barrow is so offset, and thus usually only partially preserved, that the continuity argument is hard to sustain. Newton, West Glamorgan, is a good case where the remains of a round house, seemingly of LN date with Beaker associations, is partly preserved under the edge of an early Bronze Age cairn containing multiple cists (Savory 1972). The covering by barrows of settlement remains such as pits and hearths without good structural remains, for example Avebury G55, Wiltshire (Smith 1965b), illustrates the rather hit-and-miss nature of this kind of preservation. At Storey's Bar Road, Fengate, a Bronze Age ring-ditch and burial mound probably destroyed the structures of a small LN settlement which themselves had been within a circular ditched enclosure (Pryor 1978, 65–8).[4]

Many other recorded buildings survive only because of exceptional preservation. Carn Brea, Cornwall, Crickley Hill, Gloucestershire, Clegyr Boia, Dyfed, and perhaps other sites too have never been ploughed. The first two aforementioned sites both yielded evidence of between 5 and 10 buildings in the areas excavated. Both are enclosures. The buildings at Etton, Cambridgeshire, are preserved beneath more than 0.5m of clayey alluvium, which here gives the added bonus that the largely negative evidence for buildings in most of the rest of interior is especially important (Pryor *et al*. 1985). The buildings at Gwithian were sealed below layers of blown sand (Megaw 1976).

More usually, where structures have not been protected by cover-deposits of some sort, survival depends on sympathetic land-use and/or the presence of substantial features. This of course biases the survival of buildings in favour of those types with the most robust construction. Contrasts in survival sometimes exist on the same site. At Durrington Walls, Wiltshire, the postholes of the southern circle were well-protected by a deep ploughsoil which had formed in a shallow coomb. When excavated, those relating to Phase 2 of the structure ranged in average depth from 0.42m in Ring A (outer circuit) through to 2.3m in Ring E near the centre of the building. By contrast, the northern circle, ostensibly a similar building although rather smaller in size, lay in an exposed position on higher ground. Here the average depth of the postholes was just 0.12m, and some, perhaps many, had disappeared before the time of excavation (Wainwright and Longworth 1971, 30–41). Something similar can be seen at Windmill Hill, Wiltshire. Here, five postholes, four pits, and a hearth were preserved below the outer bank. The postholes were up to 0.4m deep the pits up to 0.5m deep. By contrast, no postholes were found in the unprotected interior of the enclosure, and the only remaining pits were heavily truncated with only nine surviving to a depth of more than 0.27m.

The point here is that buildings survive in very different states of preservation, from the very favourable conditions present at a few sites through to quite appalling conditions at most. The most difficult, archaeologically, is the middle of this spectrum where tantalizing traces still survive, but not enough to allow the positive identification and recording of individual structures. Some of the sites included in the Gazetteer verge on this state: Totterdown Structure A, and Easton Down, both in Wiltshire, for example.

To this list must be added the many hundreds of sites where postholes and beam-slots have been found but cannot adequately be interpreted. The causewayed enclosure at Staines, Surrey, illustrates this very clearly. Excavations here revealed numerous postholes which can be identified with at least 11 putative structures, but not one set is recognizable as a building (Robertson-Mackay 1987, 38–44). This raises the third type of context to examine, that concerning recovery.

Context of recovery

Neolithic buildings are not easy to identify for two main reasons: scale and distinctiveness. The question of scale is especially important. Many buildings are over 5m across which means that finding them requires a substantial excavation. While large-scale open-area excavation was a feature of continental research and rescue programmes since before the Second World War, in Britain such work did no become common until the later 1960s. Figure 6.2 shows a graph depicting the discovery date of the buildings listed in the Gazetteer. From this it is clear that over 80% of all known Neolithic buildings have been found since 1955, and that about half were discovered in the period 1966–1985. This can be attributed to the results of Rescue archaeology and the widespread use of open-area excavation. The last decade has seen another rise of 10% or so in the number of buildings known, but while the opportunities for discovery have been higher than ever before

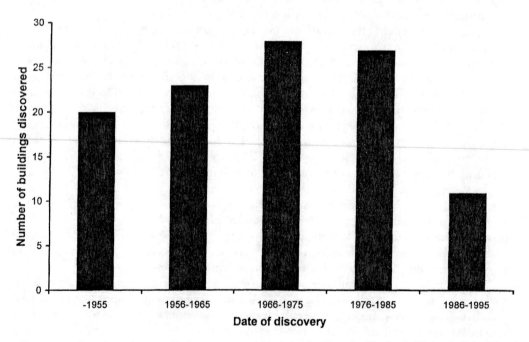

Figure 6.2: Bar chart showing the discovery rate of Neolithic buildings in England, Wales and the Isle of Man

because of the rise in developer funded field evaluations, the opportunities for large-scale investigation have diminished as a high proportion of sites are preserved in situ rather than explored and recorded through excavation.[5]

Alongside these observations should be set a certain amount of negative evidence. There are a number of major open-area excavations which have not yielded much if any evidence for Neolithic buildings. These include the 18.22ha of gravel terrace excavated at Mucking, Essex (Clark 1993), and the rather greater area of first terrace beside the River Coln west of its confluence with the Thames investigated at Claydon Pike, Gloucestershire (Miles and Palmer 1990). Such results emphasize the fact that Neolithic communities did not occupy the whole countryside; there were local as well as regional variations in settlement density.

Recognizing Neolithic buildings even when they have been uncovered is another problem. Later prehistoric structures are generally fairly regular and relatively easy to spot even when only small sections are represented. Musson (1970) has illustrated the difficulties in making sense of posthole scatters and the variety of interpretations that can be placed upon them. Most identified Neolithic buildings are known because their plan is recognizable to the modern western eye. But even well-preserved buildings need not comprise many features, so unless a complete set can be seen the chances of recognition are slim even if occupation levels are present to assist interpretation. Carn Brea, Cornwall, highlights the problem. Here, where preservation was good, the building found in Site A1 was interpreted as a lean-to against the inside face of the enclosure; its plan seems fairly straightforward. The putative buildings in Sites D and J are not nearly so easy to recognize and their ground plans remain obscure (Mercer 1981). This is a problem which bedevils the interpretation of many sites, but is in large measure a product of our own socialization that expects regularity.

EARLY AND MIDDLE NEOLITHIC BUILDINGS

There has never been a comprehensive review of early and middle Neolithic buildings for the area covered by this paper. Piggott (1954) was able to list seven sites with buildings, two of which are now known to be of later date. Now, approximately 37 buildings of this period are known, spread widely across England and Wales, although there are no certain examples in the Isle of Man (Figure 6.3).[6]

Buildings are known in two main situations, within enclosures and singly at apparently unenclosed sites.

At Hembury, Devon, and Etton, Cambridgeshire, buildings have been found just inside enclosure entrances: at Hembury to the right of anyone walking into the enclosure while at both Etton Woodgate and the main Etton enclosure the buildings lay to the left of the entrance. At Carn Brea, Cornwall, the buildings investigated were on terraces against the inner face of the enclosure boundary; other terraces were noted in the central part of the interior but were not excavated (Mercer 1981, fig. 3). At Crickley Hill, Gloucestershire, the buildings lay in the central part of the enclosure on the highest part of the hill, although some pre-enclosure structures (Phase 1A) were found below the outer causewayed bank (Dixon 1988, 75). Interim statements on the work at Crickley Hill

Timothy Darvill

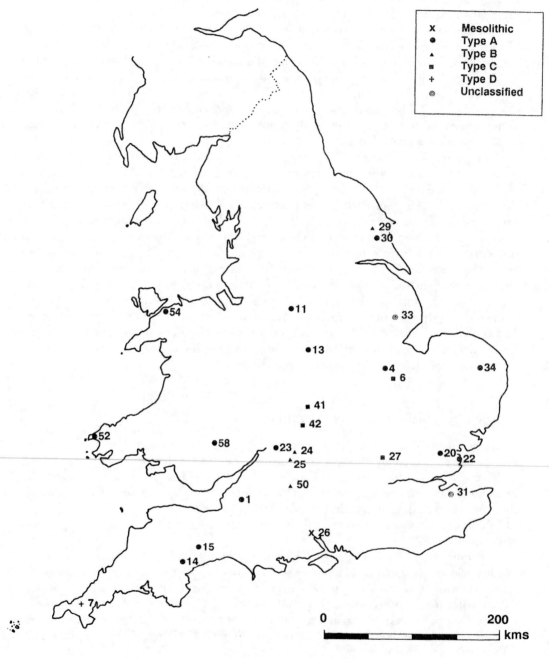

Figure 6.3: Map showing the distribution of recorded EN and MN buildings in England and Wales. The numbers refer to the list of sites set out in Appendix 1.

suggest that one of the buildings on the hilltop, set apart from the others, was used as a shrine, while the others were residences. Stake-defined fences sub-divided the interior of the enclosure and define pathways. It seems that some or all of the houses were aligned with these fences (Dixon 1988, fig. 4.30). Recent investigations in the vicinity of the well-known MN house at Haldon, Devon, suggest that this example too lay within an enclosure, although no details have yet been published (Griffith 1995).

As for the buildings not within enclosures, most are single and set on gravel terraces beside rivers, on hillslopes, or occasionally on hilltops. Most are within sight of a watercourse, or directly overlook one. Excavations generally find little sign of associated features around these structures, as well illustrated by the building at Padholme Road, Fengate (Pryor 1974).

Where it is possible to understand the plan, EN and MN buildings appear to. be mainly rectangular, although some have an almost square footprint. Figures 6.4 and 6.5 show a selection of interpretative plans based upon the excavated evidence.[7] Most are recognized through patterns of postholes, stakeholes, post-trenches, and spreads of occupation material which can be interpreted as the remains of floor levels.

Four main types of building (here nominated A-D) can be recognized archaeologically from the methods of construction employed and the footprint recoverable through excavation; originally, of course, these distinctions may have been less obvious. All seemingly rely heavily on the use of timber and all involve upright posts as major structural elements.

Type A. Post-framed buildings (Figure 6.4)

The first group comprises structures which are represented archaeologically by rectangular arrangements of postholes (some set in slots), although most must originally have included other materials in their construction, for example wattle and daub or, more likely, turf walls. In plan, the postholes suggest a sort of modular framed structure, perhaps aisles supporting purlins and rafters for a ridged roof. The group includes some of the largest EN and MN buildings known, but within the type as a whole size varies considerably. The wall-lines probably follow the outer line of postholes fairly closely. Internal postholes are sometimes present, although in lesser numbers than the outer lines of posts, for additional support and, presumably, for the definition of internal spaces. Doorways are rarely recorded, but can be suspected in either the long or the short sides. Some buildings may have two doorways. Porches may be present (eg. Figure 6.4(1)).

Type B. Ridge-roofed buildings (Figure 6.5 (1–4 & 7))

The ridge-defined buildings, generally rectangular in plan, can be recognized by the presence of a line of postholes supporting major uprights, flanked sometimes by smaller postholes and lengths of beam-slot. These are among the most difficult structures to recognize during excavation as evidence for wall-lines is sparse or non-existant unless the building was constructed in a hollow as at Kemp Knowe, Humberside. Many Type B buildings have probably gone unrecognized in the past and no doubt some structural evidence awaits reinterpretation as this kind of building in due course. Several

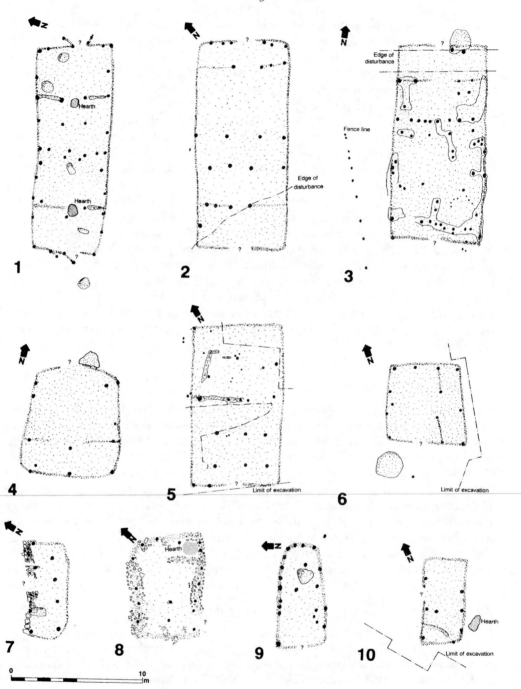

Figure 6.4: Interpretive ground plans of EN Type A and B buildings. (1) Structure A, Lismore Fields, Derbyshire; (2) Llandegai, Gwynedd; (3) Chigborough Farm, Essex; (4) Gwernvale, Powys; (5) Mill Street, Driffield, Humberside; (6) Structure B, Lismore Fields, Derbyshire; (7) Structure 1, Clegyr Boia, Dyfed; (8) Haldon, Devon; (9) Hembury, Devon; (10) Structure 2, Clegyr Boia, Dyfed. (Sources: various)

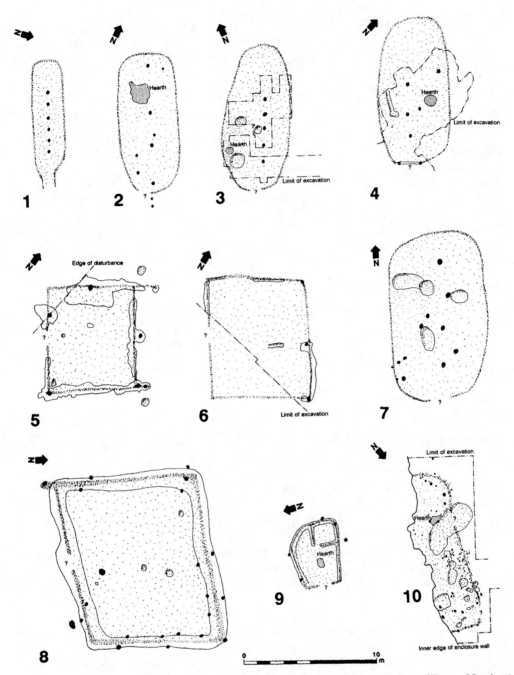

Figure 6.5: Interpretative ground plans of EN Type C and D buildings. (1) Kemp Knowe, Humberside; (2) Hazleton, Gloucestershire; (3) Windmill Hill, Wiltshire; (4) Sale's Lot, Gloucestershire; (5) Fengate, Cambridgeshire; (6) Gorhambury, Hertfordshire; (7) Structure A, Willington, Derbyshire; (8) Site C, Barford, Warwickshire; (9) Site 5, Stretton-on-Fosse, Warwickshire; (10) Carn Brea, Cornwall. (Sources: various)

interpretations of these structures are possible, including a symmetrical superstructure with the ridge at the centre, or an asymmetrical form with the highest part along one side and a flat pitched roof. Porches and elaborated entranceways may be present at some sites.

Type C. Post and wall-slot buildings (Figure 6.5 (5–6 & 8–9))

The third group comprises post and wall-slot structures. These are not very common in England and Wales (cf. Grogan this volume for Ireland), but can be reconstructed rather like North American-style log-cabins with vertically or horizontally set timbers between upright posts supporting a flat pitched roof.[8] These buildings are generally square in plan, and may have some internal postholes and wall-slots for extra support of the roof and to define internal subdivisions. Entrances are very hard to identify. The southeast side of the Fengate house (Figure 6.5(5)) may have had some sort of projecting façade or verandah to judge from the arrangement of postholes.

Type D. Stake-walled buildings (Figure 6.5(10))

The fourth group comprises structures built with a small number of major posts and numerous minor posts or stakes along the wall-lines and defining internal partitions. These are not numerous, and are best represented by the structure in Site A1, Carn Brea, Cornwall, where the building formed a lean-to against the inner face of the enclosure wall.

Size and arrangement

Figure 6.6 provides an analysis of building dimensions, from which it can be seen that all four types occur in a fairly continuous range of sizes, although the post-framed and post and wall-slot buildings tend to be the largest and, on occasion, merit the use of the term "hall" to describe what must have been fairly cavernous interiors. Overall, dimensions range from as little as 2m by 1m (Crickley Hill, Gloucestershire) up to 15m by 5m if it is accepted that Structure A at Lismore Fields, Derbyshire, is a single building (Figure 6.4(1)). Typically, EN and MN buildings are between 4m and 10m long and 3m to 7m wide. The four early fifth millennium BC structures from Bowmans Farm, Hampshire, lie on the periphery of the distribution of sizes.

Construction

Woodworking technology was of a sufficiently high calibre in the later fifth and fourth millennia BC that in constructional terms many of these buildings could have been fairly sophisticated with jointed beams and plank walls. Waterlogged timbers from the Somerset Levels illustrate the potential and the technologies available (Orme and Coles 1983) although no certain house-timbers have been found. Oak has been recognized as charcoal in buildings at Carn Brea, Cornwall (Mercer 1981) and elsewhere, but other woods were probably used too. Stone wall footings are known at Haldon, Devon, and Clegyr Boia,

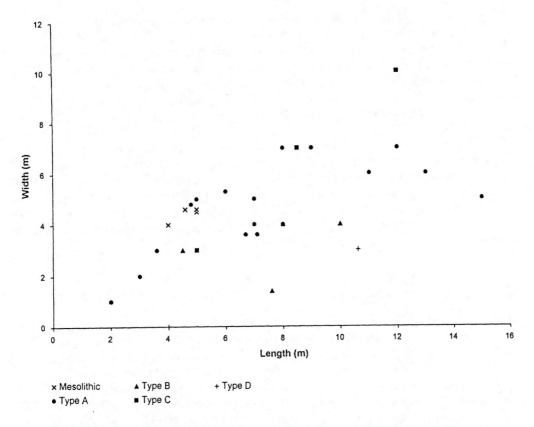

Figure 6.6: Scatter diagram showing the distribution of EN and MN Neolithic building sizes

Dyfed. Refurbishment of timber walls is suggested at Carn Brea, Cornwall, but must have featured strongly in the history of many sites.

A number of buildings are described as being within hollows or on terraces cut into a hillslope. Kemp Knowe, Humberside, is perhaps an extreme case where the structure is partially subterranean, but the buildings at Carn Brea, Cornwall, Driffield, Humberside, and Clegyr Boia, Dyfed, must have produced a similar feeling.[9] Doorways are noticeably hard to define and, where established, show no regularity in placement. Porches and elaborated entrances have already been mentioned.

Internal arrangements, associations and material culture

Internal subdivisions within EN and MN structures are typical, often with one end of the building partitioned off to provide two rooms, one rather larger than the other. This is particularly noticable in Type A buildings. Hearths, which in some cases may be covered ovens or cooking pits, occur within the buildings at several sites, including: Stretton-on-Fosse, Warwickshire, Sale's Lot, Gloucestershire, Haldon, Devon, and Carn Brea Site

A1, Cornwall. At Haldon, Devon, the hearth seems to be in a partitioned-off the corner of the building. Hearths probably lay just outside each of the two buildings at Clegyr Boia, Dyfed. Pits, gullies and shallow "working hollows" are well represented at excavated sites, the latter perhaps the result of erosion to the earthen floor by repeated sweeping and cleaning out. It is possible that some of the pits are dedicatory or symbolically significant. At Windmill Hill, Wiltshire, Pit 47 inside the putative structure contained a complete leaf-shaped arrowhead sealed between the wall of the pit and the clay lining (Smith 1965, 27).

Finds are notably scarce within and around houses, being mainly confined to the fills of associated features. Small amounts of worked flint, stone tools, broken pottery, and occasionally animal bones have been recorded. Floors sometimes comprise an accumulated "occupation soil" as at Carn Brea Site A1, Cornwall, and Mill Street, Driffield, Humberside. Pits and hollows have been found outside the buildings and these often prove more productive in terms of finds. At Hazelton, Gloucestershire, there was a midden *c*.8m north of the building (Saville 1990, 14–21).

LATE NEOLITHIC BUILDINGS

Later Neolithic structures, including those with beaker associations, have been the subject of a number of reviews, some of which focus on houses (McInnes 1971; Simpson 1971; Gibson 1982, 43–48) while others deal with large circular buildings of the period (Musson 1971). Piggott (1954) adopted a fairly conservative view of what represented a LN house and includes discussion of just three examples within the geographical area covered by this study. The large circular structures known at the time at Woodhenge and The Sanctuary were included as ritual buildings. The Gazetteer appended to this paper lists 67 buildings broadly attributable to the LN scattered widely across England, Wales, and with one example in the Isle of Man (Figure 6.7).

Archaeologically, these structures occur in a variety of situations. Some appear singly or in groups of up to seven on unenclosed sites in hilltop, valley side and valley-bottom locations. Examples range from the pair of sub-circular structures high on Trelystan Long Mountain, Powys, at 360m OD to the six structures at Willington, Derbyshire, beside the Eggington Brook on a flood-plain terrace of the River Trent at 40m OD. Others occur singly within small enclosures, walled at Little Cheney, Dorset, and Levens Park, Lancashire; ditched at Playden, East Sussex. Buildings are also known within henges, as for example at Woodhenge, Wiltshire, and within the much larger henge-enclosures as at Durrington Walls, Wiltshire, Mount Pleasant, Dorset, and Marden, Wiltshire. The building or buildings at Easton Down, Wiltshire, might be associated with flint mining. Structure F at Redhill, Hunstanton, Norfolk, lies just inside a large trapezoidal post-built enclosure, *c*.47m across, but of uncertain date (Healy *et al.* 1993, 9).

The range of footprints illustrated by LN buildings is more diverse than for EN and MN times. Rectangular buildings are still represented, but only occasionally and perhaps in the social context of extreme conservatism. More often, plans are trapezoidal, sub-rectangular, or circular in outline. Figures 6.8–6.10 show a selection of interpretative plans, based on excavated sites and information from aerial photography. As with earlier

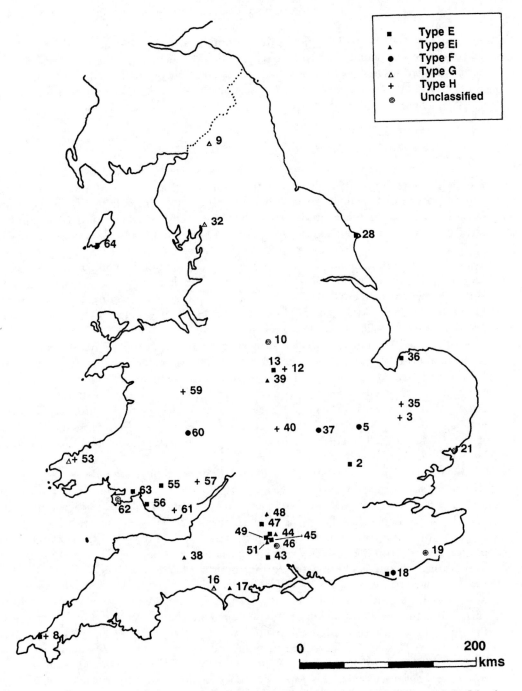

Figure 6.7: Map showing the distribution of recorded LN buildings in England, Wales and the Isle of Man. The numbers refer to the list of sites set out in Appendix 1.

buildings, most are recognized through structural components and spreads of occupation material.

Four main types of LN building (here nominated E-H) can be identified from the archaeological remains uncovered to date, although again these might be misleading in terms of their original use. Two of the types rely heavily on the availability of substantial timbers, the other two are more economical in their use of such resources and involve the greater use of stakes for support.

Type E. LN post-framed buildings (Figure 6.8 and 6.9)

This is the most hetrogeneous group of Neolithic structures and may in due course require revising. Structurally, however, these buildings fall into two kinds: those with a central post-setting, and those without. Sometimes it is difficult to tell the two apart because in isolation the central setting can look like a small version of a complete structure without a central setting. Both sorts are known in a range of shapes and sizes.

Where a central post-setting is present there are usually four or six posts arranged in a square or trapezoidal plan. Good examples include the building below the Durrington 68 round barrow, Wiltshire, and Phase 2 of the Northern Circle at Durrington Walls, Wiltshire, where elements of the wall-lines can be seen. Structure E at Willington, Derbyshire, may be similar, as too, but on a smaller scale, Structure D at Willington and Structure F at Redhill, Hunstanton, Norfolk.

Post-framed structures without substantial central settings generally have more substantial postholes along their wall-lines, although most have some internal uprights. Ronaldsway, Isle of Man, Mount Pleasant, Mid Glamorgan, and Willington Structure B, Derbyshire, are rectangular and sub-rectangular in plan, while the remainder known are circular and sub-circular. The largest, inside the henge enclosure at Marden, Wiltshire, is circular and has a diameter of *c*.10m. At Mount Pleasant, Mid Glamorgan, there were stone wall footings. The entrances to these Type E buildings are sometimes flanked by large postholes suggesting some elaboration.

One rather distinctive variation of the post-framed buildings are the very large circular structures, sometimes called timber circles (Piggott 1940), which range in size from 20m across at The Sanctuary, Wiltshire, to over 50m across at Catholme, Staffordshire (Figure 6.9). These are here called Type Ei buildings. Seven examples are currently known at six sites in southern England, five through excavation and two only through aerial photography.[10] Woodhenge, Wiltshire, and Mount Pleasant Site IV lie within henges (the later within a henge-enclosure, the former beside a henge-enclosure). Two successive examples at Durrington Walls (Southern Circle) lie within a henge-enclosure, while the remaining three are not within henges or henge enclosures.[11] Much controversy has surrounded the way these buildings should be reconstructed (see Musson 1971 for some options). Some authorities prefer an open design (eg. Barratt 1994, 20–24), some a partly open design (Musson 1971), while others, including the excavator of several examples, see them as fully-roofed buildings (Wainwright 1989, 115–161). In the context of the other buildings discussed in this paper Type Ei structures are seen here as large examples of a style of building which is widely reprsented in simpler form in smaller sizes. The matter of the use of these very large buildings is discussed further below.

Type F. LN post and wall-slot buildings (Figure 6.10(1–3))

Examples of this second group of LN buildings, of which only three are certainly known, are defined by a penannular wall-slot in which a series of upright posts and stakes were set to form a sub-circular structure. Two examples, Briar Hill, Northamptonshire, and Little Paxton, Cambridgeshire, are small, being less than 3m across, while the third example at Little Chetney, Dorset, has a maximum diameter of 8.5m. Perhaps not surprisingly, this last-mentioned example has a centrally placed posthole reflecting the need to support such a wide roof-span. The doorways are assumed to coincide with the open part of the pennanular wall-slot.

Type G. LN stone and turf walled buildings (Figure 6.10(4–6))

The third group of LN buildings is confined to the north and west of England and Wales where there are a series of LN structures with low walls of stone, soil, and turf. Some, such as those at Rhos-y-clegyrn, Dyfed, and Cefn Glas, Mid Glamorgan, are rather ephemeral and thus difficult to define. They are probably sub-rectangular in plan, and may have been seasonal structures. More regular, and probably slightly later in date, are the circular examples at Levens Park, Lancaster, and Woodhead, Cumbria. In all cases timber and thatch roofs probably rested on the low surrounding walls. Doorways seem to have been unelaborated where present. There is no evidence for internal subdivision.

Type H. LN stake-walled buildings (Figure 6.11(7–13))

The fourth group of LN buildings are those whose walls were constructed wholly or mainly from stakes, sometimes with larger posts at the doorway or in the interior to help support the roof. The plans of these buildings are sometimes hard to work out, especially when subject to replacement and refurbishment. Most, however, are circular, sub-circular, or oval in plan. Especially clear examples include those at Trelystan Long Mountain, Powys, (and see Gibson this volume), Gwithian Site XV, Cornwall, and Chippenham 5, Cambridgeshire. Less clear is Easton Down, Wiltshire, included here as one building but probably the remains of five or six stake-walled buildings,[12] Swarkeston, Derbyshire, which again probably represents several structures if only the arrangement could be unravelled, and Cefn Cilsanws, Powys. In all cases the stakes used in the construction of these buildings were presumably woven together to form a frame over which skins or some other form of temporary covering was stretched. Although structurally emphemeral, some of these structures must have been impressive buildings. Pairs of larger than usual postholes at Gwithian, Cornwall, and Chippenham 5, Cambridgeshire, suggests that some at least had porches and elaborated entrances.

Size and arrangement

Figure 6.11 provides an analysis of building dimensions. The linearity of the graph along the x=y axis, even with logrithmic scales to accommodate the large number of smaller examples, reflects the fact that the majority of houses of the LN are more or less square

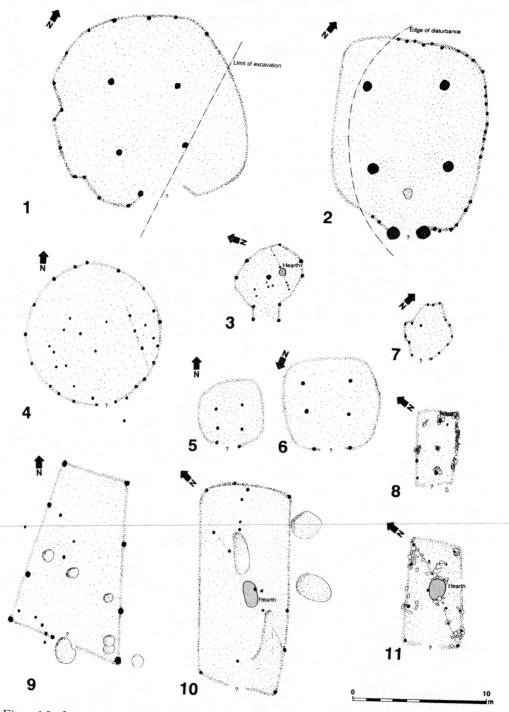

Figure 6.8: Interpretative ground plans of LN Type E buildings. (1) Northern Circle Phase 2, Durrington Walls, Wiltshire; (2) Durrington 68, Wiltshire; (3) Gwithian Phase 1, Cornwall; (4) Marden, Wiltshire; (5) Structure F, Redgate Hill, Norfolk; (6) Structure D, Willington, Derbyshire; (7) Structure 1, Belle Tout, East Sussex; (8) Mount Pleasant, Nottage, Mid Glamorgan; (9) Site E, Willington, Derbyshire; (10) Downton, Wiltshire; (11) Ronaldsway, Castletown, Isle of Man. (Sources: various)

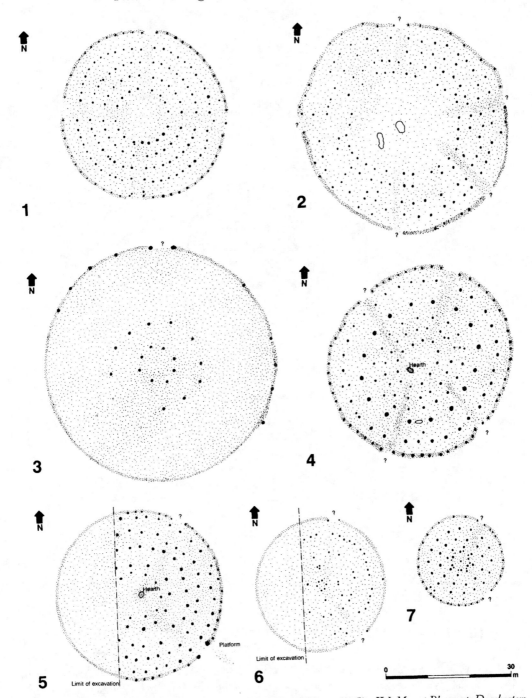

Figure 6.9: Interpretative ground plans of LN Type Ei buildings. (1) Site IV, Mount Pleasant, Dorchester; (2) Catholme, Staffordshire; (3) Norton Fitzwarren, Somerset; (4) Woodhenge, Amesbury, Wiltshire; (5) Southern Circle Phase 2, Durrington Walls, Wiltshire; (6) Southern Circle Phase 1, Durrington Walls, Wiltshire; (7) The Sanctuary, Avebury, Wiltshire. (Sources: various)

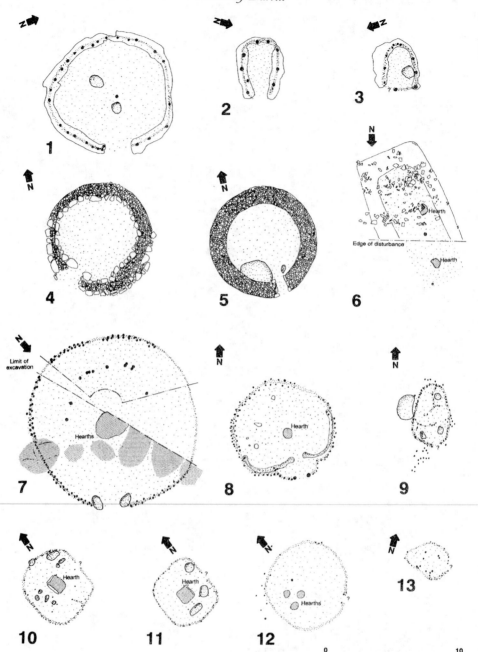

Figure 6.10: Interpretative ground plans of LN Type F, G and H buildings. (1) Little Cheney, Dorset; (2) Briar Hill, Northamptonshire; (3) Little Paxton, Cambridgeshire; (4) Levens Park, Lancashire; (5) Woodhead, Cumbria; (6) Cefn Glas, Rhondda Fach, Mid Glamorgan; (7) Chippenham 5, Cambridgeshire; (8) Phase 2, Gwithian, Cornwall; (9) Site B, Barford, Warwickshire; (10) Structure A, Trelystan, Powys; (11) Structure B, Trelystan, Powys; (12) Hockwold-cwm-Wilton, Norfolk; (13) Cefn Cilsanws, Vaynor, Powys. (Sources: various)

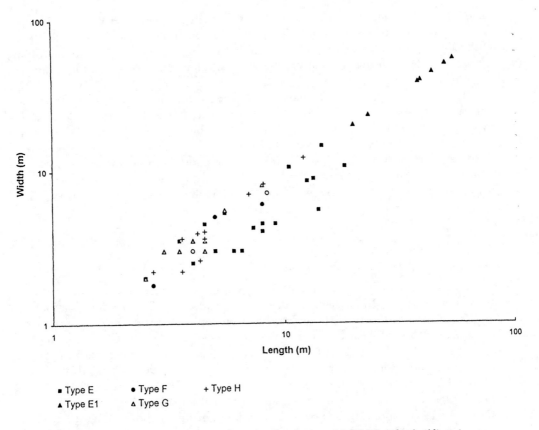

Figure 6.11: Scatter diagram showing the distribution of LN Neolithic building sizes

or round in plan. The large circular post-framed structures of Type Ei stand apart towards the top-right part of the graph as massive examples at one end of a spectrum in which there are also examples of more modest scale. As with the EN and MN buildings, the range of sizes represented is considerable and suggests that not all these buildings fulfilled the same role.

Construction

The range of construction methods appears to be greater in the LN than previously. Less use of wood in some areas has already been noted, and may be related to the dwindling availability of suitable timbers, or perhaps the reluctance on the part of the builders of these structures to spend time felling large trees and working them into usable planks and beams. The sophistication of woodworking techniques available in the LN is suggested by timbers from the Essex coast (Warren *et al.* 1936, plate xxxviiii).

In Wessex massive timbers, mainly oak, were certainly available and widely used for the large Type Ei buildings. Some of the timbers were so large that ramps had to be made to manoeuvre them into the sockets that provide their support. It has been estimated that some 260 tons of timber would be needed to construct Phase 2 of the Southern Circle at Durrington Walls; over 1036m of timber of various diameters for the uprights, and around 1524m for the purlins, ring-beams and rafters (Wainwright and Longworth 1971, 220–1).

Several LN buildings appear to have been terraced into hillslopes as at Woodhead, Cumbria, or constructed in a hollow as at Ronaldsway, Isle of Man. In some ways this kind of construction prefigures later Bronze Age round houses in northern Britain (Burgess 1984) and elsewhere (Musson 1970, 268).

Doorways seem to open in just about every direction from northeast round to the northwest with a slight preference towards the southeast (7 out of 18). The large Type Ei structures have a fairly regular set of alignments within their layout, and usually have one of several entrances opening to the northeast (see below).

Internal arrangements, associations and material culture

Internal subdivisions within LN buildings are common, even within the rather flimsy stake-built structures. Often, slight evidence of partitioning cuts diagonally across the interior with the hearth on the boundary between the two spaces and accessible from both. Where identified, hearths are often situated near the centre of LN buildings. At Trelystan Long Mountain, Powys, the hearths are fairly elaborate, square in plan and reminiscent of those found in Orkadian LN houses (Richards 1990a; Barclay this volume). Some buildings have hearths immediately outside their limits; the Southern Circle (Phase 2) Durrington Walls had both an internal and external hearth.

Little is recorded about the floors of LN buildings, mainly because so many have been lost prior to excavation. At Woodhead, Cumbria, however, flat stones were used to pave the interior, while at Rhos-y-clegyrn, Dyfed, the floors comprised hard-packed stony clay. Wooden floors may be present among the poorly-recorded structures from the Essex coast (Warren *et al.* 1936, plate xxxviii).

Rather common is the presence of pits within buildings, in some cases perhaps used for storage. Finds though are notably scarce, being mainly confined to the fills of associated features. Small amounts of worked flint, stone tools, broken pottery, and occasionally animal bones have been recorded. Pits and hollows have been found outside these buildings and they often prove more productive in terms of finds. At Durrington Walls, Wiltshire, there was a midden immediately outside the Southern Circle to the north. Enclosed within a stake-defined fence, this midden received broken pottery, animal bone, flintwork, and presumably other material too (Wainwright and Longworth 1971, 38–40).

The LN house at Ronaldsway, Isle of Man, differs from others of the period in being associated with a large quantity of finds including parts of at least 50 pottery vessels, worked flint, animal remains, seven stone axeheads, rubbers, and five incised schist plaques. It is difficult to explain the presence of this material, although one possibility is that it became incorporated into the fill of the hollow in which the house was set through having originally been incorporated in external midden material revetted by the walls.

DISCUSSION

> "So Windmill Hill folk did not live exclusively in causewayed camps nor in one type of dwelling, even in southern England." (Childe 1949, 36)

Gordon Childe's comment cited above may have been regarded as precocious when first delivered, yet now far more acceptable. A range of Neolithic building forms can be recognized in England, Wales and the Isle of Man, many of them not dissimilar to structures identified in other parts of the British Isles and northern Europe. It is too early yet to discuss regional trends and distinctive styles of architecture, although doubtless some exist to be defined. Currently, in matching archaeological evidence to the range of basic house-types described here there are three key points that deserve attention.

First is that some buildings are difficult to classify because of their size and irregular form. This should cause no great difficulty as the examination of almost any settlement will reveal the presence of various sheds or outbuildings used for storage, as livestock shelters, and so on, together with a range of props for all sorts of purposes. The latter represent background noise masking the recognition of coherent buildings, the former represent just one dimension to the great range of archaeological evidence that can be called a "building".

Second, is the matter of settlement systems. If the sample of buildings discussed above is at all representative then the proportion of rather ephemeral stake-built structures and stone and turf walled buildings known from the later Neolithic is rather greater than for earlier times. Moreover, they are often found in upland areas, as for example at Trelystan, Powys, and Woodhead, Cumbria. While it is difficult to be sure from archaeological evidence alone, these structures may represent the beginnings of a transhumant settlement system in which communities exploited both upland and lowland at different times of the year. The nature and origin of the finds recovered from Trelystan Long Mountain appear to support such an interpretation (Britnell 1982). In Wales, a transhumant subsistence economy remained active until the mid 18th century AD if not later (Lloyd 1928).

Third is the matter of how Neolithic buildings are interpreted and understood both in the past and the present. Many attempts have been made to impose an essentially ritual use on some structures. In the case of the large timber buildings in henges and henge-enclosures this is understandable (eg. Richards and Thomas 1984), but in cases like Ronaldsway, Mount Pleasant, and Fengate the argument is less clear and is based on flimsy evidence. The supposed ritual deposit under a stone at Ronaldsway, for example, has been radiocarbon dated to AD 620–880 (GU-2695) and is clearly either a later intrusion or has become contaminated. The Fengate pattern is contingent on there being common alignments in the way the wider landscape is structured, a phenomenon that should surely be seen as typical rather than exceptional (see papers by Richards and Hugh-Jones in this volume). As indicated in the introduction to this Chapter, a binary division between ritual and domestic is not helpful in viewing the sort of evidence represented in the British Neolithic. Superficially similar structures may play different roles yet embody common themes in their layout, structure and use. This has been touched upon with reference to Crickley Hill, Gloucestershire, where the excavator has postulated that one building represents a shrine while others were dwellings.

Work by Julian Thomas and Colin Richards on the finds from Durrington Walls provides another example of possible differences in the way buildings within a single site were used. At the northern circle cattle predominate, while at the southern circle pig bones dominate the faunal assemblage. Bone pins are found in the southern circle but not the northern circle, while heavily decorated Grooved Ware is more far more common at the southern circle than the northern circle. Despite sharing certain structural similarities, the distribution of material culture within and between the two buildings is quite different. As a result, it can be suggested that while the massive southern circle may have been a rather special place of some sort, perhaps a communal meeting building for feasting, ceremonial, and social activities, the northern circle was a residential unit. Clearly, the context of construction and use is critical here, as it is with understanding all buildings. Through the kind of analysis that Richards and Thomas present it is possible to begin exploring the way that space was used and given meaning within sites, and this in turn can lead to fresh insights about what people did in the past. However, such analysis takes us beyond the basic recognition the buildings themselves, the focus of this paper, and into a wider world of belief systems, settlements, landscapes, and society to which research attention now needs to turn.

APPENDIX 1 – GAZETTEER OF NEOLITHIC BUILDINGS IN ENGLAND, WALES, AND THE ISLE OF MAN

England

AVON

1. Chew Park, Chew Valley, Stowey Sutton [ST 568593]. Excavations in 1953–55 revealed an irregular group of postholes forming a structure *c.*3.6m by 3m with a doorway opening to the south. Finds include small amounts of pottery, a leaf-shaped arrowhead, flintwork, and a hammerstone. Disturbed by Roman features. Dated by association to MN. Type A. (Rahtz and Greenfield 1977, 26–7)

BEDFORDSHIRE

2. Waulud's Bank, Luton [TL 061246]. Excavations in 1953 revealed traces of a circular or sub-rectangular building outside the enclosure earthwork. Approximately 2.5m by 2.0m, the building was defined by postholes and gullies. Loosely dated to the LN. Type E. (Dyer 1964; Simpson 1971, fig. 27.A; Selkirk 1972)

CAMBRIDGESHIRE

3. Chippenham Barrow 5 [TL 662713]. Excavations in the 1930s revealed a series of stakeholes and domestic debris beneath a Bronze Age round barrow. The stakeholes have been re-interpreted as the remains of a round building *c.*12.1m in diameter with an outer wall of paired stakes supporting a wattle and daub wall. Internal postholes contained freestanding posts supporting the roof. The door opened to the northeast. There were probably internal hearths. Finds included abundant beaker pottery. Dated by association to the LN. Type H. (Leaf 1936; Leaf 1940; Gibson 1980)

4. Etton [TF 138073]. Excavations in 1982–84 revealed traces of several structures at Etton Woodgate and the main Etton causewayed enclosure. One at Etton Woodgate appears to be post-built, rectangular in plan, *c*.7m long by 4m wide, and set only 20m inside the main entrance to the enclosure. Type ?A. A structure at the main Etton enclosure, also rectangular in plan, lay just inside causeway B. Type ?A. Both provisionally dated to the MN by association. A full report on the excavations is in preparation. (Pryor *et al.* 1985; Pryor 1988)

5. Little Paxton [TL 183627]. A watching brief in 1967 revealed traces of a small post-in-slot structure. Sub-rectangular in plan, internally *c*.2.7m by 1.8m, three sides are defined by small postholes and stakeholes in a shallow gulley while the fourth is defined only by a posthole. It is considered that the structure originally had turf walls supported by posts and stakes. The door opened to the northwest. Finds included worked flints and Peterborough style pottery. Loosely dated by association to the LN. Type F. (Rudd 1968)

6. Padholm Road, Fengate, Peterborough [TL 213989]. Excavations in 1971–72 revealed a single square structure of plank and post construction, *c*.8.5m by 7m. Radiocarbon dated to the MN: 3900–3696 BC (GaK-4196) and 3096–2923 BC (GaK-4197). Type C. Finds include plain pottery, a flake of greenstone axe, a flint sickle blade, scrapers, and knives, a stone pounder, and a jet bead. Initially interpreted by the excavator as a house, later reported as a ritual structure. (Pryor 1974; 1991, 51)

CORNWALL

7. Carn Brea (Eastern Summit), Illogan [SW 684408]. Excavations in 1970–73 revealed three fairly certain structures set immediately behind the enclosure wall, and other possible structures within the enclosure. The structure in Site A1 was a post- and stake-built lean-to, *c*.10.6m by 3m, constructed against the rear of the enclosure wall. Some evidence of reconstruction and repair. Possible internal dividing wall. Internal pits towards north end; working hollow and fire pit in the centre, the hollow extending outside the structure to the west. Associated finds include pottery and flintwork in a recognized occupation level. Type D. Structure on Site D was of post- and stake construction but of indeterminate plan. Associated with a spread of occupation debris. Structure on Site J was post- and stake-built as a lean-to against the enclosure wall, of indeterminable plan, associated with a spread of occupation debris and a putatively internal fire-pit. All three structures dated by association to EN-MN: Oak charcoal from posthole F63 in Structure D yielded a radiocarbon date of 3940–3704 BC (BM-825). EN (Mercer 1981)

8. Gwithian [SW 591423]. Excavations in 1960 revealed two successive post-built structures. The first was circular in plan, 4.5m in diameter, with a large central post. A hearth was off-set near the centre. The door, which opened to the southwest, was defined by a porch of more substantial posts. Type E. The second house was constructed over the top of the filled-in postholes of the earlier one. It was larger, 8.1m in diameter, of sub-circular plan, with a double line of stakeholes defining the wall. The door set within a small porch opened to the southwest. Two curving gulleys flanked the entrance on the inside. There was a central hearth. Type H. The house was set within a rectangular palisaded enclosure. Finds included querns, Beaker pottery and animal bones. Dated by association to the LN. (Simpson 1971, 138; Megaw 1976; Gibson 1982, 43–44)

CUMBRIA

9. Woodhead, near Bewcastle [NY 585740]. Excavations in 1939 revealed a circular stone bank 0.7m wide, with an internal diameter of 5.5m, possibly wall footings. The structure had been cut back into the hillslope. There was an entrance *c*.0.8m wide to the southeast defined by larger stones. Inside the structure were two postholes, a shallow depression filled with occupation soil, and a hearthstone immediately inside the entrance. The floor was covered by flattish stones over an irregular layer of clay. Finds included a jet button, a pulley ring of Beaker type, and struck flint from the internal hollow. Very loosely dated by association to the LN. Type G. Similarities to certain styles of ring-cairn have been raised as a question mark over the interpretation as a building. (Hodgson 1939, 162–66; Simpson 1971, 136; Ritchie and MacLaren 1973, 7)

DERBYSHIRE

10. Aleck Low [SK 175595]. Excavations in the late 1970s are reported to have revealed the remains of five rectangular structures below a late Neolithic surface scatter. Finds included Grooved Ware. Tentatively dated to LN. Excavation not published. (Vine 1982, 81)

11. Lismore Fields, Buxton [SK 050731]. Excavations in 1984–86 revealed the remains of up to three structures. Building I, found in 1985, may be two buildings each *c.*7.5m by 5m or one structure 15m by 5m. Type A. Building II, found in 1986, is roughly square in plan, *c.*5m by 5m. Type A. Building I is dated to 3800–3650 BC (pooled means of OxA-2434, OxA-2436, OxA-2437, OxA-2438 and UB-3290) and Building II to 3650–3350 BC (mean of OxA-2435 and UB-3289). MN. Full publication in preparation. (Garton 1986; 1987; 1991; Barnatt 1995)

12. Swarkeston [SK 369295]. Excavations in 1956 revealed two partly overlapping arrangements of postholes and stakeholes preserved beneath a Bronze Age round barrow. One group has been interpreted as the remains of a roughly square-shaped building about 3.6m across with a small rectangular extension to the southeast. A hearth and three pits are associated with the structure. Type H. Finds include Beaker pottery. Loosely dated by association to the LN. (Greenfield 1960; Simpson 1971, 136)

13. Willington [SK 285278]. Excavations in 1970–72 revealed seven groups of postholes that have been interpreted as the remains of buildings. Structure A: possibly a rectangular building represented by a line of three postholes over *c.*8m by 4m with flanking postholes, pits and gullies. Type B. Structure B: sub-rectangular building *c.*8m by 4m defined by postholes. Internal pits. Type E. Structure C: possibly a sub-circular building *c.*3.5m across defined by postholes. Type E. Structure D: trapezoidal building *c.*5m by 3m, defined by postholes. Type E. Structure E; large trapezoidal building *c.*12.5m by 8.5m at the wider end and 5m at the narrow end. Type E. Structure F: possibly a sub-circular structure but rather ill-defined. Structure G: possibly a square or rectangular building but rather ill-defined. Finds from the site included plain Grimston-Lyles Hill pottery, but was dominated by a Grooved Ware and Beaker assemblage. Structure A was associated with EN pottery; Structures B, C and F were associated with LN pottery; Structures D and E contained no associated datable material. There are no radiocarbon dates from the houses themselves but a date of 2888–2510 BC (HAR-957) was obtained from material in a (?post-Neolithic) pit. (Wheeler 1972; 1979; Vine 1982, 80–1)

DEVON

14. Haldon [SX 8786]. Excavations in 1935 revealed the remains of a house of trapezoidal plan *c.*6m long by 5.3m wide at the east end and 4.4m wide at the west. Construction combined a stone wall up to 0.3m wide, perhaps the footings for a timber superstructure, with upright posts. Two postholes on the central axis suggest a pitched roof. There are slight traces of an internal partition. A hearth or fire-pit lay in the southeast corner. Finds include plain pottery, struck flintwork, daub, and at least two spreads of occupation debris. Dated to the MN by association. Type A. Recent evaluations in the area suggest that this site lay within an enclosure. (Willock 1936; 1937; Piggott 1954, 32–6: Griffith 1995)

15. Hembury [ST 113031]. Excavations in 1931 revealed the remains of a post-built timber structure immediately inside the boundary earthwork of a causewayed enclosure near a gateway. Sub-rectangular in plan, 7.1m long by 3.6m wide, its sides were defined by postholes which were closer set at the rather rounded eastern end. The entrance may have been to the west. Finds included plain Hembury style pottery and flintwork. Dated by association to the EN/MN. Type A. (Liddle 1931; Piggott 1954, 24–5)

DORSET

16. Little Cheney [SY 556917]. Excavations in 1974 revealed a sub-circular post-in-slot construction building set within a penannular enclosure bounded by a bank and ditch. The building is approximately 8.4m by 7.1m. The foundation trench was up to 1m wide and a maximum of 0.1m deep. The postholes within it were set at fairly regular intervals of 0.8–0.9m. There was a single roughly central posthole and two internal scoops. The doorway opened to the southeast. Outside the building to the south, but within the enclosure, was a small cairn containing cremated human bone of between 3 and 6 individuals. Finds were few, but included late Neolithic flintwork, Bronze Age urns from the cairn, and some probable Iron Age sherds. Very loosely dated to the LN or EBA. Type G. (Catherall 1976)

17. Mount Pleasant Site IV, Dorchester [SY 710899]. Excavations in 1970–71 revealed the remains of a large post-built structure, circular in plan, with an maximum diameter of 38m. Five concentric rings of posts were present with what appear to be two pairs of opposed entrances opening to the northeast and southwest, and southeast and northwest. Finds included abundant Grooved Ware, flintwork, a chalk ball, antler picks, and animal bones. Dated by association to the LN. Type Ei. The structure was set within a penannular ditched enclosure like a henge, itself within the large henge-enclosure of Mount Pleasant. In the EBA the structure was replaced by a stone setting. (Wainwright 1979)

EAST SUSSEX

18. Belle Tout, Eastbourne [TV 557956]. Excavations in 1968–69 revealed the remains of seven heavily eroded structures; later reconsideration of the site reduced the number of acceptable Neolithic structures to four. Structure 1 was oval in plan, *c.*4m by 2.5m, and of post construction. Door possibly opened to the southeast. Type E. Structure 2 was of post-in-slot construction, roughly rectangular in plan, *c.*8m by 6m overall. Possible internal divisions. Type F. Structure 5 was probably rectangular or slightly oval in plan, *c.*6.5m by 3m, defined by a series of postholes. Type E. Structure 6 was sub-circular in plan, *c.*4.5m in diameter, defined by a setting of postholes. Type E. All the structures were associated with Beaker pottery and flintwork. Structure 1 was cut by the ditch of the enclosure and therefore pre-dated it. All the structures can be loosely dated by association to the LN. (Bradley 1970b; Simpson 1971, 140; Bradley 1982)

19. Playden [TQ 921226]. Excavations in the early 1930s, reinterpreted in 1978 and again in 1982, suggest the possibility of a small rectangular post-in-slot structure sealed beneath a later round barrow. A single radiocarbon determination dates the structure to the LN: 2280–1930 BC (BM-450). (Cheney 1935; McInnes 1971, 123 and 130; Bradley 1978; Cleal 1982)

ESSEX

20. Chigborough Farm, Maldon [TL 8708]. Excavations in ?1990 revealed the remains of a rectangular building. Published as two possibly overlapping buildings, the arrangement of postholes and gulleys is more plausibly interpreted as a single structure *c.*12m by 7m. Type A. (Adkins and Adkins 1991)

21. Stone Point, Walton on Naze [TM 249257]. Observations in the 1930s recorded one or two waterlogged structures in the inter-tidal zone. They appear to be square-shaped buildings of stake and wattle construction. Very loosely associated with MN and LN finds and stratified below layers of peat. (Warren *et al.* 1936, 183 and plate xxxvii)

22. *The Stumble, Goldhanger (Blackwater Site 28) [TL 901072]*. Excavations in the inter-tidal zone in 1986–87 revealed the remains of a post-built structure. Probably of rectangular plan and approximately *c.*7m by 5m, defined by postholes and the distribution of occupation debris. Finds included plain Neolithic pottery and flintwork. Loosely dated to the MN. Type A. Final publication in preparation. (Wilkinson and Murphy 1985, 27–35; 1986, 19–54; 1987, 100–121)

GLOUCESTERSHIRE

23. *Crickley Hill, Coberley [SO 928161]*. Excavations between 1969 and 1993 revealed a number of Neolithic buildings. Three or four small oval posthole structures ranging in size from *c.*2m by 1m up to *c.*3m by 2m were assigned to the earliest pre-enclosure phases of occupation on the hill top, putatively EN. Type ?A. During the use of the two successive phases of the enclosure, rectangular post-built houses stood on the highest part of the hill. A rectangular building constructed of timber and stone stood apart from the other structures and is interpreted as a shrine. Full report on the Neolithic phases in preparation. (Dixon 1988)

24. *Hazleton North, Hazleton [SP 07271889]*. Excavation of a Cotswold-Severn long barrow in 1979–82 revealed traces of a pre-barrow structure and midden. The structure comprised 13 postholes and stakeholes set more or less along a northwest-southeast line over a distance of *c.*10m (building possibly *c.*10m by 4m). A hearth lay on the west side of this alignment. Flints and plain pottery were found in the vicinity of the features which can be associated with a midden 8m to the north. A date of 3780–3690 BC was obtained from the mean of three determinations (OxA-646; OxA-738; OxA-739) on samples derived from the buried soil around the putative house and loosely dates the structure to the EN/MN. Type ?B. (Saville 1990, 14–21)

25. *Sale's Lot, Withington [SP 048157]*. Excavation of a Cotswold-Severn long barrow in 1964–65 revealed traces of a timber structure partly sealed beneath the cairn. Not all the cairn was removed so the complete plan is not known, but available evidence suggests a post-built rectangular structure at least 8m long and 4m wide. There was a hearth in the central area. Finds included leaf-shaped arrowheads, plain pottery, and stone artifacts. Loosely dated by stratigraphic relationships to the EN or MN. Type B. (O'Neil 1966; Darvill 1982, 60–1; Darvill 1987, 52; Darvill and Grinsell 1989, 51–2)

HAMPSHIRE

26. *Bowman's Farm [SU 334170]*. A watching brief in 1990 revealed four structures. Structures 1, 2 and 4 are of sub-rectangular plan, 4m by 4m, 5m by 4.5m, and 5m by 4.5m respectively. Structure 3 is of sub-circular plan, 4.5m by 4.5m internally. Ring-slot and post construction. Doors open to the southeast. Structure 3 has given a radiocarbon date of 4934–4721 BC (OxA-263). Associated finds reported as of Mesolithic character. (Green 1991; Green this volume)

HERTFORDSHIRE

27. *Gorhambury [TL 117079]*. Excavations 1972–1983 revealed part of a beam and post-built structure cut by later features. Probably rectangular in plan, at least 9m long and *c.*7m wide, there was evidence of wattle and daub wall construction and at least one internal partition. Finds included plain pottery and worked flint. A radiocarbon determination on charcoal from the fill of one of the wall-slots gave a date of 3696–3389 BC (HAR-3484). MN. Type C. (Neal *et al.* 1990, 7–9)

HUMBERSIDE

28. Beacon Hill, Bulford, Flamborough [TA 225694]. Excavations in 1963 revealed one end of a roughly oval post-built structure, *c.*4.5m wide but of unknown length. A hearth lay outside. Finds include Beaker pottery. Loosely dated by association to the LN. Type ?E. (Moore 1964; Simpson 1971, 151; Gibson 1982, 44)

29. Kemp Knowe, Cowlam [SE 9665]. Excavations in 1878 revealed a partly subterranean rectangular structure dug into a hillslope, sealed below a later round barrow. The structure was *c.*7.6m by 1.4m with an entrance to the northeast. Along the centre-line was a row of posts. Occupation debris in the hollow included plain pottery and animal bones. Very loosely dated by association to the MN. Type B. (Mortimer 1905, 336–8; Piggott 1935, 124; Piggott 1954, 113)

30. Mill Street, Driffield,[TA 025594]. A field evaluation in 1989 revealed a hollow in the natural chalk surface in which were the remains of a post-built rectangular building *c.*8m by 7m. An area of occupation soil corresponded with the area defined by the postholes. Finds included arrowheads, scrapers, and abundant worked flints. Provisionally dated to the MN. Type A. (Dent no date)

KENT

31. Grovehurst, Sittingbourne [TQ 9066]. Excavations last century revealed floors, perhaps the remains of buildings, but details are vague. One seems to have been of broadly circular plan, *c.*3m across, and definable as a slight hollow in the ground filled with occupation debris. Daub suggests that the walls were of wattle and daub construction. Finds include plain pottery, a flint sickle, scrapers, a leaf-shaped arrowhead, and stone and flint axes. Possibly MN. Type ? (Payne 1880; Jessup 1930, 42–3; Clarke 1982, 25–6)

LANCASHIRE

32. Levens Park [SD 505862]. Excavations in 1968 revealed a circular stone structure *c.*8m in diameter set off-centre within a larger walled enclosure *c.*25m in diameter. The central structure had an entrance to the southwest. Finds included extensive traces of ash and flint-waste. The structure was later used as a burial place, a cairn associated with Beaker burials being heaped over the central structure. Tentatively dated to the LN on stratigraphic grounds. Type G. (Sturdy 1972)

LINCOLNSHIRE

33. Tattershall Thorpe [TF 235608]. Excavations in 1981 and 1984 revealed slight traces of part of a post-in-slot construction structure. Possibly originally square or rectangular in plan, but heavily truncated. Abundant other pits and settlement features in the general area. Finds included plain round-bottomed pottery in Grimston and Mildenhall styles, some Grooved Ware, and worked flint. A radiocarbon determination on charcoal from one of the posts in the beam slot dates this structure to the EN: 4782–4609 BC (HAR-4639). (Chowne *et al.* 1993, 87–88)

NORFOLK

34. Eaton Heath, Norwich [TG 209060]. Excavations in 1971 over an area in excess of 6500 square metres revealed two groups of postholes that might be interpreted as the remains of buildings. The first comprises eight postholes arranged in a roughly trapezoidal plan, *c.*8m by 4m, with a slightly off-centre pit. Not dated, although the trapezoidal form suggests a LN date. Type ?A or E. The smaller group of five postholes defines a rectangular area *c.*3m by 2m. Type ?A. Finds include struck flint and sherds from a plain round-based pottery. Tentatively dated by association to the MN. (Wainwright and Donaldson 1972; Wainwright 1973, 9)

35. Hockwold-cum-Wilton [TL 694875]. Excavations in 1962–66 revealed a circular floor of occupation debris *c.*7m across, around which were stakeholes. Three heaths lay off-centre within the structure. Finds include animal bones, flints, a fragment of stone axe, and Beaker pottery. Dated by association to the LN. Type H. (Bamford 1982, 9–12)

36. Redgate Hill, Hunstanton [TF 678398]. Excavations in 1970–71 revealed a large trapezoidal enclosure within and around which were numerous alignments and the remains of post-built structures. One structure, Structure F, can be assigned to the LN on the basis of associated Grooved Ware. Structure F is of trapezoidal plan *c.*5.5m by 5.3m, and probably associated with nearby pits. Type E. (Healy *et al.* 1993)

NORTHAMPTONSHIRE

37. Briar Hill [SP 736592]. Excavations in 1974–78 revealed a sub-circular structure of post-in-slot construction, *c.*4.5m by 3m internally. Door opened to the east. Finds included Grooved Ware pottery. Loosely dated by association to the LN. Type F. (Bamford 1985, 42–5)

SOMERSET

38. Norton Fitzwarren [ST 193273]. A vertical aerial photograph taken in 1947 shows three concentric rings of cropmarks that can be interpreted as the remains of a post-built timber structure *c.*54m in external diameter. Very loosely dated by structural analogy to the LN. Type Ei. (Ellis 1986)

STAFFORDSHIRE

39. Catholme, Barton-under-Needham [SK 195167]. Aerial photographs show cropmarks suggestive of a large post-built structure *c.*50m in overall diameter. Very loosely dated by structural analogy to the LN. Type Ei. (Harding and Lee 1987, 268–71)

WARWICKSHIRE

40. Barford Site B [SP 289624]. Excavations in 1965–66 revealed an oval-shaped structure *c* 4.3m by 2.6m defined by stakeholes. Possibly some internal partitions. Finds include pottery, a quernstone and some animal bone. Tentatively dated to the LN by association. Type H. Possibly overlain by a second square-shaped structure. (Oswald 1969, 16–19 and fig. 8)

41. Barford Site C [SP 289624]. Excavations in 1965–66 revealed a sub-rectangular structure *c.*12m by 10m of post and slot construction. Finds possibly included Peterborough Ware. MN or LN. Type ?C. Possibly the latest of a series of four successive structures. (Oswald 1969, 19–27 and figs. 10–11; but see also Loveday 1989, 71 for alternative interpretation)

42. Stretton-on-Fosse Site 5 [SP 2238]. Excavations in 1971–76 revealed a sub-rectangular structure *c.*5m by 3m, defined by a wall-slot, incomplete on the west, with occasional postholes. Internal partitions and possible central hearth. Finds included worked flint. Dating uncertain, but probably MN. Type C. (Gardiner *et al.* 1980, 9–13 and fig. 6)

WILTSHIRE

43. Downton [ST 180211]. Excavations in 1955–57 revealed traces of a rectangular building *c.*14m by 5.5m. Central hearth and internal hollows. Possible internal partitions. Finds included pottery and worked flint. Dated by association with Beaker pottery to the LN. Type E. (Rahtz and ApSimon 1962, 123–127 and figs. 9–10)

44. Durrington Walls, Durrington [SU 150437]. Extensive excavations in 1966–68 revealed two substantial buildings, each of two main phases; other similar structures are believed to lie within the unexcavated part of the henge-enclosure. The Northern Circle has two phases, the first of which cannot be satisfactorily interpreted. The second phase is represented by two rings of postholes reconstructable as the structural elements of a circular building about 14.5m in overall diameter perhaps with a central "lantern roof" raised above the general line of the main conical roof. The entrance probably opened to the southwest and was approached along a path edged by posts. Finds included Grooved Ware pottery, flintwork, two antler picks, and small amounts of animal bone. A single radiocarbon determination allows the structure to be dated to the LN: 2580–2148 BC (NPL-240). Type E. The Southern Circle also has two main phases to it, both of Type Ei. Phase 1 comprised five broadly concentric rings of postholes that are considered to be the remains of a series of freestanding timber circles up to 23m in diameter. In phase 2 this was replaced by a series of six concentric rings of postholes which can be reconstructed as the foundations for the structural elements of a large circular building with an external diameter of about 39m. There is an entrance to the southeast marked by large posts on the outer ring. Near the centre of the circle was a small hearth; a second hearth lay on a platform immediately outside the entrance, on the right for anyone entering the building. To the northeast of the building was a midden. Finds included pottery, bone, and flintwork. Three radiocarbon determinations date this building to the LN: 2469–2331 BC (average of BM-395, BM-396 and BM-397). Various interpretations as to the use of this structure have been presented. (Wainwright and Longworth 1971; Musson 1971; Richards and Thomas 1984)

45. Durrington 68 [SU 151433]. Excavations of a ring-ditch south of Woodhenge in 1928 revealed the remains of a post-built structure, although its true character was not recognized until 1995. A roughly trapezoidal setting of six large postholes is surrounded by a possible wall-line defined by smaller postholes delimiting an area *c.*13.3m by 8.8m. There is a possible doorway opening to the southeast defined by two of the large postholes. Finds include Grooved Ware and LN flintwork. Dated by association to the LN. Type E. (Cunnington 1929, 41; Pollard 1995)

46. Easton Down, Winterslow [SU 236356]. Excavations in 1931–2 revealed part of a stake- and beam-built structure putatively of rectangular plan. More plausible as buildings are some of the groups of stakeholes thought by the excavators to form part of one large building. Finds of Windmill Hill pottery and Beaker ware were only loosely associated. Dating is uncertain, probably LN. (Stone 1933, 228–232; Simpson 1971, 135–7; Whittle 1977, 48; Gibson 1982, 44)

47. Marden [SU 090583]. Excavations in 1966–67 revealed the remains of a post-built structure 14m inside the northern entrance of the henge-enclosure. The outer wall was represented by a single ring of posts 10.5m in diameter. Inside was a general scatter of postholes with no particular arrangement except a triangular setting in the centre. A possible hearth-pit lay outside the building to the south. Finds included Grooved Ware pottery and worked flint. Dated by association to the LN. Type E. (Wainwright 1971)

48. The Sanctuary, Overton Hill, Avebury [SU 118679]. Excavations in 1930 revealed the remains of one or more successive post-built circular structures. Various phasing has been suggested for the structure, although recent studies suggest that the six concentric rings of postholes represent a circular timber building with a diameter of 19.8m, of unitary construction. The main entrance was probably to the northeast, although other portals may have existed. Finds include Grooved Ware, Beaker, animal bone, flintwork, and some human bone. The final building was replaced by two concentric rings of upright stones, the outer of which was linked, via the West Kennet Avenue, to Avebury. Type Ei. (Cunnington 1931; Piggott 1940; Musson 1971; Pollard 1992)

49. Totterdown (Structure A), Durrington [SU 150435]. South of Durrington Walls, outside the henge-enclosure, excavations in 1966 revealed a set of pits or postholes that might be the remains of a rectangular building 18.2m by 10.6m. Finds include Grooves Ware pottery, struck flintwork, and animal bones. Dated to the LN by association. Type ?E. (Wainwright and Longworth 1971, 44–7)

50. Windmill Hill, Avebury [SU 987715]. Excavations in 1925–29 revealed the remains of a simple building partly sealed by the outer bank on the southeast side of the enclosure. A line of five postholes over a distance of *c.*4.5m with a hearth to the east. Building possibly *c.*4.5m by 3m. Finds included Windmill Hill style pottery. Tentatively dated to the EN/MN. Type B. (Smith 1965a, 25–7)

51. Woodhenge, Durrington [SU 150434]. Excavations in 1926–7, following the discovery of the site from aerial photography, revealed the remains of a post-built structure of egg-shaped plan, with a series of six concentric rings of postholes with a maximum diameter of 44m. Finds include Grooved Ware, flintwork, some Beaker, human and animal bones, and the burial of a child. Dated by association to the LN. Type Ei. (Cunnington 1929; Piggott 1940; Musson 1971)

Wales

DYFED

52. Clegyr Boia, St David's [SM 737252]. Excavations in 1943 revealed two structures on the top of the hill; one further possible structure had been found previously during excavations in 1902. Structure 1 is rectangular in plan, 6.7m by 3.6m, post-built, but with traces of a low wall on the northwest side. The area of the structure was marked by an occupation level which included broken pottery, charcoal, daub, and animal bones. Probable entrance mid-way along the northwest side. One internal pit. No internal hearth but a fire-pit *c.*3.6m to the west. Type A. Structure 2 was partly sealed below the rampart surrounding the top of the hill (putatively of later prehistoric date and loosely associated with radiocarbon dates of 408–398 BC (BM-1109) and 100 BC – AD 140 (BM-1110)). Probably of sub-circular plan, *c.*4.8m across, post-built, although lacking a coherent structural design. An internal gulley was interpreted by the excavator as a drain. A circular spread of occupation debris included charcoal, pottery and animal bone. An external hearth was believed to lie immediately outside the wall to the southeast side. Possibly an incompletely explored rectangular house. Type ?A. Both dated by association to the EN or MN. (Williams 1953; Barker 1992, 68–9)

53. Rhos-y-clegyrn, St Nicholas [SM 916356]. Excavations in 1962–68 revealed the remains of at least seven structures, not all contemporary, stratified below an activity horizon associated with a pair of standing stones. All the structures were of square or sub-rectangular outline with rounded corners, defined by low stone and clay footings. Structure I was 4.5m by 3.5m; II was 2.5m by 2.0m; III was 3.0m by 3.0m; IV was 3.5m by 3.0m; V was 4.9m by 3.0m; and VII was 4.5m by 3.0m. An eighth building some 15m away from the others comprised a stake-built structure of roughly rectangular plan 1.7m by 2.5m. Finds were mainly flint flakes and dating is uncertain; possibly LN. I-VII, Type G; VIII Type H. (Lewis 1974)

GWYNEDD

54. Llandegai, Bangor [SH 594711]. Excavations in 1966–67 revealed the remains of a post-built structure 13m long by up to 6m wide. Orientation southwest-northeast; possible doorway at the northeast end. Pits and fire-pits were found around about. Finds included Grimston-Lyles Hill style pottery, flintwork, an axe polishing stone, and flakes of Graig Lwyd rock. A single radiocarbon determination dates the structure to the EN/MN: 4240–3824 BC (NPL-223). Type A. (Houlder 1968; Lynch no date)

MID GLAMORGAN

55. Cefn Glas, Rhondda Fach [SN 931025]. Excavations in 1971–74 revealed the remains of a trapezoidal structure, 9.1m long by 4.5m wide, recessed into a slope. Constructed with some posts possibly supporting a ridged roof and stone wall footings. A radiocarbon determination on charcoal in the floor date the structure to the LN: 2875–2579 BC (HAR-744). Type E. (Savory 1980, 227; Clayton and Savory 1990)

56. Mount Pleasant, Nottage [SS 833795]. Excavations in 1951 revealed the remains of a wall- and post-built structure beneath a Bronze Age cairn. The structure, rectangular in plan, *c.*6m by 3m, was built in a shallow natural hollow. A central line of three postholes presumably supported a ridged roof; wall footings up to eight courses high marked the eastern and southern walls. On the north side the footings seem to have supported posts. The west wall was mainly destroyed by the construction of the later cairn. The doorway was to the east, marked by a pair of postholes. Finds included Peterborough style pottery and flintwork from around about. Loosely dated by association to the LN. Type E. (Savory 1952; McInnes 1971, 113; Lane 1986)

POWYS

57. Cefn Cilsanws, Vaynor [SO 025099]. Excavations in 1957 revealed the remains of a small oval stake-built structure *c.* 3.6m long by 2.2m wide partly sealed beneath a Bronze Age cairn. No evidence of a hearth, although abundant charcoal in the area. Finds included some worked flints and Peterborough style pottery from the general vicinity. Loosely dated by association to the LN. Type H. (Webley 1958; Savory 1980, 227–8)

58. Gwernvale, Talgarth [SO 211192]. Excavation of a Cotswold-Severn long barrow in 1977–78 revealed a series of postholes and bedding trenches which can be interpreted as the remains of a rectangular building *c.*11m by 6m. Pottery and struck flints were found in the fills of the features representing the structure. Pits and other cut features lay to the west. An alternative interpretation would see the features as the remains of two structures, one associated with the forecourt of the long barrow, the other, quite separate, pre-dating the barrow by some time. Loosely dated to EN/ MN. Type A. (Britnell and Savory 1984, 139–142 for discussion)

59. Trelystan [SJ 277070]. Excavations in 1979 revealed the remains of two roughly square post- and stake-built structures sealed below a pair of round barrows. Structure A was *c.*4.5m by 4m with a central hearth and eight internal pits. The door probably opened to the east. Structure B was *c.*4.2m by 3.9m with a central hearth and three internal pits, possibly cooking pits. The door opened to the east. Finds included Grooved Ware pottery and flintwork. LN. Structure A is dated by two radiocarbon determinations which average 2585–2468 BC (CAR-275 and CAR-276); Structure B is dated by three determinations which average 2872–2614 BC (CAR-272, CAR-273, and CAR-274). Both Type H. (Britnell 1981; 1982; Gibson this volume)

60. Hindwell Farm, Walton [SO 252613]. Excavations in 1993–94 revealed the remains of a post- and stake-walled structure of circular plan about 5m in diameter sealed below a later mound. There was a central hearth and pit. Peterborough Ware was present. Adjacent was a circular enclosure, 10m in diameter, also defined by postholes. A radiocarbon determination of 2279–2036 BC (CAR-1480) was obtained from charcoal in one of the postholes. LN. Type ?F. (Gibson 1993; 1995; this volume)

SOUTH GLAMORGAN

61. Sant-y-Nyll, St. Brides-Super-Ely [ST 100782]. Excavations in 1958 revealed the remains of three post- and stake-built structures sealed below the remains of a Bronze Age round barrow. Structure

A was of oval plan *c*.4.5m long by 3.6m wide, orientated roughly southwest-northeast. Posts were set at intervals of 1.2m around the edge of the structure and there was at least one central posthole suggesting a longitudinally ridged roof. The area of the structure was marked by a layer of occupation debris. Type H. Structure B partly overlaid A. It too was of oval plan, 2.7m by 2.2m, and on a southwest-northeast axis. The postholes were about 0.6m apart and in places were set in a shallow gully. There were two internal roof supports. Structure C was only partly uncovered but appeared to be the same as Structure B. The date of the structures is not known, although it is suggested that they represent a sequence of use, perhaps A, B, C. Pottery from within and around the structures includes round-based plain Neolithic ware and fragments of Food Vessels and also EBA urns. Finds also included flintwork and animal bone. Possibly LN. (Savory 1959)

WEST GLAMORGAN

62. Cefn Bryn, Gower [SS 490905]. Excavations in 1983–85 revealed evidence of a post- and beam-construction structure sealed beneath a large Bronze Age cairn. Evidence includes a bedding trench 3.2m long, a posthole, a pit and a hearth. These were associated with Peterborough related pottery and worked flints over an area of approximately 35 square metres. Four radiocarbon determinations ranging between 3094–2898 BC (Birm-1237) and 2590–2340 BC (Birm-1236) indicate a LN date. (Ward 1987; Barker 1992, 69)

63. Newton (Mumbles), Colts Hill, Swansea [SS 605887]. Excavations in 1969 revealed part of the outer wall of a circular post-built structure sealed beneath a Bronze Age barrow. Possible central hearth. Loosely associated with Beaker pottery: LN. Type ?E. (Savory 1972, 125–7)

Isle of Man

64. Ronaldsway, Castletown [SC 280680]. Excavations in 1943 revealed a hollow in the natural bedrock surface in which was the remains of a rectangular post-built structure *c*.7.3m by 4.2m. The postholes form a slightly irregular plan, some being in the central area (perhaps a double line), others on the periphery to form walls with stone footings and upright posts. Some evidence for internal partitions. The entrance was probably to either the southeast or southwest. Central hearth. An occupation soil covered the floor and filled the hollow in which the structure lay; perhaps collapse from a surrounding midden. Finds include Ronaldsway style pottery, Grooved Ware, abundant flintwork, some animal bone, stone axes, and decorated stone plaques. Three AMS radiocarbon determinations on residues on pottery from inside the house average at 2558–2466 BC (OxA-5328, OxA-5329 and OxA-5330). Conventional dates of 2030–1640 BC (GU-2694) and AD 620–880 (GU-2695) were obtained from animal bone. LN. Type E. (Bruce *et al.* 1947; Piggott 1954, 346–7; McInnes 1971, 113–5).

Acknowledgements

Grateful thanks are extended to Miles Russell, Liz McCimmon, Stephen Burrow, John Gale, and Nicola King for help in tracking down information about Neolithic buildings in the areas covered by this paper.

Notes

1. Throughout this paper dates BC refer to calendar years Before Christ based on the calibration of radiocarbon ages using the University of Washington Radiocarbon Calibration Programme (Version 2.0. 1987) with calibration data from Pearson and Stuiver (1986). Three broad chronological subdivisions of the period are used: early Neolithic (EN), *c.*4400-3700 BC, middle Neolithic (MN) *c.*3700-3000 BC, and late Neolithic (LN) *c.*3000-2100 BC (see Figure 6.1).

2. This has also been suggested at Site A, Carn Brae, Cornwall, to explain the large number of stakeholes and postholes.

3. This situation is similar to that obtaining in Denmark (see Midgeley 1992, Chapter 7).

4. Case (1964) discusses the possibility raised by Leeds (1936) and Childe (1949, 158) that some of the Oxfordshire ring-ditches were Neolithic settlement sites. He concludes that a small proportion of what are recognized as ring-ditches were probably settlements. The same sharing of form between burial monuments and settlements can be found in areas where ring-ditches are less common (eg. Catherall 1976; Sturdy 1972).

5. Because of the slow speed of publication it is likely that discoveries have been made which are not yet widely known about; thus the figure of 11 buildings found this decade may be artificially low.

6. The recent discovery of a line of postholes at Billown Quarry, Castletown, may betoken the existence of buildings at this site.

7. Figures 6.4, 6.5, 6.8, 6.9 and 6.0 are intended as provisional interpretations of recorded evidence to stimulate future debate and perhaps prompt questions in the minds of excavators dealing with future discoveries. In general, information from better-preserved examples of a given type has been used to guide possible reconstructions of less well preserved examples.

8. In this view there may be similarities with the appearance of portal dolmens in western Britain.

9. Although the idea of "pit-dwellings" in the Neolithic has been well and truly put to rest in respect of the ditches of causewayed enclosures, it may be worth re-considering some of the other reported pit-dwellings to see whether they represent the floor-areas of sunken or terraced buildings.

10. It is notable here that both Woodhenge and The Sanctuary were located through aerial photography prior to excavation.

11. The Sanctuary is loosely associated with Avebury, although not formally until the construction of the stone circle and West Kennet Avenue which probably post-dates the timber building.

12. The linear gulleys at Easton Down may be less important than the patterns of stakeholes around the hollows.

Chapter 7

Mesolithic or later houses at Bowmans Farm, Romsey Extra, Hampshire, England?

Francis J Green

INTRODUCTION

It is the intention of this paper to consider whether the structures recorded on the Bowmans Farm site constitute dwellings or evidence of habitation, and to discuss briefly this structural evidence in relation to the artefactual and environmental assemblages and the dating of the site. It must be stressed that the analysis of the evidence is only at a preliminary stage.

THE SITE

The site is situated on a shallow southern facing slope some 70m from the present course of the river Blackwater, a tributary of the river Test (Figures 7.1 and 7.2). The edge of the flood plain is marked by the field boundary and shallow lynchet to the south of the excavated structures. This boundary also marks the division between the flood plain area of permanent unimproved pasture and the present land-use of the site itself as temporary pasture. The underlying geology consists of Bracklesham beds of the Hampshire basin formations: mixed sand, gravel and clay. The site is situated predominantly on a silty sand B horizon with some pebble and gravel inclusions. Soil surfaces exposed during excavation rapidly broke down. The fine silt or clay component was blown clear of the site as a fine dust leaving a whitish sand behind which wind action blew into hollows on the excavated areas.

The modern vegetation present at the interface between the flood plain and the cultivated areas is diverse and is marked by mature oaks within the hedgerows along the edge of the flood plain. This is associated with extensive areas of bracken and scrub vegetation. The flood plain exhibits a much richer flora, with the river Blackwater fringed by alder, hazel and oak. Bowmans Farm and this western part of the parish of Romsey Extra have, by tradition, been on the edge of the New Forest, but have not been within the forest boundary since at least the early medieval period.

The site at Bowmans Farm was located during a watching brief on the construction of a gas pipeline between Braishfield and Ower in June 1990. British Gas provided sufficient funding for one full time observer for the approx 15km of the pipe's route. This site was only located at a late stage in the pipeline programme, and it was impossible to re-route

Francis J Green

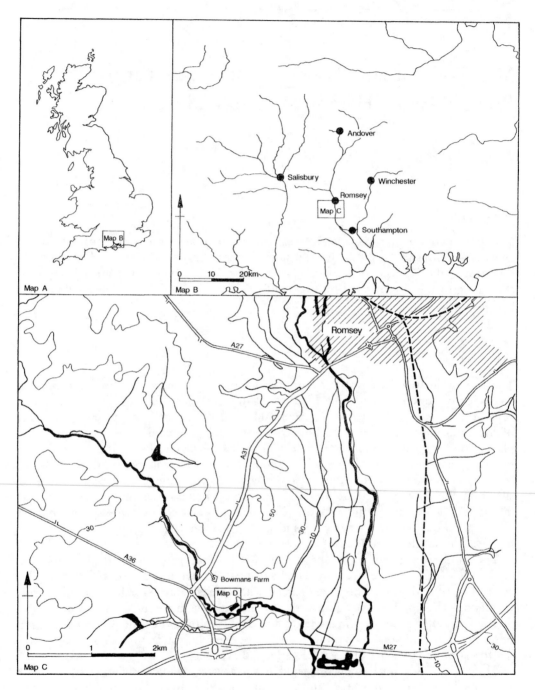

Figure 7.1: Map showing the general location of the Mesolithic / Neolithic site at Bowmans Farm, Hampshire

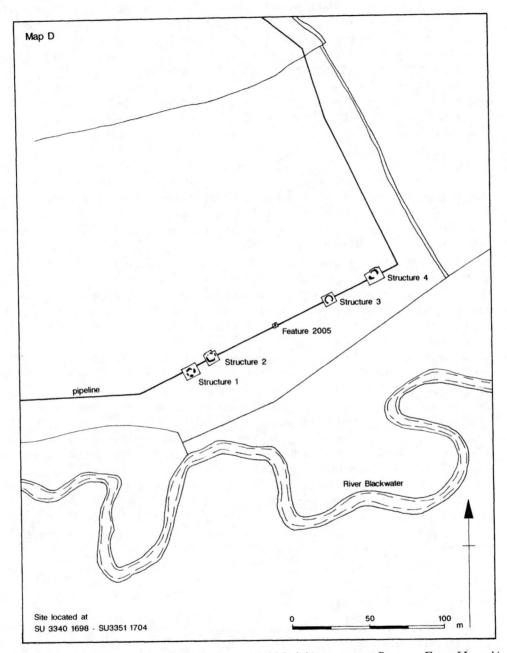

Figure 7.2: Plan showing the arrangement of Mesolithic / Neolithic structures at Bowmans Farm, Hampshire

the pipe to avoid it. Negotiations with British Gas Southern resulted in a total period of 10 days access for full excavation of the structures to take place. The significance of this short time scale will become apparent at a later stage in this discussion.

Whilst it is not the aim of this paper to discuss the philosophical concept of what constitutes a house or dwelling, it has been necessary to define terminology, pending additional dating and other evidence that will result from full post-excavation analysis. Until such time as the post-excavation work is completed the present author has approached the work in a conservative fashion, using terminology such as structures which may possibly be dwellings which we might consider as habitations. The reason for this will become evident.

It is perhaps worth noting that when the structures at Bowmans Farm were first discovered the present author, whilst fully recognizing the significance of the lithic assemblage as Mesolithic, was concerned to establish contemporaneity between the lithics and the structures. This concern resulted from the analysis of structures at Lismore Fields, Derbyshire (Garton 1987; 1991) where there might possibly be two or more quite separate phases of activity present. It could be that the structures were coincidental with the lithic scatters, although this seemed quite improbable, and that the two events might be of widely different date ranges. Thus from the outset of the project it was fundamental to the retrieval programme to obtain the maximum amount of information. Running through the present author's mind at that time was the distinct possibility that the structures as observed prior to excavation, consisting of slots characterized by high concentrations of wood charcoal, might just possibly be the remains of charcoal burners' huts or even annular shallow ditches left from the charcoal burning clamps. The manufacture of charcoal by semi-migrant workers in this part of Hampshire was widespread even as late as the early 20th century.

The structures at Bowmans Farm were preserved beneath approximately 0.3m of plough soil. The recent history of the site's utilization as temporary pasture ploughed infrequently became apparent during excavation. Deep scars were visible cutting across the structures and filled with partially decayed vegetation. The closeness to the present field surface and the shallow nature of the surviving structural evidence clearly demonstrates the vulnerability of such evidence within intensively farmed landscapes in lowland Britain. It is also clear that if intensive cereal cultivation had occurred, as on adjacent fields, in the period after the Second World War, then it is doubtful if the site at Bowmans Farm would have yielded anything other than a thin lithic scatter associated with high concentrations of comminuted charcoal.

EXCAVATION TECHNIQUES

Before discussing the structural evidence it is necessary to mention briefly the excavation techniques and sampling programme imposed. Given the limited excavation time it was determined by discussion between the lithic consultant Francis Wenban-Smith, the archaeological computing consultant Kris Lockyear, the site manager Dave Bonner and the present author acting as project director and archaeobotanist, that the site would be excavated stratigraphically but within 0.25m by 0.25m boxes within features and 0.5m by

0.5m boxes elsewhere and that the layers and observable horizons would themselves be excavated stratigraphically within the grid and be further subdivided into 50mm spits.

Since the surface of the site had been damaged by site vehicles to a depth of some 0.1m, and due to pressure of time, the surfaces of the structures were cleaned and finds considered as unstratified. By excavating within the grid system and removing all soil within each box it was possible for the entire soil contents to be bagged and removed for off site processing at a later stage. All large easily observable artefacts located during excavation were placed in marked self seal bags but stored within the larger sample bags, to be retrieved when the soil was processed. This was undertaken to minimize damage which might possibly preclude edge ware analysis of the lithic material.

It was considered that the method of excavation and recording, and the provenancing of finds, would be somewhat cruder than excavation in an ideal situation would allow, but that the potential loss of information would be minimal and that detailed spatial plotting and study of all the finds would still be possible. Theoretically, 100% of the finds contained within the site would ultimately be retrievable and that a fully detailed integrated computer analysis would be possible, which would be essential for determining the precise relationship between the structures, the lithics and the environmental data. The methodology to be applied had been developed by Green and Lockyear (1992). It was from this earlier work that specific lessons had been learned and allowed for the rapid formulation of strategy to be applied to the Bowmans Farm excavation. From the outset it was decided by the present author that this detailed analysis would lead to a full site history. The sampling strategy would allow for the recovery of all small and possibly intrusive items and this could provide important data about site utilization and site formation processes. This was particularly relevant bearing in mind the very shallow nature of the site and the fact that during the preliminary site cleaning it was observed that rodent or mole activity had caused considerable damage to the site in antiquity, with the potential mixing of materials. Due to the limited excavation period it was virtually impossible to isolate such burrows and deal with their contents separately. No modern materials were observed in these burrows and their contents were compressed. Invariably, they were only recognized where B horizon material had been redeposited within darker more humic archaeological fills and/or where humic fills extended into the B horizon.

DATING

From the outset, examination of the lithic assemblage has clearly indicated that this material is of late Mesolithic date. The first AMS determination (OxA-263) obtained in November 1991 gave an uncalibrated date of 5910±90 BP, *c.*4800–4900 BC. This was well within the expected date range for the site. It was obtained from a piece of oak of no greater than 20 years growth according to the wood anatomist (Gale pers. comm.). This piece of round wood was typical of the material filling the pennanular slot of Structure 3 (See Figure 7.3). This led to the conclusion that these structures were indeed of late Mesolithic date. Partial funding for post-excavation work on this site was obtained from British Gas in September 1991. As a consequence, processing the excavated soil was only completed in early 1992. After about one-third of the environmental soil samples

Table 7.1: AMS determinations on material from Bowmans Farm, Romsey Extra, Hampshire

Structure	Laboratory Number	Material	Uncalibrated date bp	Calibrated date*
4	OxA-4145	Charred *Hordeum vulgare var. nudem*	675±80	AD 1266 (1284) 1391
4	OxA-4146	Charred Hazel-nut fragment	415±65	AD 1431 (1450) 1510
3	OxA-4147	Charred Oak cupule/acorn	400±65	AD 1435 (1460) 1620
3	OxA-4148	*Triticum dicoccum* (Grain)	2160±70	366 (196) 109 BC

* Computed using University of Washington Radiocarbon Calibration Programme (Version 2.0. 1987) with calibration data from Stuever and Pearson (1986, 805-838), ranges expressed at 1 sigma

had been processed a single charred cereal grain was retrieved. To date some six charred cereal grains have been located from 2000 sample units. A sequence of four AMS determinations was financed by SERC, to try to establish if the plant macrofossils were contemporary with the structures. The calibrated dates set out in Table 7.1 are from material which on other criteria were considered by the present author to be intrusive or most probably intrusive, clearly relate to later periods of activity on the site.

When the processing of the soil was finally completed, some 25 small and highly abraided fragments of fired clay and pottery had been recovered. The bulk of the pottery is prehistoric, possibly representative of the late Bronze Age, late Iron Age and Romano-British periods. Only two small fragments of medieval pottery and one small (medieval/post medieval) tile fragment were found.

Whilst this detailed discussion of dating might not seem relevant to a discussion of the structures the two cannot be divorced. It is now clear that the structures at Bowmans farm are most likely to be of late Mesolithic date but that more recent land-use activities have resulted in small fragments of later materials becoming incorporated into archaeologically earlier contexts. This is not perceived as a specific problem; it is hoped that a further programme of conventional radiocarbon dates will indicate from which periods the different botanical and other components originate. Plotting this information in conjunction with ceramic and other intrusive evidence may itself reveal spatial patterning and provide invaluable information not only about the site's more recent history but also about post-Mesolithic depositional site formation processes. It is a salutary lesson that if the site had been excavated in a traditional way with a dry sieving sampling programme and not 100% processing, then these very small quantities of intrusive material might have been missed. It is probably true that the charred cereal grains and some other intrusive botanical components would not have been found and that fundamental questions about the site's Mesolithic integrity might never have been asked. In the author's opinion this is a major justification for completion of the work on this site, for which future funding has yet to be secured from British Gas.

Only a view of Structure 3 has been published to date (Green 1991). This structure, as can be seen from Figure 7.3, is more circular in plan than the other structures. Structures 1, 2 and 4 can be described as sub-rectangular being perhaps more circular on

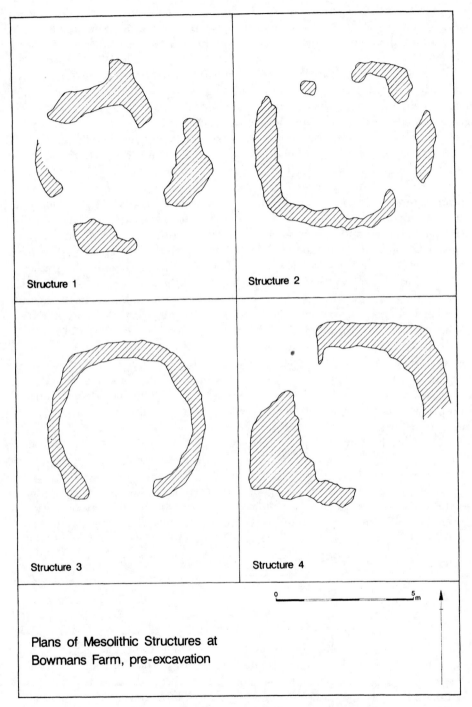

Structure 1

Structure 2

Structure 3

Structure 4

0   5 m

Plans of Mesolithic Structures at Bowmans Farm, pre-excavation

Figure 7.3: Pre-excavation ground plans of Mesolithic / Neolithic structures at Bowmans Farm, Hampshire

their inner faces than externally. Bearing in mind the shallowness of the site, the potential loss of both internal floor surfaces and the upper part of the slots due to ploughing, then the shape of the slots on the original Mesolithic land surface might have been quite different.

Before discussing the nature of the structures that might have existed on this site, it is first of all necessary to examine the function of the slots and to try and understand how and why they may have become filled with the charred material which to date has been assumed to originate from their superstructures.

The charred material in the slots showed no specific patterning or orientation. In the normal course of events when buildings are entirely destroyed by fire they collapse and continue to burn, with decreased levels of oxygen present, the material becomes charred rather than being entirely turned to ash. It is not uncommon to find on the surface beneath a modern domestic bonfire unburnt wood and paper. Thus quite large fires, even where people do not intervene to extinguish them, can result in large quantities of partially combusted and uncombusted materials. In other cases fires may continue to burn slowly consuming all material and resulting in ash and a deep area of scorched soil beneath the fire. The latter clearly was not the case with the Bowmans Farm structures. No deep scorched soil was visible, and while most of this could have been distributed by later ploughing it is unlikely to have been entirely removed. The large quantities of charred material present argue against this. The evidence suggests that the charred material only entered the slots by one of the following mechanisms. The slots were either empty at the time of the destruction of the structures, or the charred material does not reflect structural evidence at all, but relates to some other activity pre-dating the structures which has been incorporated into the slots during construction rather than during their destruction. With this in mind it is perhaps unwise until further detailed analysis has taken place to jump to the conclusion that the charred evidence must represent burnt structural material.

Thus it is perhaps more likely that the charred round wood reflects site clearance involving cutting and burning of material prior to the creation of a settlement; that the slots were excavated shortly afterwards and the charred material inadvertently incorporated as a part of the slots' filling. This could have occurred even during the dismantling of the structures. Detailed wood analysis will no doubt show the range of species involved and might indicate if there is any patterning within the slot fills which might reflect structural evidence. Of course, the absence of a clear indication of timber selection would not itself prove the argument but would assist a clearer resolution and limit the possibilities.

THE STRUCTURES

At this preliminary stage in the analysis of the evidence from Bowmans Farm, and without the detailed specialist reports on the lithics, wood and plant macrofossils it is not possible to make more than some tentative conclusions. The evidence as presented and argued here suggests that the slots containing charred round wood associated with late Mesolithic flint work may simply be bedding trenches for the covering of a shelter. The principles involved may not be very different from those associated with modern polythene tunnels used for temporary horticultural purposes, frequently adapted to archaeological use. Such structures usually require a bedding trench in which the roof covering can be placed and upon which soil is placed onto the ends of the roof covering in the slot to hold it down. The roof covering, if a continuous membrane and fully stretched, needs no specific attachment to the light framework over which it is stretched, with the possible exception of some form of binding around the door or entrance. The framework for such a structure could be very light weight and the supporting structure need not itself be bedded into the ground, but could simply sit on the ground surface.

As to the shape of the structures above ground level, the evidence from Bowmans Farm is perhaps not quite so helpful. The presence of Structure 3 which is virtually circular suggests that in this particular case the building might have consisted of something akin to a north American Indian tepee, or may even have been domed shape such as frequently recorded in many ethnographic examples, and used as the basis of reconstruction, like the shape at Mount Sandel (Woodman 1985). It may even have had a cylindrical base and a domed roof.

Real problems arise in interpreting the other structures from this site. Structures 1,2 and 4 give an impression from the evidence that they were externally more sub-rectangular than circular. The variation in ground plans therefore may suggest structures of different periods, though this is improbable given the similarity of artefact assemblages and the charred content of the ring trenches. It is possible that these structures may have had different functions and thus their form may have varied. It is possible that the results of the lithic analysis may indicate that Structures 1, 2 and 4 may have had a different function to Structure 3. It is possible that these externally sub-rectangular structures may have consisted of two layers of covering, providing an inner circular structure and a slightly larger external sub-rectangular one with an air space between. This would have certainly provided better insulation value than a single covering, with possible additional storage between the two coverings. These are merely preliminary suggestions. After all, pigs and other animals frequently burrow around structures leaving intermittent trenches or slots. This might account for the evidence from Structures 1, 2, and 4, but the evidence from Structure 3 is perhaps once again too neat to be accommodated by such an argument.

These ideas are quite different from those originally proposed by the present author (Green 1991). Then it was suggested that the charred wood and other materials resulted from structures that had been consumed by fire. Without further evidence it is difficult to decide between these and other possibilities.

CONCLUSION

It is to be hoped that British Gas will be able to find the necessary funding which will allow the post-excavation work on this very important site to be completed and that in due course other agencies will provide funding to allow further excavation and investigation to take place so that the structures can properly be viewed within their landscape, since other structural evidence might also be preserved on the site, which could be excavated without the pressure imposed by the salvage nature of the excavation in 1990. There is always the possibility that anaerobically preserved deposits, or at the very least deposits containing faunal remains might be located within the adjacent flood plain of the River Test. The Bowmans Farm site may have more to tell us about late Mesolithic structures and thus developments prior to the Neolithic.

Acknowledgements

The author would like to acknowledge Clive Gamble, Rupert Housley, Gordon Hillman, Jon Hather and staff of English Heritage, in particular Steve Trow and Andy Payne, without whose assistance much of the information discussed here would not have been available. Particular thanks are due to Arthur ApSimon for all his assistance during the various phases of this project and for his comments on an early draft of the text. The author accepts sole responsibility for all errors and omissions.

Chapter 8

The Ballygalley houses, Co. Antrim, Ireland

Derek Simpson
With a note on the reconstruction by Cia McConway

INTRODUCTION

The Neolithic settlement site at Ballygalley was located by field walking in August 1989, its existence indicated by a surface scatter of flint and pottery spread over two fields and covering several acres. The material lay between 10m and 20m ASL some 500m inland from Ballygalley Bay which is 7km north of Larne, Co. Antrim (D/373405). The initial exposure was the result of topsoil stripping in advance of a housing development and in view of this threat a small scale exploratory excavation was undertaken on behalf of the Historic Monuments and Buildings Branch, DoE (NI) in September 1989. The preliminary results were encouraging and this has led to four further seasons of excavation on behalf of the Branch.

The site(s) divide naturally into two areas separated by a culvert and were designated Site 1 in the north field and Site 2 in the south (Figure 8.1). The main thrust of the excavations was on Site 1 where the major concentration of surface finds occurred at the highest point in the field. It was in this area that the first house was located in 1991 and its excavation completed in the following season. In October 1993 part of what may be a second house was located on Site 2. A preliminary report was published on the first season's work (Simpson *et al.* 1990) and the work to date was summarized in Simpson 1993. A general account of the settlement will appear elsewhere (Simpson in press) and the present paper will concentrate on the two houses, their structure and associated material.

HOUSE 1, SITE 1

The complete plan of this building was recovered. It consisted of a principal rectangular room defined by beam slots with paired internal postholes, orientated northwest to southeast and measuring 8m long by 4m wide (Figures 8.2 and 8.3). The precise position of the entrance is uncertain but it may have existed at the southwest and be marked by a large posthole at the terminal of the bedding trench at this point although this area of the house had been considerably truncated by machine clearance by the developers. To the northeast was an annexe represented by a shallower beam slot, apsidal in plan and 4m long. This could only be traced with any certainty on the north side, the southern length may have been partially obliterated by the subsequent digging of an irregular pit and

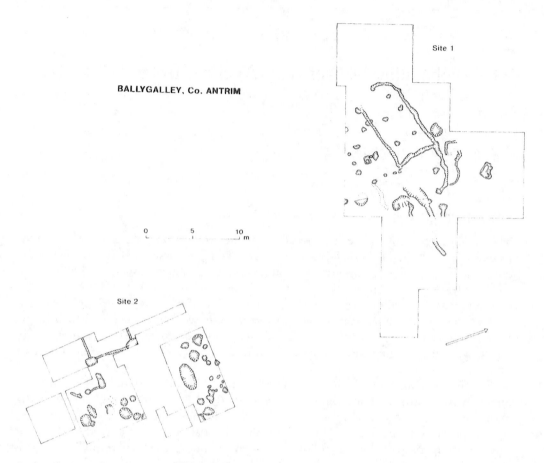

BALLYGALLEY, Co. ANTRIM

Site 1

Site 2

0　　　5　　　10
　　　　　　　　m

Figure 8.1: General plan of the excavated area at Ballygalley, Ireland

gulley; within this area was found an inverted saddle quern. Four stakeholes in an irregular row may be part of the internal fittings of the house.

The house was not the first structure on the site. The beam slots both on the north and south sides had cut through existing pits and the internal postholes had similarly superseded pits and an irregular sub-rectangular structure defined by trench slots. Many other slots and gulleys lay outside the area of the house although it could not be demonstrated stratigraphically whether these were contemporary with or pre- or post-dated the building. Where these produced artefacts and particularly pottery this belonged to the "western" tradition in the Lyles Hill and Ballymarlagh styles (Case 1961).

No postpipes or ghosts of horizontal timbers or indeed the carbonized remains of the timbers themselves, as recorded in other Irish Neolithic houses, survived and it would appear that the building had been systematically dismantled and the beam slots packed with water worn stairs, presumably beach derived and large quantities (78kg) of flint nodules.

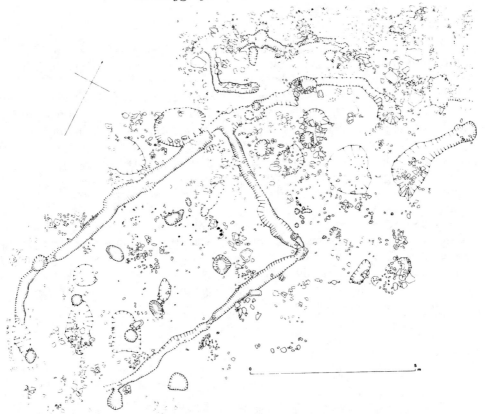

Figure 8.3: House 1 at Ballygalley under excavation. View from the southwest

Figure 8.2: Ground plan of House 1 at Ballygalley

POSSIBLE RECONSTRUCTION OF HOUSE 1 *By Cia McConway*

The basic ground plan of House 1 consists of a sub-rectangular bedding trench, continuous but for a break on the northeast corner, where a shorter curved bedding trench runs off eastwards where a terminal posthole indicates the entrance.

Unlike the house excavated at Tankardstown, Co. Limerick, which had one median line of postholes (Gowen 1988b), Ballygalley House 1 has six substantial postholes divided neatly into two rows and located equidistant within the ground plan to form a three aisled effect. A similar plan has been found at Lough Gur House 1, Co. Limerick (O'Riordain 1954) and at Ballyglass, Co. Mayo (O'Nuaillain 1972a).

The absence of any external features associated with the house, indicates that the house must have been stabilized by the interior postholes and those postholes within the bedding trenches.

The simplest, though by no means a primitive method of creating a stable superstructure, given the above ground plan is to use a trestle option, whereby an internal rectangular framework is built up using tiebeams – transversely placed horizontal beams which connect two paired postholes, and long ties (Wallace 1992). While this forms a strong framework, it does not require a knowledge of joinery, as all the joints could be lashed together with rope (Figure 8.4).

Figure 8.4: Isometric reconstruction of House 1, Ballygalley. (Drawn by Cia McConway)

It has been assumed that roughly split planks were used for walls, evidence for *in situ* timber stumps have been found at Ballynagilly (ApSimon 1969) and also at Tankardstown (Gowen 1988b). Gaps between planks would probably have been filled with a mixture of clay, dung and straw (Grogan 1992). Stones and boulders were used in the bedding trenches for packing.

The pronounced curve in the bedding trench along the northwest area, its total absence at the southwest (the entrance) and the absence of corner postholes, suggests that the roof was hipped. This would, in effect, produce a pyramidal-like shaped roof. The weight of such a roof would be supported by both the internal framework and the sturdy split plank walls with their random posts.

Rafters, regularly spaced along the long ties, would support the light horizontal batons on which the thatch roof would be placed.

A roof pitch of 40 degrees has been used. This angle has come about by the relative difference between the depths of the internal postholes and that of the bedding trenches. Unfortunately, these features have all been truncated by an unknown depth, due to pre-excavation topsoil stripping by the developer. We must assume therefore, that the walls would have stood in the region of 2m, with 3m high internal posts, allowing a feeling of space within an otherwise cramped interior.

The annexe to the east of the house has not been roofed due to the absence of supporting postholes in that area where the bedding trench does not exist. However, at the time of going to press, several charcoal flecked spreads were uncovered in this area. Should these develop into postholes, then the above reconstruction will perhaps have to be modified to accommodate the new information.

FINDS FROM HOUSE 1

All the soil component of the bedding trench fill, consisting of some 850kg of material was removed for wet sieving and floatation in the laboratory. The flint material recovered from this work and from the excavation of the feature is summarized in Table 8.1.

In addition there were two cores, twelve flakes and five fragments of pitchstone. Preliminary XRF analysis of this material would suggest a source at Corrygills on the island of Arran in the Firth of Clyde (Thorpe and Thorpe 1984; Slater 1991).

Flotation also produced a considerable quantity of carbonized grain with what appear to be an unusually high percentage of Einkorn (*Tricitum Monococcum*) (Figure 8.5). The cereals from the house slot are more fragmentary than samples from elsewhere on the

Table 8.1: Flint material from the beam slot in House 1, Ballygalley, Co. Antrim, Ireland

Unworked burnt flint (weight: kg)	Flint flakes (count)	Flint flakes (weight: kg)	Debitage (count)	Debitage (weight: gms)	Burnt flint (weight: gms)	Cores (count)
78	219	3.2	95	72	325	33

Figure 8.5: Carbonized grain from beam slot, House 1, Ballygalley

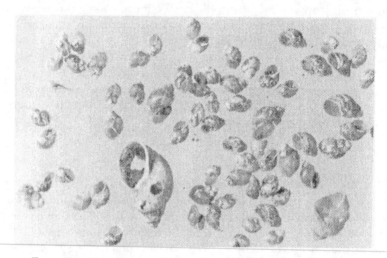

Figure 8.6: Liver fluke snails from beam slot, House 1, Ballygalley

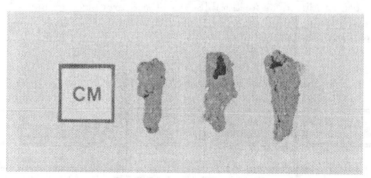

Figure 8.7: Caddis fly larval cases from House 1, Ballygalley

site and may be the result of trampling and brushing of floor waste. No processing waste was recovered from the house in contrast to finds elsewhere, notably from pits on Site 2, which included spikelets and chaff. The only evidence for animal husbandry again came from Site 2 in the form of adult cattle teeth, perhaps representing a butchering area.

Also from the beamslots were considerable numbers of juvenile and a few adult specimens of the liver fluke snail (*Lymnaea Truncatula*) (Figure 8.6) and two caddis fly cases of the family *Limnephilidae* of the genus Stenophylax or Limnephilus, the former indicating wet pasture and the latter standing water (Figure 8.7). Other species of caddis fly larval cases are represented elsewhere on the site and indicate generally wet conditions. It is not clear, however, whether these wet conditions are an aspect of the initial phase of construction or are to be related to the period of abandonment and infilling. The latter would appear to be more plausible and may be the reason for the abandonment of the structure and the raising of the surface by the building of a stone and flint "platform" which covered both the house and the other pits and gulleys dug into the subsoil.

Two radiocarbon dates have so far been obtained from wood charcoal in the bedding trenches. The first is a bulk sample from sieving many kilos of soil gave a date of 4226–3829 BC (UB-3471) and a second of 3776–3386 BC (UB-3491) from a more concentrated sample. The latter date would appear to be more acceptable.

HOUSE 2, SITE 2

A part of what may be a second house was recovered in October 1993 (Figure 8.1). It shows the same northeast to southwest orientation as House 1. Only the southwest end has so far been exposed for a length of 2m. The second building would appear to be more strictly rectangular in plan with two large posts at the eastern gable corners for support. The length of the second house is at present unknown but its internal dimensions are 5m in breadth, slightly greater than House 1. Nothing more can be said of this house, if such it is, at present as there are several layers of redeposited material, overlying, underlying and cut by the house slot. Pre-house features may be represented by stakeholes.

DISCUSSION

Other Irish Neolithic houses are surveyed by Grogan in this volume and detailed discussion would be inappropriate here. Two points should, however, be stressed. First, the high incidence of raw materials from non-local sources. Clearly flint, whether beach derived or mined on Ballygalley Hill 1.3km to the northeast (Collins 1978) forms the principal source of inorganic raw material with over 2000 artefacts, primarily scrapers, axes and projectile points, tens of thousands of struck flakes (Figure 8.8) and over 800 cores, mostly polyhedral. More distant locations are associated with 150 axes, roughouts and flakes of porcellanite from Tievebulliagh and Rathlin Island (Jope 1952; Sheridan 1986; Mallory 1990; Sheridan *et al.* 1992) (Figure 8.9). Further afield, two axes of Group VI, from Great Langdale, Cumbria, have been macroscopically identified, presumably introduced in a finished state, and in 1993 a possible Cornish greenstone axe was also

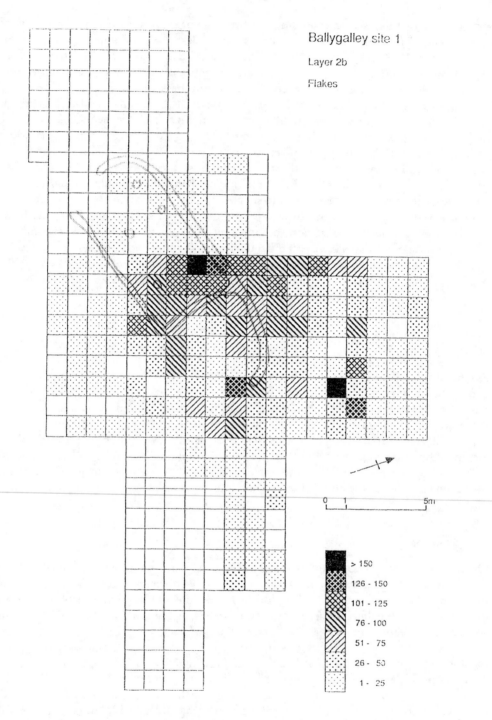

Ballygalley site 1

Layer 2b

Flakes

> 150

126 - 150

101 - 125

76 - 100

51 - 75

26 - 50

1 - 25

Figure 8.8: Plan showing the distribution of flint flakes at Site 1, Ballygalley

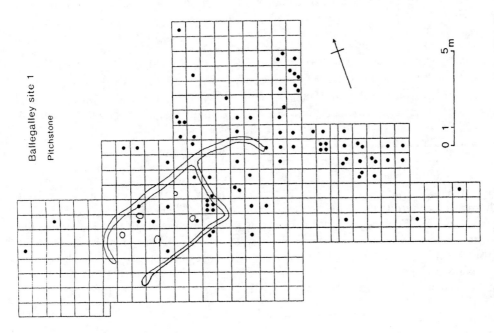

Figure 8.10: Plan showing the distribution of pitchstone at Site 1, Ballygalley

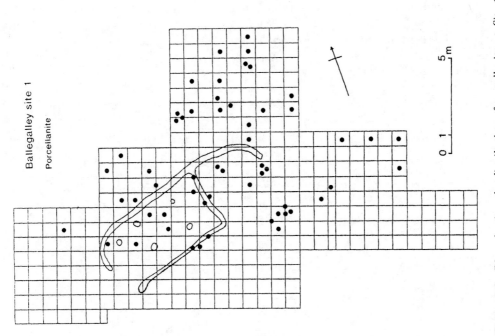

Figure 8.9: Plan showing the distribution of porcellanite at Site 1, Ballygalley

tentatively identified. Rock crystal, quartz and serpentine was amongst the other non-local material brought to the site. Perhaps, however, the most significant of the exotic raw materials is pitchstone, represented by over two hundred pieces (Figure 8.10). The majority of the finds are fragments, many of which show no trace of working but there are a number of cores and one horseshoe scraper and one end scraper. Seven other sites in east Antrim have yielded pitchstone but in no case more than two pieces.

It is clear therefore that the Ballygalley site was a major redistribution centre for a considerable variety of products both insular and imported. This inevitably raises the question of the status of the site as a straightforward farmstead associated with cereal cultivation and cattle raising.

The second point concerns the pattern of Neolithic settlement in Ireland. It is generally assumed that the norm was the isolated farmstead (Gowen and Halpin 1992) as in England. This, however, may be a reflection on the limited nature of many excavations rather than a time reflection of the settlement pattern. Where large area excaations are undertaken as at Ballygalley and Tankardstown (Gowen and Tarbett 1988) more than one structure is recovered and the same may be true of Britain as at Lismore Fields, Derbyshire (Garton 1987). The true picture may be that of dispersed rather than isolated settlement similar to that which prevails in some areas of the west of Ireland today and also preserved in the Scottish system of crofts.

Acknowledgements

Malachy Conway and Dermot Moore assisted in the direction of the excavation which was undertaken by undergraduates and graduates of the Department of Archaeology, Queen's University, Belfast. Analysis of material is currently being undertaken by Ian Meighan (pitchstone and rock sources), Finbar McCormick (animal remains), David Weir (seeds) and Roy Anderson (insects). Sieving and floatation was supervised by John Davison. The author and editors gratefully acknowledge a grant towards the cost of publication of this paper by the Historic Monuments and Buildings Branch, Department of the Environment (Northern Ireland).

Chapter 9

The later Neolithic structures at Trelystan, Powys, Wales: Ten years on

Alex Gibson

INTRODUCTION

Houses of the Neolithic/Bronze Age transition have been a "Holy Grail" of prehistorians for almost 30 years. In the early 1970s, with a shift in emphasis from sepulchral to domestic archaeology, reviews of the settlement evidence were able to draw on only a handful of sites (Simpson 1971) and prehistorians gave a sympathetic ear to Bradley's cry of "where have all the houses gone?" (Bradley 1970a). In the ensuing quest for things structural, tentative houses were reconstructed from posthole arrangements with varying degrees of plausibility (Belle Tout: Bradley 1970b; Molenaarsgraaf: Louwe Kooijmans 1974; Willington: Wheeler 1979). Consequently finds of convincing structures such as the two sites at Trelystan were enthusiastically greeted.

The Trelystan structures were excavated in 1979 and published in detail shortly afterwards (Britnell 1981; 1982). They were small flimsy stake-built structures, the remarkable survival of which was due to their protection by a buried soil in turn protected by the slipped material of two substantial round barrows. A considerable period of time appears to have elapsed between the abandonment of the structures and the construction of the barrows. Radiocarbon dates suggest that this may have been as much as 1000–500 years (Britnell 1982, Appendix 1). Both structures were clearly marked in the subsoil/bedrock by their stakehole walls; some stakeholes actually surviving as voids (Figure 9.1).

THE STRUCTURES

Structure A

This structure was defined by a perimeter of 35 stakeholes or possible stakeholes set between 0.2m and 0.8m apart and delimiting an area 4m by 4.5m. The stakeholes were between 40mm and 60mm in diameter and between 40mm and 200mm deep. Further stakeholes of unknown function were found within the structure. Central to the floor area was a hearth bounded on two sides by shallow slots which had probably originally held edge-set stones. Seven pits lay within the structure while an eighth lay on the line of the wall. These pits contained charcoal and black soil. Pits 1–4 and 6 were *c*.60–120mm deep while pits 5 and 7–8 were slightly deeper. The duplication of some stakeholes in the perimeter wall suggest an element of rebuilding or repair.

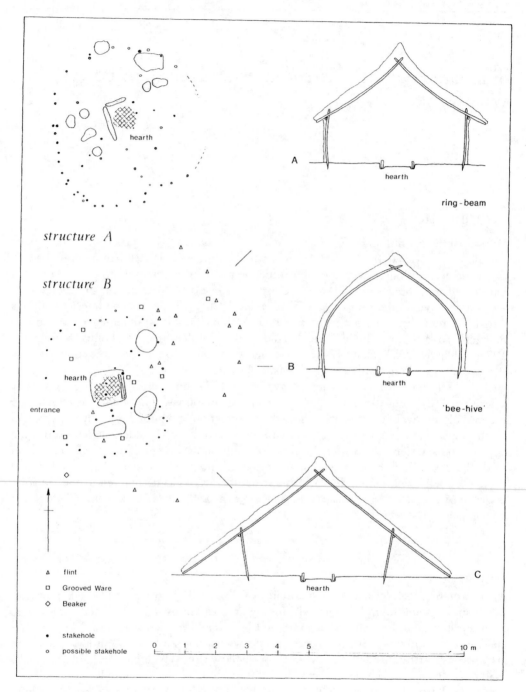

Figure 9.1: Ground plans and possible reconstructions of the Trelystan structures. (Plans after Britnell 1982; Reconstructions A and B after Britnell 1981)

Structure B

This was similar to Structure A. Twenty-seven stakeholes defined the perimeter and enclosed an area 3.9m by 4.2m. The stakeholes averaged 60mm in diameter, 130mm deep and were spaced at 0.6m intervals. Many stakes sloped outwards, 10 degrees from vertical. A slightly larger gap on the west side may well have been the entrance. The rectangular central hearth was defined by shallow gullies, the northern of which contained edge-set stones. Three small rock-cut pits also lay within the structure. Pit 13 was 0.7m in diameter and 0.31m deep and contained heat-cracked stones in an arc around the southern half of the pit. Pit 14, 0.65–0.8m across and 0.43m deep, also contained charcoal and fire-cracked stones. Similar stones were encountered in pit 15, an elongated pit measuring 1.10m by 0.48m by 0.12m deep.

DATING

Grooved Ware and Beaker sherds and contemporary flintwork were found in the buried soil which overlay the structures and Grooved Ware was associated with the hearth and pits in Structure B. Furthermore a suite of five radiocarbon dates were obtained from charcoal from the associated hearths and pits (Britnell 1982, Appendix 1). The two radiocarbon dates from Structure A range from 4050±70 BP (CAR-275) to 3955±70 BP (CAR-276). Both dates are statistically indistinguishable and average to 4003±50 BP or *c*.2574–2462 BC (Figure 9.2) (Stuiver and Reimer 1993).

   The dates from Structure B similarly range from 4260±70 BP (CAR-272) to 3985±70 BP (CAR-274). The three dates average to 4127±40 BP or *c*.2865–2589 BC (Figure 9.2). Both houses are therefore broadly contemporary though obviously need not have co-existed.

RECONSTRUCTION

Structure B, the better preserved, provides more information on the possible reconstruction of the buildings. Important in this consideration are the observations that the stakes had been pointed, forced into the ground rather than dug in, and had been pushed in at an angle of 10 degrees from the vertical to ensure that the walls were splayed outwards. No internal stakeholes can be positively identified as roof supports.

   If the structures were roofed then, at face value, the ground plan appears to suggest that the roof and walls were self-supporting. Britnell (1981) suggested that a ring-beam may have been employed to support a pitched roof without the need for internal supports (Figure 9.1, Reconstruction A). Alternatively, it was also suggested that the stakes may have been bent inwards after they had been stuck in the ground; walls and roof perhaps gaining their strength from the tension in the bent stakes (Figure 9.1; Reconstruction B). A similar reconstruction had also been suggested for the late Neolithic structures on the Goldberg (Simpson 1971, 149).

   Both reconstructions produce structures with very small floor areas. In the case of

Structure B, this would be in the region of 14 square metres total area with *c.*2.21 square metres taken up by pits and hearths leaving *c.*11.8 square metres living space. This puts the Trelystan structures amongst the smallest presumed domestic buildings of the period in Britain and Ireland (Figure 9.3). It nevertheless remains a possibility that the Trelystan structures represent a common type, their apparent uniqueness resulting from the flimsiness of the type and the consequent susceptibility to destruction from ploughing.

A third option may be to regard the surviving remains as part of a larger whole, perhaps only representing the internal structural features of a larger building (Figure 9.1; Reconstruction C). Thus the stakes might support longer poles which sloped up from the ground to form a conical structure. Any traces of the seatings for these longer poles would have been destroyed at the time of the Bronze Age disturbance of the old soil and turfline when the barrows were constructed. The survival of the inner stakes is a result of them being the only subsoil-penetrating structural components. A similar reconstruction was proposed for the slightly sunken structure at Monknewtown (Sweetman 1976) and possibly also the sunken houses at Northton (Simpson 1976) and Rosinish (Shepherd 1976).

The closeness of the stakeholes suggest that access to this outer area may have been restricted since not all the gaps between the stakes are wide enough to allow free-passage. Nevertheless the spacing of the stakes is somewhat irregular in places and larger gaps can be detected in the north, northeast, east, south-southeast, south-southwest and west which were clearly large enough to allow human passage.

Support for this hypothesis may be drawn from the distribution of finds within the buried soil (Britnell 1982, fig. 6; Figure 9.1). There would appear to be a "clean" area, largely devoid of finds, of *c.*2.5–3m wide around Structure B. On the assumption that people do not live on their rubbish (except at Skara Brae and other Orkney sites where they appear to have lived IN it), this may represent additional otherwise undetected floor-space. An arc of flints and, to a lesser extent pottery, to the east and south of the stake wall may well, therefore, represent the vestigial traces of the outer limits of the structure. This pattern does not exist round the entire circumference of the house since the remnant soil was eroded in the western and northern arcs.

If the interpretation of this observation is correct, then the ground area and floor space increase dramatically (Figure 9.3) to a total area of *c.*63.6 square metres if circular or *c.*80 square metres if rectangular. Clearly in a conical structure such as this, not all the floor area would be usable as a living space (though it would be usable for storage) therefore we may assume that headroom below 1m was for storage only, then, the total living area could be estimated as 31 square metres if circular and 40 square metres if rectangular.

These estimated figures, particularly for the circular structure, are much more in keeping with the areas of broadly contemporary houses such as *inter alia* Monknewtown (Sweetman 1976), Northton 2 (Simpson 1976), Gwithian (Megaw 1976), and Hockwold cum Wilton (Bamford 1982). Indeed, this broad uniformity of size and the presence of internal hearths and pits are common features of all houses of the late third and early second millennia BC (Gibson 1987), particularly in the north and west of Britain where their remains tend to be better preserved.

DISCUSSION

A Domestic Interpretation

Surviving later Neolithic settlement activity fortuitously preserved in protected contexts such as below barrow mounds is well-paralleled (Gibson 1982). In many cases the evidence is comparatively flimsy suggesting that similar data in a non-protected context would be unlikely to survive ploughing. Furthermore, even if structural data were to survive, it would probably escape detection, leaving no surface features to hint at its presence.

At Trelystan, over 500 years (*c*.400 radiocarbon years) seem to have elapsed between the use of the structures and the construction of the barrows. This suggests that they are far enough divorced chronologically from the Bronze Age sepulchro-ritual activity not to be directly related to it. Furthermore, the distribution of flint and finds from the buried soil is consistent with the presence of a settlement.

Countering this argument, however, is the presence of a burial pit between the two structures (Britnell 1982, 187). With a radiocarbon date of 4345±65 BP (CAR-282). This date is statistically similar to CAR-272 from pit 13 in Structure B (Figure 9.2) and although it is earlier than the other two dates from the structure, there is overlap in their 2–sigma ranges (Stuiver and Reimer 1993). When considerations such as old wood or charcoal are taken into account, then it remains a possibility that the two structures are associated with this sepulchral activity. Might the large number of heat-cracked stones suggest ritual sweat-houses already proposed by Barfield and Hodder (1987) for some burnt mound sites?

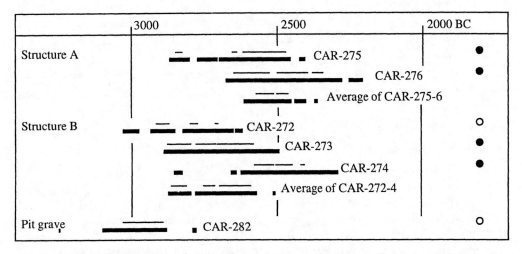

Figure 9.2: Plot of the radiocarbon dates for the pre-barrow contexts at Trelystan. Calibration using University of Washington calibration programme CALIB 3, Rev. 3.0.3 (Stuiver and Reimer 1993). Circles indicate dates which are statistically similar

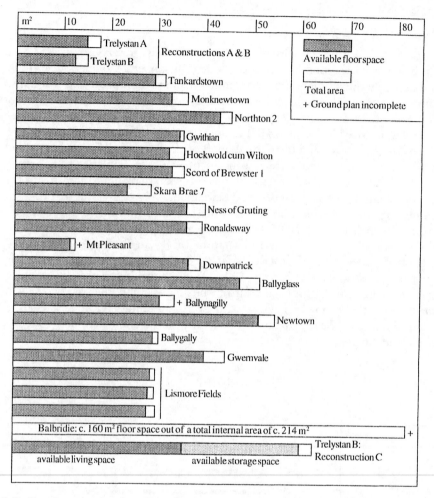

Figure 9.3: Bar chart showing the estimated floor area compared with available living space for a selection of Neolithic houses

Permanent or Temporary?

The answer to this question depends very much on the envisaged reconstruction. Taken at face value (Figure 9.1; Reconstructions A and B) the structures are quite small (about equal to the size of the lounge in a modern "starter home") and flimsy; the stakes were only *c.*60mm in diameter. However, bending the stakes inward and wattling together the uprights would have considerably increased the structures' strength and rigidity. Nevertheless the structures occupy exposed positions on the top of Long Mountain susceptible today to deeply drifting snow and strong southwesterly gales. The houses seem too flimsy for their exposed position and while they may well have been sited in a clearing and have gained protection from the trees, this environment is not suggested by the charcoal taxa from associated contexts which rather point to mixed open woodland or scrub (Britnell 1982, Appendix 4). On surviving ground plan alone, the smallness of the structures and flimsiness of the stake walls may suggest that permanence was not foremost in the minds of the builders. Consequently, perhaps temporary, seasonal occupation is the best interpretation here.

Reconstruction as larger structures (Figure 9.1; Reconstruction C) may be better suited to permanent settlement. Certainly a larger living space, more in keeping with contemporary highland houses, would be obtained. Cooking and other domestic activities would be confined to the central area, while sleeping and storage could take place in the peripheral living space. Roof poles extending to the ground would also afford better protection against wind-damage, offering no vertical obstruction to the airflow.

Are these sites domestic? Do they represent a permanent settlement? On balance, the answer to the first question would appear to be "yes", particularly if the reconstruction proposed here is accepted. The answer to the second question is more open.

POSTSCRIPT: A NEOLITHIC HOUSE FROM WALTON, RADNORSHIRE, POWYS

In the summer of 1994, a putative Bronze Age round barrow was excavated in Upper Ninepence Field, Hindwell Farm, Walton (SO 252613). The mound was suffering severe degradation from periodic ploughing and had already yielded *c.*700 flints from the topsoil which had been collected by Chris Dunn when a schoolboy living in the area. Dunn had also tested the site by excavation and had concluded by sondage and from pottery and calcined bone in the topsoil that secondary collared urn burials had been disturbed and that the mound was indeed less than 0.3m high.

The present excavations have failed to determine the nature of the mound and it may indeed be a 19th century rabbit warren. Radiocarbon dates from a hearth on top of the mound will provide a *terminus ante quem*. There were no burials beneath or within the mound and the Collared Urn identified by Dunn has been re-interpreted as Peterborough Ware which occurred in the mound material and old ground surface in considerable quantities.

Below the mound and the well-preserved old ground surface lay a number of subsoil pits and postholes presumably representing the traces of a pre-mound settlement. Peterborough Ware, Grooved Ware and associated flint artefacts were recovered from these pits but spatial and quantitative analysis remains to be done.

Stakeholes were noted to delineate two distinct features, a circular enclosure of close-set posts measuring 10m in diameter, and a stake-walled house measuring 5m in diameter. Both features were badly damaged by rabbit burrowing.

The house (Figure 9.4) comprised an arc of 13 stakeholes *c.*0.1–0.25m in diameter. It was cut by a later arc of ditch which was in turn cut by a Grooved Ware pit. Central to the house was a hearth and adjacent pit, the latter containing a large shoulder and bodysherd of Peterborough Ware. Neither this pit nor the hearth can be tied stratigraphically to the perimeter though their central position makes the association possible if not probable: radiocarbon dating will hopefully resolve this.

The house bears comparison with Trelystan hence this interim statement here. The

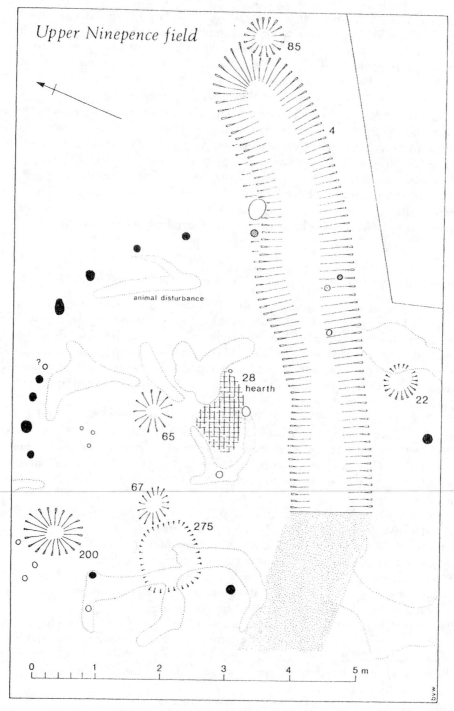

Upper Ninepence field

85

4

animal disturbance

?

28
hearth

65

22

67

275

200

0   1   2   3   4   5 m

bvw

Figure 9.4: Ground plan of the excavated LN house in Upper Ninepence Field, Walton, Powys

uprights of the Walton house were rather more robust than the Trelystan structures, and the posts more widespread, but the size and internal features, especially the central hearth, are common points.

There is a certain amount of evidence also at Walton to support the Trelystan re-interpretation suggested here, namely that the posts are internal supporting a roof which sloped to ground level. Around the best preserved arc of the Walton house was a slightly gleyed "halo" of subsoil 3m wide. Does this represent house floor? In which case the overall diameter of the house would be 11m and not 5m. Walton may, therefore, have been a tent-like structure, albeit solidly built, with a considerable floor area of some 90 square metres. Soil micromorphology may well elucidate this point.

Acknowledgements
Thanks are extended to Bill Britnell for commenting on the original text and discussions of the site and excavation. B V Williams drew Figures 9.1 and 9.4.

Chapter 10

The life, times and works of House 59, Tell Ovcharovo, Bulgaria

Douglass W Bailey

INTRODUCTION

Archaeologists have neglected the interpretation of house remains and the search for the meaning of the numerous Neolithic and Chalcolithic houses of southeastern Europe. Several recent studies have kindled a debate (Hodder 1990; Tringham 1991a; 1991b; 1994; Bailey 1990). The work of Ian Hodder and Ruth Tringham exemplify the flavour of this research: Hodder's high-level generalizing and Tringham's house-specific analyses illustrate the gap which exists between macro- and micro-level approaches to the interpretation of prehistoric houses. The present paper approaches houses on an alternative level, which, while taking the best parts of Hodder and Tringham's work, bridges the gap between micro- and macro-level work.

In producing the alternative I employ Amos Rapoport's writings about systems of activities (Rapoport 1990) and my own conception of living houses (Bailey 1990). In building an explicit definition of what we term houses, I question the implicit association, accepted by many, whereby dwelling activities fill the wattle and daub houses of southeastern Europe and whereby self-contained functions of eating, sleeping and sheltering are assigned to houses. It will become clear that a vacillating range of activities occurred in the Neolithic and Chalcolithic houses of southeastern Europe. As an example, I will examine the life, functions and meaning of a house at the settlement Tell Ovcharovo in northeastern Bulgaria. The example will reveal the importance of non-dwelling activities (ie. elements of the built environment not dominated by sleeping, eating and sheltering such as work stations and activity-specific structures) in fifth and fourth millennia BC society at Ovcharovo as well as in our reconstruction of social strategies at this time. As the association between "house" and habitation comes into question, so also, unavoidably, will I illuminate the fact that prehistoric house users, and modern excavators, must see houses as having multiple functions and meanings.

Therefore, by beginning house analysis on the micro level (the house at Ovcharovo) and then placing the results of the analysis in the medium level (the house in the context of the settlement) it will be possible to move securely to the macro-level of trans-regional generalizations and interpretation. By moving step by step from the micro-level to the macro-level, House 59 from Ovcharovo emerges as a metaphor for the composure and agenda of late Neolithic and Chalcolithic society in southeastern Europe.

The domus

In his recent European study, Ian Hodder nominated the house as the most important social, economic, symbolic and ideological entity of the Neolithic in southeastern Europe (Hodder 1990). Hodder defines the Neolithic in terms of the house, or domus as he chooses to call it, and he contends that the domus is of paramount importance to social structure and action.

Hodder's work dwells on the generalizing macro-scale; he deals not with the actual remains of a series of houses through time at one site, but with the concept of the house; a concept he draws from modern western philosophical traditions. The root of the generalization is betrayed by the scale of the data analysis which he makes the basis of his study. Hodder mistakenly believes that the amount of data from individual sites in most areas of Europe is inadequate for rigorous theorizing and that progress in interpretation is only possible if one "pools" the information from many sites (Hodder 1990, 47). Few would agree that no parts of Europe offer an adequate body of site-specific evidence for a rigorous study of prehistoric social action and ideology, or that pooling of information is necessary. Hodder has assumed, mistakenly, that the absence of the built environment from the archaeological record equals an absence of data required for interpretation. In southeastern Europe, evidence for the built environment is abundant in the Neolithic and Copper Age (ie. thousands of Neolithic and Copper Age sites exist) and completely excavated and published sites are available to those willing to make the effort to study them; there is no need to pool information in southeastern Europe from these periods. By ignoring the site specific evidence in archaeologically rich regions, Hodder's generalizations over-emphasize broad cross-regional trends at the expense of site specific (and "domus"-specific) information.

While Hodder's study is valuable as an attempt to trace a high-level model through time and space, and while he may be correct in applying broad ideas and concepts in some parts of Europe where evidence is thin on the ground, certainly he is mistaken in not investigating the site- and house-specific data from Bulgaria, Romania, former Yugoslavia, Hungary and Greece. Thus Hodder has approached houses at a macro-level, from a region-wide or, at best, site-wide perspective. In doing so he has missed the details which are of most value to the archaeology of houses.

The engendered house

While Hodder dealt with houses on the macro-scale, Ruth Tringham has focused on the micro-scale of analysis. Using her excavations of Neolithic settlements at Opovo-Ugar Bajbuk (Tringham *et al.* 1985; Tringham *et al.* 1992), Selevac (Tringham and Krstić 1990) and Robert McPherron's investigations at Divostin (McPherron and Srejović 1988), all in Serbia, Tringham has offered an archaeology of the engendered house (Tringham 1991a; 1991b; 1994). Following a feminist critique of science, Tringham has aimed to illuminate gender in and around the built environment. Most of all, Tringham writes a prehistory of people, of social actors who have gender, personalities and biographies. Tringham's method of illuminating gender highlights the ambiguity of interpretation and the plurality of plausible views. Tringham suggests that the archaeologist needs to use her imagination and anthropological experience to envisage the prehistoric significance of material culture, such as houses. In her analysis of the houses at Opovo, Tringham presents a feminist interpretation of the site's archaeological record. The Opovo houses had "life-histories": the tangible expressions of the continuity of place. Social actors use these life-histories and the houses' inhabitants assign different meanings to the houses. Tringham is writing an intertwining biography of places. In focusing her attention on the micro-scale of the single house and the single village, Tringham justifies her belief that no hamlet, nor any man or woman is marginal to the larger social picture.

In her analysis of social trends at Opovo, Tringham suggests that the settlement experienced a rapid decrease in the pooling of labour between households and extra-kin support, especially that involving female members of households. In reaching this conclusion, Tringham experiences the village of Opovo from as many different levels of analysis as is possible (eg. from the perspectives of a continent, a region, an archaeological culture, an archaeological site, a millennium, an archaeological phase, a generation, a lifetime, an event). Tringham uses different levels of consensus and ambiguity to formulate an interpretation in which scientific demonstration is interwoven with a more interpretive strategy, using creative imagination and alternative forms of textual and visual expression.

Tringham's interpretation of the Opovo house is three-fold (although she admits that any additional number of folds may be relevant). The interpretation weaves the archaeologist's perception of the house as it was being excavated with the perceptions held by two Neolithic woman (one an exogamous wife, the other the daughter of the wife and a local man) as the house was being destroyed.

> Archaeologist's day-book (June 10–July 17, 1985):
> "Excavation of house floor called Feature 4 (a BH1 house). We notice a circular area in the NE corner of this feature where there was no burned clay daub rubble – mystery! ... a later tree? ... or a later pit". (Tringham 1994)
>
> Exogamous wife/widow:
> "It's burning nicely now. What a crummy house they built. Nothing but kindling for its bones. I'm surprised the loft didn't fall down on our heads ... Here it goes! Watch the flame! Look at it burn!... Mustn't let the fire die, or he'll come back. More wood. A house must die to breathe. Burn his pots! Kill his stuff! Now I'm in charge." (Tringham 1991a, 124)
>
> Daughter of exogamous wife and local man:
> "She's killed the house, as though she killed us all. But she can't kill this place! Now she's run off, back to her mother's house. It's always a problem bringing them here from so far away. They aren't the same as us." (Tringham, in press).

Thus the excavation field notes are woven into the reconstructed perceptions of two female prehistoric inhabitants. Tringham's goal is to use narrative and visual imagery to introduce the prehistoric actors and their prehistoric perceptions. The result is an interpretation which is alive with people and their perspectives of the house. In an earlier version of the argument, Tringham presented architecture in terms of the dominance relations and tensions between males and females. She humanized a house at the Neolithic settlement of Divostin in central Serbia in terms of three viewers: an archaeologist with her Goddess-like view of space; a male visitor to the house; and the house's female resident (Tringham 1991b, 19–21). Although the archaeologist sees, in one glance, all of the Divostin house (ie. a two-roomed structure with hearths, pots, figurines and pots) her perception is external to the views of the social actors and the action. Thus, from another perspective the male visitor sees, in the open foreground of the outer room of the house, a display of artefacts characterized by elaborate and overt symbols (female figurines, fine pottery, an elaborately decorated oven, brightly painted walls). He can see much less clearly a dark inaccessible area, guarded by a half drawn curtain, a dimly lit back room. The female resident of the house spends most of her time in this dark space which contains other women and children yet includes few if any of the highly decorated symbols of display common in the front public room. The female resident perceives the undecorated oven of the inner room as the true source of energy, death, fortune and misfortune of her household and life (Tringham 1991b, 18–20).

Two points run through Tringham's work. The first is that modern archaeological perceptions of houses must take into account as many different perspectives of the house as are reasonably imaginable, be they based on gender, age, lineage, nationality or another archaeologically plausible dimension. The second point is that archaeological interpretations of social actions and perspectives must begin their analysis on the micro-scale of the room or the house.

The living house

In a previous article I have argued that a variety of different perspectives on houses from fifth millennium BC tell settlements in northeast Bulgaria helps us to understand houses and architecture in social terms (Bailey 1990). The perspectives include not only those of the archaeologist, the house's occupants and visitors but also the perspectives held by the house itself as a living element in society. By investing each house with the status of a living being, I have suggested that houses had biographies and genealogies. And just as with human genealogies and biographies, one can trace the life of a house through the long-term development of inter-house village life. In practice, house biographies can be traced by studying the repetition of house floorplans through each rebuilding phase of a settlement mound (Figure 10.1). In tracing house biographies, it became clear that while some houses "lived" for no more than one generation, others lived for two, three, four or five generations as they were built and rebuilt in exact replication in precisely the same location in the tell village over hundreds of years. I concluded that the repetition of houses in multi-generational rebuildings was a powerful means to legitimate the continuity of occupation after episodes of abandonment at the tell settlement of Ovcharovo.

The repetition of houses and the use of the living house in strategies of continuity maintenance at settlement mounds in the southeast European Neolithic and Chalcolithic complement the contemporary context of the fifth millennium BC social strategies. At this time, tell-based communities were defined by the increasing intensification of resource exploitation, and of agricultural and material production. In these societies, classes of elite individuals arose and dominated settlement, burial and production activity (Bailey 1991; 1993; 1994). A consequence of these developments was the rise in the value of settlement space and the need to legitimate one's occupation of a settlement and the particular houses within the settlement. Patterns of house repetition and the display, destruction and deposition of house-shaped figurines were parts of the processes by which occupation was legitimated (see Bailey 1990; 1991 for further details).

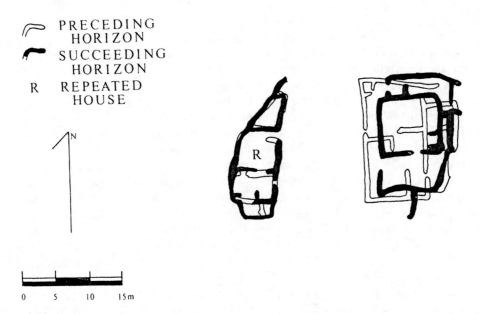

PRECEDING
    HORIZON

SUCCEEDING
    HORIZON

R   REPEATED
    HOUSE

Figure 10.1: Ground plans of repeated and non-repeated houses from the Ovcharovo tell, northeastern Bulgaria

My earlier work on house occupation focused on the biography and active power of houses on a settlement-wide basis through a 500 year period at one site. It is clear from Tringham's work that I must expand my analysis to focus as well on the micro-scale of a single house and its life through the multi-century development of the settlement tell. It is clear from Hodder's lack of specifics that I must explicitly offer an archaeologically relevant definition of a house and follow that definition into the analysis of a specific building. The remainder of the present paper addresses these three tasks.

An accurate interpretation of a prehistoric house moves from the micro-scale to the macro-scale of analysis. Thus the first concern is with an explicit definition of a house; definition identifies the parameters of the analysis. Next, the analysis of one particular house from a settlement documents the house's architecture, its contents and suggests possible activities which took place in the house. Next, attention is paid to the relationship of this house with those which preceded it and those which came after. Differences in form, contents or use are noted. Once the house itself is firmly in hand, then the project places the house, its form and uses in the site-wide context of the village or immediate community. Next the house, embedded in the village, is placed in the regional context of wider and more general social, economic and technological trends.

By building the analysis from the micro- to the macro-scale the project leads to meaning and interpretation. The remainder of the present paper offers a multi-level analysis and interpretation of a fifth millennium BC house. Thus we begin with Tringham on the house particular level, move with Bailey through the life of the house in the settlement and eventually catch up with Hodder and the high level of regional model building.

WHAT IS A HOUSE?

Three elements define a house. In the first place a house is conspicuous. It is readily seen, often unavoidably so. It is an environ which is tangibly built, used and destroyed. It can be seen, touched and experienced. Second, a house is the setting for systems of activities (Rapoport 1990). People perform actions, carry out tasks, bake bread, make love, eat breakfast, grind grain, give birth, and perform a myriad of activities within and around houses. Although the variety of potential activities is large, it is possible to isolate particular activities as primary in importance for particular houses at particular times. Third, systems of activities occur in a chronological sequence. Activities, be they frequently repeated (such as sleeping or grinding grain) or unique (such as the one-off use of a building as a place to repair a flint knife), occur in patterns through time. Thus in the morning of one day grain is parched, on the morning of the next day the grain is ground, on the third morning a child is born. In the first afternoon a woman sleeps, in the second afternoon the house is empty, on the third afternoon three men sit gossiping. The scale of time expands and the house is used and reused over many days, weeks, months and perhaps years. A house, therefore is the conspicuous, spatial focus of systems of selected activities through time.

A house is also active. Its role in village life is not only as a frame for activities or the setting of behaviour; houses also act and behave. Houses play a prominent role in the creation, maintenance and alternation of social reality. As visual, tangible things they separate individual from individual or individual from group or group from group; they establish and maintain distinct identities. A house is also an active participant in the maintenance of occupation rights (see Bailey 1990) and the rebuilding and replications of house-form through time are statements of rights to reoccupy locations. Indeed it is legitimate to think of houses as living things which participate in the daily, routine maintenance and alteration of social reality. In engaging houses as alive and active it is important not to limit the archaeological definition to traditionally perceived functions (ie. places of shelter, sleeping and eating). Instead one must accept alternative functions within houses (ie. work stations, textile processing rooms, animal butchering huts).

As active members of society, houses have biographies. They are conceived, born, live, die, are inhumed or cremated, and are remembered after death (Bailey 1990; 1991). Houses also have genealogies; they are related to houses which preceded them and they are related to houses which succeeded them. Thus, to write a relevant, accurate archaeology of a house from southeastern Europe is to trace the house's biography and genealogy. A house biography and genealogy reveal information about the function of the house (and how that function may have changed over time) as well as about the meaning of the house as perceived by its inhabitants and by its exhabitants. Let us turn to the example of a house from southeastern Europe.

HOUSES IN THE FIFTH MILLENNIUM BC SETTLEMENT TELLS

Houses in the Neolithic and Copper Age settlement tells of southeastern Europe are made of timber post and wattle frames upon which is packed mud, clay and straw building material. Most houses have internal hearths and many have complex layouts of two, three, four or more rooms. Houses congregate in villages of up to 20 houses and develop, through long-term use, into substantial multi-layered settlement mounds, or tells. The tells, which can reach over 10m in height and over 100m in diameter, contain many layers of house building activity and were in use, according the radiocarbon dates, for up to, and beyond, 500 years.

The Ovcharovo Tell

The fifth millennium BC mound at Ovcharovo, in northeastern Bulgaria, is a tell typical of the Neolithic and Chalcolithic settlement patterns and provides the houses for study here. Ovcharovo sat in the northern floodplains of the Stara Planina Mountains, 60km south of the Danube and 100km west from the Black Sea. Before excavation it stood almost 5m high and 100m in diameter. Occupation at Ovcharovo began at the beginning of the fifth millennium BC (the third lowest horizon yielded a date of 5990±80 BP (Bln-1546) and continued for more than 500 years (the youngest radiocarbon date, 5420±60 BP (Bln-1357), is from Horizon XII). In terms of regional culture chronology the occupation of Ovcharovo spans Todorova's early Eneolithic (Polyanitsa III), middle Eneolithic (Polyanitsa IVb) and late Eneolithic (Kodjaderman-Gumelnitsa-Karanovo VI: 2–3) (Todorova *et al.* 1983; Todorova 1986).

From 1971–1973, Professor-Dr. Henrietta Todorova of the Archaeological Institute of the Bulgarian Academy of Sciences completely excavated the tell and satisfactory publication has followed (Todorova 1976a; Vasilev 1985; Todorova *et al.* 1983). More recently I have produced an English language review of the excavation incorporating unpublished archive information (Bailey 1991).

Ovcharovo is but one of hundreds of contemporary settlement tells in Bulgaria. The vast majority of these remain unexcavated. Of those which have been completely excavated, a significant proportion come from the same region as Ovcharovo (ie. northeastern Bulgaria). Two of these sites have been published in full: Golyamo Delchevo (Todorova 1976a; Todorova *et al.* 1975) and Vinitsa (Raduncheva 1976). Golyamo Delchevo has also featured in the English review of the region's archaeology (Bailey 1991). Three other tells from the region have been completely excavated and published in part: Radingrad (Ivanov 1981; 1982; 1984); Polyanitsa (Todorova 1976b; 1982); and Turgovishte (Angelova 1981; 1982a; 1982b; 1986a; 1986b). Thus, northeastern Bulgaria supplies a more than adequate inventory of information on settlements and houses from the fifth millennium BC. Furthermore, the similarity of tell structure and content between the northeast Bulgarian tells and those located further to the south from the same and earlier periods (the fifth and sixth millennia BC) makes the study of Ovcharovo and its neighbours relevant to an understanding of settlement and houses from most of the regions of southeastern Europe in the Neolithic and Copper Age.

THE BIOGRAPHY OF HOUSE 59 AT OVCHAROVO

House 59 is one of a population of 112 houses from the Ovcharovo tell. Originating in

Horizon VII (5745±60 BP (Bln- 1366)), House 59 lived through four of the 13 horizons of the Ovcharovo tell being rebuilt in Horizons VIII, IX and X. The first generation of the house was built as a single roomed structure with a small internal wall division and two doors (one to the east and one to the west) (Figure 10.2a). During its original construction builders probably recycled timber from ruins of houses in the previous habitation horizon. In its first generation, House 59 did not have a hearth or any stationary furniture (such as a clay platform). Two main activity areas are evident in the house at this time: an area of textile production or textile working in the southeastern corner (defined by piercing tools, a spindle whorl and cutting implements); and, near the western door, an area dominated by digging and chopping tools (Figure 10.2). Other individual finds of chopping, digging and cutting tools were recovered scattered about the house. Two reconstructible fineware pots (one of 900cc and the other 1600cc) were found, both near the western entrance of the house. Conclusions about house function are difficult to draw; perhaps the house was used for a range of temporary activities related to textile production and possibly agricultural (eg. planting and digging) or house building activities. The first generation of the house collapsed or was pulled down thirty or forty years after its original construction and the house was reborn in an expanded form in the succeeding habitation level, Horizon VIII (Figure 10.2b).

While the main floorplan of the Horizon VII house was incorporated in the rebuilding of the house in Horizon VIII, substantial architectural changes are evident. The house now has one main room surrounded by three subsidiary rooms and a grain silo. It is also possible that the addition of internal divisions (here interpreted as rooms) is evidence for a second storey. Access to, and egress from, the house is via a single door to the south and the largest room lies two rooms (and two doorways) deep in the house. The house now contains a hearth, on the east wall, and a clay platform or bench, on the northern wall. Between the main room and the doorway lies a large grain silo. In Horizon VIII three main activity areas define the house: an area around the hearth in the main room dominated by grinding stones; an area in the long thin western room containing cutting, digging and textile working tools and fragments of a sieve (most probably used for dairying); and a more dispersed area in the southern outer room consisting of cutting, digging and grinding tools as well as a sieve fragment and a bone ornament.

The grinding stones, the oven and the grain silo are important keys to the activities carried out in the house. They suggest that, in the main, the house served as a work station (for the storage, parching and grinding of cereal grains) in a village increasingly concerned with (and dependent on) the cultivation and processing of cereals. The collection of fourteen reconstructible pots (ranging from 500cc to 2100cc) two of which had prestige graphite decoration, the bone pendant and the small sizes of the majority of the pots (11 of 14 are a litre or less in capacity) as well as the arrangement of the rooms, and the depth and inaccessibility of the grinding, parching and processing area, suggest that in level VIII the house's main function was that of a small scale redistribution centre for cereal grain. Redistribution may have occurred on a settlement wide basis with many different individuals bringing their small quantities of grain to be processed in the house before storing the grain in their own houses. Part of Horizon VIII was burned down and the cause of the fire may have been nothing more than a consequence of an increase in the production and processing (particularly the parching) of cereal grains (on the

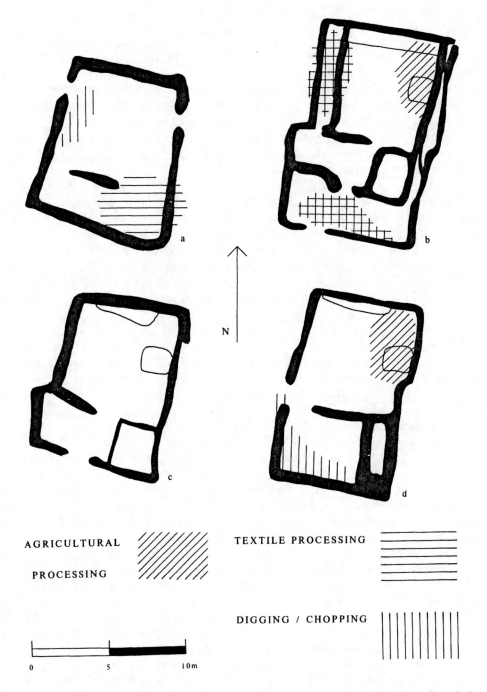

N

AGRICULTURAL

PROCESSING

TEXTILE PROCESSING

DIGGING / CHOPPING

0   5   10m

Figure 10.2: Ground plans showing the evolution of House 59 at the Ovcharovo tell, northeast Bulgaria. (a) The first generation from Horizon VII. (b) Horizon VIII. (c) Horizon IX. (d) Horizon X

connection between tell fires and cereal production see Tringham and Krstić 1990, 609–10).

When the house is rebuilt in Horizon IX (Figure 10.2c) the most important architectural elements are retained although the overall layout is simplified. Only two rooms are rebuilt (the main northern room and the southern foyer) and the silo is retained. The hearth remains as does the platform-bench along the northern wall. While the structure of the house remains intact there is little similarity in the artefacts recovered from the house. Where the level VIII house was a hive of activity centred on the processing and redistribution or sale of cereal grain, the house in level IX appears as a ghost: only two finds are recorded (a piercing tool in the northeast corner of the main room and a 1200cc pot in or near the silo).

There are two possible reasons for the discrepancy in the house contents between the two horizons. On the one hand the house may have lain empty and out of use. If this were the case, then why was it rebuilt? It is more likely that the sparse inventory reflects a stage in the house's life after it had been built but before it had come into use or that it reflects a period of the house's life when it was not in use. The latter suggestions fit securely in the model, built for the function of the house in the previous horizon, that the house was a station for the processing of grain. As a grain processing station, the house would have been used for its primary function only at specific times of the year after harvest. At other times of the year it may have served a variety of temporary and unique purposes, no records of which have survived. The absence of finds in the house in Horizon IX parallels the general low density of finds in the horizon as a whole (third least dense for the 13 horizons; Bailey 1991). The finds which were recovered from Horizon IX concentrate in the houses in the eastern half of the settlement and match the description of houses used for the processing, storage and redistribution of cereal grain. All of the houses in Horizon IX were destroyed by fire, which again may have started from grain parching activity in the other houses of the horizon.

In Horizon X, the house's fourth generation, the pattern of activity returns to the previous design. Architecturally the house retains the simple two-room-plus-silo structure, although the door is now in the western wall (Figure 10.2d). The oven and platform-bench remain as they were in the previous generation of the house. The house contains three main activity areas: an area of cereal grain processing around the hearth in the northern room (many grinding stones and ten pots, four of which are graphite decorated); an area in the southern room containing chopping and digging tools; and the grain silo (containing a mixture of wheats). The range in size of pots found around the oven differs from the size range found in earlier horizons. The Horizon X pots range from 500cc to 10,500cc in volume. Four pots are 600cc or less, five pots range from 1500cc to 3500cc and one is 10,500cc. If one assumes that the house is functioning, in the main, as it had in previous Horizons, as a grain processing station, then the shift to larger pots (ie. those 1500cc and larger, especially the 10.5 litre pot) documents a shift in the scale and organization of the production and processing strategies of cereal cultivation and redistribution. The shift in pot capacity in the house is mirrored by increases in pot sizes in other houses in Horizon X. Combine the increase in large pots in individual houses with the decrease in size and eventual disappearance of silos in the settlement and the result is a shift in the control of resources and their processing and redistribution. Where in earlier horizons, the processing, storage and redistribution of resources such as cereals were open-ended and spread evenly throughout the settlement, in the later horizons of the settlement (eg. Horizons IX and X) longer-term storage (ie. the purpose of the larger pots) and cereal redistribution are closed and linked to specific houses. Thus the shift is one from small-scale to large-scale processing of cereal produce.

Fire destroyed all of the houses in Horizon X and the site is abandoned for a substantial period of time. When the tell is reoccupied in Horizon XI, there is no sign of continuity with the earlier occupation: no architectural contiguity or similarity exists and the ceramics exhibit striking dissimilarity with the previous types.

HOUSE 59 IN CONTEXT

House 59 at Ovcharovo lived through four generations of the settlement's half millennium duration. While the house was rebuilt in Horizons VIII, IX and X with continuity in mind (the maintenance of architectural form and main activities) changes in the pattern of artefacts reflects both shifts in the settlement-wide social strategies of resource control as well as different moments in the life of the house. Thus in Horizons VIII and X the house is busy at work; in Horizon IX it is at rest. In Horizon VIII it is part of a small-scale grain processing and redistribution activity, in Horizon X it is part of a large-scale processing and redistribution activity.

The span of House 59's complete four-horizon genealogy corresponds to interesting developments in settlement life at Ovcharovo. Chapman has suggested that Horizons VII – X were a time of increased inter-household competition marked by an expansion of house complexity and a decline in the ease of access to houses (Chapman 1990, 75). Indeed these horizons document an increase in the number and range of prestige items (*Spondylus gaederopus*, stone and bone jewellery, graphite decorated pots) as well as an increasing emphasis on house-based storage of dry goods (most probably cereals) in increasingly large pots, some of which have twenty to thirty litre capacities (Bailey 1991). The late Chalcolithic increase in valuable goods is mirrored by the increasing representation of individuals in society as documented in anthropomorphic figurines and rich inhumations placed in newly developed extramural cemeteries (Bailey 1991; 1994). The increase in the destruction of houses by fire is also a phenomenon which developed in the life time of House 59; only one horizon (Horizon II) earlier than Horizon VII was destroyed by fire while all but two (Horizons XI and XIII) of the last seven horizons revealed evidence of burning after Horizon VII. The appearance of horizon-destroying fires corresponds to the attempts to increase cereal production. It is highly likely that the rise of the individual in Ovcharovo society, the increase in production, acquisition and display of prestige goods and the increase in inter-house competition are linked to an increased pressure to intensify agricultural production and processing.

It is not a coincidence therefore that it is the period in question (the middle and later occupation of Ovcharovo) that loom weights disappear from the site: Horizons I – VIII contained 84 loom weights, or 10.5 per horizon, while Horizons IX – XIII contained 13, or 2.6 per horizon. Clearly a shift in production practices took place from the earlier phases when the management of animals for primary and secondary products (sheep and goat for wool and meat; cattle and pig for meat) to one which concentrated on cereal production and the use of cattle for traction (pack animals and possible plough traction) (Bailey 1991). The trend to more mature animals and an increase in the proportion of wild to domestic animals is also seen at the contemporary, neighbouring site of Polyanitsa (Bokonyi 1986).

Having detailed the archaeology of House 59 in its micro-context and in relation to the multiple horizons of the tell, it is necessary now to fit these patterns into the wider macro-scale of the late Chalcolithic of northeast Bulgaria. In the late Chalcolithic the spectacular finds of gold, copper and *Spondylus* in the Varna and Durankulak cemeteries on the Black Sea coast dominate the archaeological record. I suggest that the appearance of these ostentatiously rich graves is linked to, and probably supported by, the house-based agricultural production of the inland tell sites, such as Ovcharovo.

The inland regions are populated by tell-based settlement producing cereal products as well as textiles and animal by-products. While the landscape of northeast Bulgaria at this time is visually dominated by the presence of the tell settlements, it is becoming clear that it is also a landscape riven with group mobility and temporary settlement. Mobility is documented by an increase in the seasonal and longer term movement of populations through the landscape (see Bailey in press). The use of animals for the transportation of goods (as documented by the figurines of pack animals from Ovcharovo and the south-central Bulgarian site of Drama (Bertemes and Krastev 1988), the probable seasonal movement of sheep, goat and cattle to summer uplands, the hydrographic consequences of flood-plain agriculture and the abundant evidence of seasonal or annual house repair and rebuilding combine to argue forcefully that late Chalcolithic societies may not have been the self-sufficient, independent, permanently settled farmers that they are traditionally portrayed to be. Indeed, it may be more accurate to reconstruct the late Chalcolithic communities which used tells (such as Ovcharovo) as groups of farmers and herders who moved among a range of settlement and work sites, producing agricultural and livestock products. These groups may have sent these products to the Black Sea coasts in exchange for prestige goods. Indeed, it is not beyond reason to hypothesis that the metal-based prestige goods system exemplified by the Varna cemetery was supported by the inland agriculturalists.

The new picture emerging of society at this time therefore is mirrored in the life and times of House 59, a house dominated by the increase in the production and processing of cereal grain. Indeed the social importance and focus directed on House 59 by its creators and users' rebuilding of the house in four consecutive horizons is understandable when the house is placed in its wider macro-level context. House 59 meant a great deal to its inhabitants, for it signified and literally contained the increasingly important activities surrounding grain production and processing. Hence its precise repetition through the Ovcharovo horizons. House 59 means a great deal to the interpreters of the Chalcolithic of southeastern Europe, for it documents not only the activities taking place at this time but also, through its repetition, the importance of these activities to the communities which inhabited the settlement mounds.

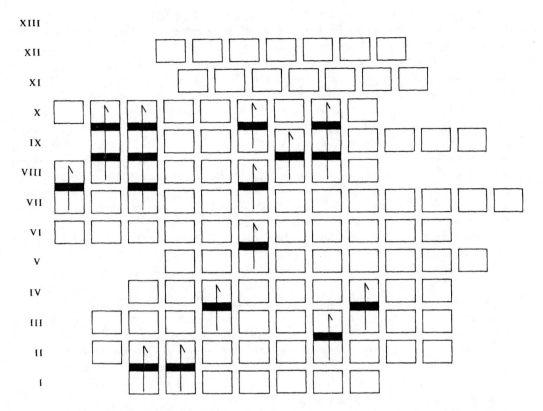

XIII
XII
XI
X
IX
VIII
VII
VI
V
IV
III
II
I

Figure 10.3: A complete genealogy of houses from the Ovcharovo tell. Clear blocks represent individual houses; solid blocks represent repition of houses from one horizon to the next

CONCLUSIONS

Micro-level analysis of houses at the tell settlement Ovcharovo documents the interpretive success in reconstructing house functions and meaning through the micro- and macro-levels. To build interpretation from the house specific to the macro-level is to look at the changes in house use though time and in turn to link these changes to the geographically and chronologically wider trends of social action and belief. The increasing importance of cereal production and the potential link between the house-based cereal producing economies of the inland tells (the cemeteries of which seldom have rich graves) and the coastal elite burials are but two of the consequences of a micro-level study of houses from the fifth and sixth millennia BC in southeast Europe. The analysis of House 59 suggests that some structures may better be understood, primarily, not as habitations (ie. places of dwelling used for shelter, living, sleeping or eating) but as components in other systems of activities, such as cereal production, processing, storage and redistribution. This conclusion raises important questions for our interpretation of settlement sites in southeastern Europe during the Neolithic and Chalcolithic. Are we not mistaken, for example, to think of all houses as having one similar function? Assigning functions to structures is not a straightforward exercise; it must proceed in unison with the understanding that a structure may have several different functions which operate at different times or on different scales of time (ie. the repetition of grain parching after each harvest or the one-off use of a room to repair a knife).

An additional consequence of the biography of House 59 is that once one understands a single house, and its development through its generation and regenerations, one must map that genealogy against the genealogies of the other houses from the same site (Figure 10.3). Concepts such as genealogies, and their visual representation, force archaeologists to place the micro-level analysis in the medium-level context of settlement. Only once the house and its life are located in the medium inter-house context is it possible to accurately understand the function and meaning of houses within their settlement. And it is only once the intra-settlement meaning is located can one move to the macro-level context and to the off-tell activities.

If one intends to understand the function of houses on the tell settlements of southeastern Europe than it is paramount that research also consider the use of structures built off the site. To date few if any studies have focused on off-tell components of the landscape. Those archaeologists who have looked beyond the walls of the houses and settlements, such as Hodder with his ideas about the "agrios", have assumed that the function of on-site houses is distinct from off-site houses. In truth we know so little about off-site structures in southeastern Europe that it is impossible to build any model about these areas (Bailey in press). Certainly this is the focus for future research: to build our knowledge of the Neolithic and Chalcolithic exploitation of the landscape around and between the tell sites. Such knowledge will allow the complete understanding of prehistoric houses in their complete contexts.

Chapter 11

Structure and ritual in the Neolithic house: Some examples from Britain and Ireland

Peter Topping

INTRODUCTION

This paper seeks to discuss certain questions relating to the size and structure of Neolithic houses in Britain, and to contrast some of the findings with sites in Ireland and mainland Europe. A review of the structural layout and artefact deposition in several Neolithic houses is explored in an attempt to determine whether aspects of ritual behaviour can be recognized in the archaeological record.

THE DIMENSIONS OF NEOLITHIC BUILDINGS

For the purposes of this discussion a sample of 31 British sites, 9 Irish, and 31 European sites has been reviewed (Table 11.1). In general the British and Irish longhouses tend to be smaller than their European counterparts, although there is an overlap in size between the smaller European houses and the larger British and Irish examples (Figure 11.1). Not surprisingly, the European longhouses show a preponderance for the rectangular form, while there is a noticeable grouping of sub-rectangular, almost square British buildings ranging between 4.0m to 8.0m long by 3.0m to 6.0m transversely. Some of these structures may represent ancillary buildings adjacent to rectangular longhouses, for example at Lismore Fields (Garton 1991) or in Ireland at Tankardstown (Gowen and Tarbett 1988) and Newtown (Gowen and Halpin 1992). In addition, the British corpus also includes a minority of circular or sub-circular types such as Bowman's Farm (this volume) or Trelystan (this volume). Some of these circular or sub-rectangular buildings may have satisfied more specialist non-residential requirements.

In general, the European rectangular structures are much longer than the British and Irish examples, and range from 7.8m to 44.8m in length by 4.1m to 10.0m transversely; the British sites span 5.3m to 24.6m in length by 2.6m to 13.4m transversely. Both of the greater dimensions in the British sequence are from Balbridie. Balbridie (Fairwether and Ralston 1993), the longest house by far from Britain and Ireland to date, remains modest by European standards (see Figure 11.1). However, it is notable that Balbridie is wider by over 3m than any of the European examples in the sample of 31 sites chosen for this study.[1] The larger size of longhouses in mainland Europe may imply that a wider range of activities was carried out within the house than in Britain or Ireland, or perhaps that

Table 11.1: Neolithic house dimensions

Site	Dimensions[1]	Area	References
BRITAIN			
Balbridie	24.6m x 13.4m	329.6sq m	Reynolds 1980; Fairweather and Ralston 1993
Barnhouse 1	3.9m x 2.8m	10.9sq m	Richards 1992
Barnhouse 2	9.7m x 6.7m	64.9sq m	Richards 1992
Barnhouse 3	5.4m x 4.7m	25.3sq m	Richards 1992
Barnhouse 8	8.0m x 7.5m	60.0sq m	Richards 1992
Carn Brea A1	10.6m x 3.0m	31.8sq m	Mercer 1981
Chigborough Farm	? 8.7m x 7.6m	c. 66.12sq m	Adkins and Adkins 1991
Clegyr Boia	7.3m x 3.6m	26.28sq m	Williams 1953
Fengate	7.5m x 8.0m	60.0sq m	Pryor 1974
Haldon	7.6m x 4.8m	36.4sq m	Willock 1936; 1937
Hembury	8.5m x 3.6m	30.6sq m	Piggott 1954, 25
Knap of Howar 1	9.9m x 9.5m int	94.05sq m	Ritchie 1983
Knap of Howar 2	7.5m x 3.6m int	27.0sq m	Ritchie 1983
Links of Noltland	6.0m x 4.2m	25.2sq m	Clarke and Sharples 1990
Links of Noltland	7.2m x 2.7m	19.4sq m	Clarke and Sharples 1990
Lismore Fields 1	c. 15.0m x 5.0m	c. 77.0 sq m	Garton 1991
Lismore Fields 2	c. 7.5m x 5.5m	c. 41.2sq m	Garton 1991
Llandegai	c. 13.0m x 6.0m	c. 78.0sq m	Lynch 1989
Mount Pleasant, Glam	5.3m x 2.6m	13.7sq m	McInnes 1971
Ness of Gruting	5.5m x 4.5m	24.7sq m	Calder 1956
Rinyo A	4.6m x 3.4m	15.6sq m	Childe and Grant 1947
Rinyo G	4.7m x 5.0m	23.5sq m	Childe and Grant 1947
Ronaldsway, IOM	7.5m x 4.1m	30.75sq m	Bruce *et al.* 1947
Scord of Brouster 1	7.0m x 5.4m	37.8sq m	Whittle *et al.* 1986
Scord of Brouster 2	5.2m x 3.8m	19.7sq m	Whittle *et al.* 1986
Scord of Brouster 3	5.1m x 4.5m	22.9sq m	Whittle *et al.* 1986
Skara Brae (House 9: early)	4.5m x 3.5m	15.7sq m	Childe 1950
Skara Brae (House 1: late)	6.2 x 5.9m	36.5sq m	Childe 1950
Stanydale	6.8m x 4.7m	31.9sq m	Calder 1956
Trelystan A (L Neo)	4.5m x 4.0m	18.0sq m	Britnell 1982
Trelystan B (L Neo)	4.2m x 3.9m	16.38sq m	Britnell 1982
IRELAND			
Ballygalley	13.1m x 5.1m	66.8sq m	Simpson 1993
Ballyglass	13.1m x 5.8m	75.9sq m	Ó' Nualláin 1972a
Ballynagilly	6.5m x 6.0m	39.0sq m	ApSimon 1969
Lough Gur, Circle K, House 2	6.5m x 5.6m	36.4sq m	Grogan and Eogan 1987
Lough Gur, Circle L, Central house, 2nd phase	5.3m x 2.6m	13.7sq m	Grogan and Eogan 1987
Lough Gur, Site A	10.1m x 5.4m	54.5sq m	Ó'Ríordáin 1954
Newtown	c. 12m x 6.5m	c78.0sq m	Gowen and Halpin 1992
Tankardstown 1	7.4m x 6.4m	47.3sq m	Gowen 1987
Tankardstown 2	15.0m x 7.5m	112.5sq m	Gowen and Tarbett 198

EUROPE: ATLANTIC PERIPHERY			
Berry-au-Bac (NE France)	20.0m x 10.0m	200.0sq m	Dubouloz *et al.* 1988
Berry-au-Bac (NE France)	9.5m x 8.25m	78.3sq m	Dubouloz *et al.* 1988
Cuiry-les-Chaudardes (NE France)	12.5m x 6.5m	81.2sq m	Illett *et al.* 1982
Cuiry-les-Chaudardes (NE France)	24.0m x 8.5m	204.0sq m	Illett *et al.* 1982
Darion M1 (Belgium)	31.7m x 6.8m	215.5sq m	Keeley and Cahen 1989
Darion M2 (Belgium)	16.5m x 5.8m	95.7sq m	Keeley and Cahen 1989
Darion M3 (Belgium)	8.3m x 5.0m	41.5sq m	Keeley and Cahen 1989
Darion M4 (Belgium)	16.8m x 7.0m	117.6sq m	Keeley and Cahen 1989
Diverhoj I (Denmark)	18.0m x 6.0m	108.0sq m	Asingh 1987
Diverhoj II (Denmark)	13.5m x 5.0m	67.5sq m	Asingh 1987
Elsloo (Holland)	28.5m x 7.5m	213.7sq m	Modderman 1970
Elsloo (Holland)	15.6m x 6.9m	107.6sq m	Modderman 1970
Grodbygard A (Denmark)	10.2m x 7.6m	77.5sq m	Kempfner-Jorgensen and Watt 1985
Gug (Denmark)	9.0m x 5.0m	45.0sq m	Simonsen 1983
Larzicourt (NE France)	37.5m x 7.0m	262.5sq m	Chertier 1980
Limensgard Y (Denmark)	c. 19m x 6.2m	c. 117.8sq m	Nielsen and Nielsen 1985
Limensgard R (Denmark)	c. 28m x 6.5m	182.0sq m	Nielsen and Nielsen 1985
Limensgard S (Denmark)	40.0m x 8.0m	320.0sq m	Nielsen and Nielsen 1985
Limensgard T (Denmark)	32.0m x 7.0m	224.0sq m	Nielsen and Nielsen 1985
Limensgard AB (Denmark)	44.8m x 9.3m	416.6sq m	Nielsen and Nielsen 1985
Longchamps H1 (Belgium)	16.0m x 8.5m	136.0sq m	Keeley and Cahen 1989
Longchamps H2 (Belgium)	13.0m x 6.0m	78.0sq m	Keeley and Cahen 1989
Myrhoj EAB (Denmark)	14.0m x 7.0m	98.0sq m	Simonsen 1983
Myrhoj GAB (Denmark)	12.5m x 6.0m	75.0sq m	Simonsen 1983
Myrhoj D (Denmark)	14.0m x 7.0m	98.0sq m	Simonsen 1983
Oleye M1 (Belgium)	28.5m x 7.6m	216.6sq m	Keeley and Cahen 1989
Oleye M2 (Belgium)	14.3m x 6.0m	85.8sq m	Keeley and Cahen 1989
Oleye M4 (Belgium)	24.5m x 6.5m	159.2sq m	Keeley and Cahen 1989
Oleye M7 (Belgium)	7.8m x 4.1m	31.98sq m	Keeley and Cahen 1989
Ornehus (Denmark)	15.3m x 6.5m	99.45sq m	Eriksen 1988
Oster Nibstrup (Denmark)	19.5m x 7.0m	136.5sq m	Michaelsen 1988

(1) Dimensions of stone buildings are internal; those of timber maximum overall measurements

a differing social structure required larger houses. It is still a major difference between the European evidence and Britain and Ireland that there are still as yet no Neolithic villages on the scale of the European model; even Skara Brae (Childe 1950) or Barnhouse (Richards 1992) are much smaller than the majority of those of the *Bandkeramik* horizon for example.

The internal area of the British rectangular longhouses ranges from 16.3 square metres at Trelystan B up to 94.0 square metres at Knap of Howar 1 (see Figure 11.1), with Balbridie an outlier at 329.6 square metres. In Ireland the parameters are very similar, ranging from 13.7 square metres at Lough Gur Circle L (central house), to 112.5 square

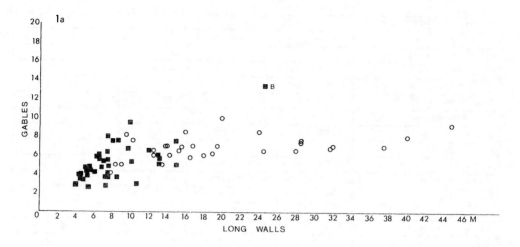

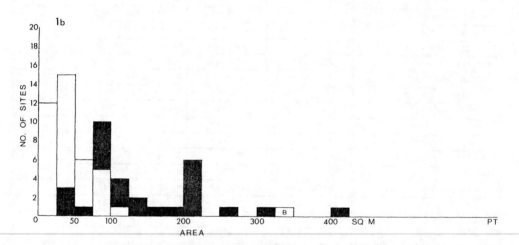

Figure 11.1: Neolithic house dimensions and areas. Top. Scatter diagram of Neolithic house dimensions shown in metres. Black squares represent the British and Irish houses; open circles are the Europen examples. Balbridie is marked B. Below. Bar graph illustrating the range of internal areas of Neolithic houses in 25 square metre intervals. The British and Irish examples are shown white; the European are superimposed in black. Balbridie is marked B

metres at Tankardstown 2. The mean area of the sample corpus is 45.4 square metres. The exceptional size of Balbridie is illustrated in Figure 11.3, where it is shown in comparison with two more modest buildings at Ronaldsway (30.7 square metres) and Ballyglass (75.9 square metres), both of which are close to the norm. The fact that recent writers have been able to find only one possible parallel for the Balbridie hall (Fairweather and Ralston 1993, 316), and that in relation to its design rather than its huge scale, lends weight to the suggestion that in a British context the structure is unique in its scale and probably its function.

THE ORIENTATION AND INTERNAL STRUCTURE OF NEOLITHIC BUILDINGS

The orientation of Neolithic houses has previously been explored (eg. Marshall 1981), and these studies have largely suggested environmentally-determined stimuli were responsible. In Europe it was found that the trapezoidal longhouses were generally aligned with their narrower end to the northwest, and this was mirrored to some extent by the rectilinear longhouses (Marshall 1981, 112). It was suggested on the basis of ethnographic data that the narrower gables were pointed into the wind to give greater structural stability against the prevailing air flow. However, other factors such as solar radiation and the direct absorption of heat by and through the roof could only be maximized if a roughly east to west alignment was chosen and the largest possible roof area faced the longest period of the sun's declination (*cf.* Oswald 1991), with the long wall facing roughly to the south (Figure 11.2). In addition light penetration may have played a role in the location and orientation of doorways (*cf.* Bourdieu 1973). External and non-environmental factors appear to have produced a correllation between the orientation of certain central European longhouses and those of contemporary tombs, which implies that forces other than wind direction lay behind some orientational choices (Hodder 1990, 171–2).

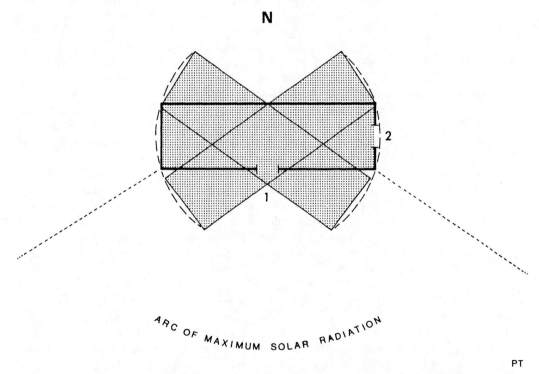

Figure 11.2: Diagram illustrating the optimum longhouse orientation. 1 indicates optimum doorway orientation for maximum sunlight penetration. 2 shows position of limited light penetration, thus internal illumination was of secondary importance

The majority of British and Irish Neolithic houses conform to the European pattern. The predominant alignments fall within a range between northeast to southwest and east-southeast to west-northwest, producing a long wall facing roughly to the south or southeast, as may be expected for maximum solar heat absorption. However, this cannot explain the aberrant alignments of certain houses such as Lough Gur A (Ó'Ríordáin 1954), Trelystan A and B (Britnell 1982), Ballyglass (Ó'Nualláin 1972a), or Hembury (Piggott 1954). These sites all share alignments nearly north to south, and thus must have been influenced by other considerations such as topographic variation, social, locational or symbolic factors. It has been suggested that, in the case of the Danubian longhouses, orientation was controlled to such an extent that variation to counteract locational problems did not occur (Hodder 1990, 170), implying that topographic factors could be of secondary consideration to certain communities, and that symbolic or social influences were of greater importance.

That other environmental stimuli were involved is suggested by the location of doorways. Although access is the basic function of a doorway, a major consideration is the degree of light penetration which can define potential activity areas immediately within the building. It has recently been suggested that the orientation of Bronze Age houses made greater use of sunlight and daylight penetration than those of the Iron Age (Oswald 1991). It is certainly noticeable that many longhouses in Britain and Ireland, where the evidence survives, do feature an entrance in the southern long wall which would have allowed the maximum daylight penetration into the immediate interior. Such zones would have been expected to have been utilized for activities such as weaving, leather, bone and wood working as has been suggested for the Bronze Age houses at Black Patch (Drewett 1982, 339). By contrast light is relatively unimportant for storage and even detrimental to the storage of certain vegetable substances, so that this generally occurs in the darker areas away from the doorways. As a rider it is perhaps worth considering the possibility of alternative natural light sources such as windows or open gable apexes, which could have had a considerable impact on the internal layout of the longhouses; in addition, considering the general lack of evidence in Britain and Ireland for wall coverings such as daub, it may be possible that prepared animal skins could have been used which would have allowed translucent light to penetrate the interior.

Unfortunately, few Neolithic houses have surviving floor deposits to provide evidence for structures and artefact deposition in the interiors, although certain sites do provide an insight. At Trelystan A, a central hearth is flanked by a group of postholes on the west and what may be a later pit with two or three postholes in the northeast, perhaps suggesting specialized activities requiring light from the hearth (Britnell 1982, 140). Trelystan B also had a central hearth (Britnell 1982, 142), but in this case no posthole grouping, only one cooking pit and two further pits in the east side of the building, possibly indicating a greater storage facility in this house. Both Trelystan sites are problematical in that the precise location of the doorways is unclear, although in the case of House B it would appear to have been in the southwest, thus allowing light to reach the cooking pit but keeping the other pits in shadow, which would be especially useful if they were being used for storage of perishable produce.

Other sites such as Ballynagilly (ApSimon 1969) and Ronaldsway (Bruce *et al.* 1947) feature central hearths with pits closely adjacent, which in the case of Ronaldsway contained a "votive" deposit (see below). Ronaldsway also had a series of irregularly scattered postholes which may not have had an economic function (see below). Although again the locations of the entrances at both of these sites are unclear, the central position of the hearths does imply a need for even light and heat distribution. At Ballyglass (Ó'Nualláin 1972a) the entrance was probably located in the northwest-facing gable and pointing away from direct sunlight, while the hearth was found immediately adjacent to the opposite gable suggesting the need to illuminate the innermost areas away from natural light sources (Figure 11.3).

The building at Balbridie (Reynolds 1980; Fairweather and Ralston 1993) like Ballyglass, also illustrates the fact that entrance location need not be determined by the optimum natural lighting. Here the entrance is prominently situated in the east gable which would have limited the amount of natural light penetration into the interior, and implies that in this case it was of secondary importance (see below). This observation is reinforced by the fact that no more than 1m within the entrance lies what appears to have been a linear barrier which would effectively have blocked what light did penetrate the interior.

To summarize, although there was a general trend in orientation with a long side facing to the south suggesting a desire to maximize heat absorption and light penetration where doors were located in this long side, the fact that door positions were variable and unusual house alignments exist, implies that other considerations were also entertained within house design which may reflect a range of social, symbolic or functional requirements. It is probable that certain aspects of house design reflect the perceived cultural identities of their inhabitants in a way that artefact design and communal monuments can do, creating a tangible sign of group membership.

THE POSSIBLE RITUAL USE OF NEOLITHIC BUILDINGS

The question of the ritual use of Neolithic houses is an intriguing one made more so by the paucity of relevant evidence. There is an inherent problem in the identification of the interplay of different levels of ritual and symbolic remains. The identification of ritual on a domestic scale, which might be indistinguishable from the ordinary repertoire of activity debris, contrasts with the more tangible range of evidence in certain purpose-built structures where the nature of the putative ritual is more overtly displayed in terms of a distinctive or unusual building style or a range of structured deposits.

Although comparatively few floor levels have been preserved together with evidence for the superstructure, several sites do display certain structural traits or are associated with deposits which appear to be unusual in comparison with other sites, and which could be suggested were of a ritual nature or at least outside the norm. It is possible that the apparently "normal" house sites in fact followed an equally rigid framework of contemporary symbolic reference, and therefore incorporated a more fundamental level of ritual behaviour than those associated with unusual ground plans or novel artefacts. This all leads to the question of whether it is genuinely possible to be able to detect a difference between secular and ritual behaviour, and how far a house can be seen as simply a residence and not also a repository of ritual behaviour. Should the Neolithic longhouse not be more appropriately viewed as a domestic ritual monument?

If overtly ritual/ceremonial activities can be legitimately correlated with the unusual in the archaeological record, then probably one of the prime examples of Neolithic houses of an unusual form is Balbridie (Reynolds 1980; Fairweather and Ralston 1993). This single large hall is longer and wider than any other in Britain, and has few parallels in continental Europe. In addition its ground plan illustrates a degree of structural elaboration and complexity which is currently unique. The fact that the plant macrofossils recovered at the site exhibit a distinct similarity to European contexts rather than those in Britain underlines the exceptional nature of the Balbridie hall.

The layout at Balbridie has a symmetry to its design (Figure 11.3), with its long axis aligned east to west, and a construction trench, only broken by an entrance in the east gable, enclosing a series of regularly spaced vertical roof supports and linear construction trenches. The unusual length and single entrance to the Balbridie hall may have been purposefully combined to create a "directionality" (*cf.* Hodder 1990, 170) to the building in the way in which it was used and the direction of the access routes into its interior. The internal plan suggests a series of three continuous barriers which are deliberately laid across the direct axial access route from the door in the east gable to the opposite end of the building. These barriers take the form of linear construction trenches which may have held vertical partitions of various heights.

Anyone entering is faced with a barrier only roughly a metre from the entrance, and deviating around this is then faced with a second which creates a narrow area some two metres wide. Again, access past this second barrier is possible around either end where gaps of roughly one metre have been left between the barrier and the house wall. Once beyond this second barrier the structural layout becomes more open, and apart from the roof supports only two groups of paired pits and postholes break up the interior before a further barrier cuts across the interior. This central open area may have been the principal activity area of the building, the pits and postholes having held sets of paired vertical fittings, perhaps for a ritual structure. The barrier which defines the west perimeter of the central area has two slight returns at either end, emphasizing the impression that it enclosed the activity area to its east. At both ends of this barrier gaps of approximately 1m have been left for access.

The area between the third linear barrier and the west gable is probably the most interesting of all. Here a centrally-positioned posthole, significantly the only central example in the whole building, lies immediately behind the barrier. Parallel with the west gable lay two corner roof supports between which were two further postholes and an irregular bulbous trench which may have held some form of ritual feature which was non-structural. Although some plough-damage has occurred in the northwest part of the building which may have disfigured the sub-surface features, its overall layout does suggest that having negotiated the various linear barriers laid out across the interior, once beyond the third barrier there was a distinctly separate area with a range of different features which may have been some form of ritual sanctum to which direct access was impossible, and only attainable once the barriers had been bypassed.

The area between the third barrier and the west gable may have functioned as a repository for significant or ancestral relics, hidden from general display by the interior layout of the hall, but still indirectly accessible to specific individuals or restricted castes by association within the same building. The area between the second and third barriers,

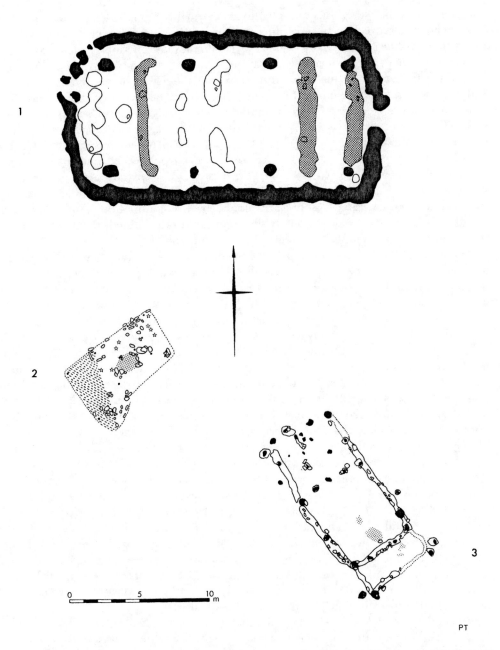

Figure 11.3: Ground plans of three Neolithic houses shown at the same scale and orientation. (1) Balbridie with possible linear barriers shown stippled, and main structural components in black (Based on Fairweather and Ralston 1993, 317). (2) Ronaldsway with its hearth shown by stipple, artefact location by stars, and machine disturbance by dashes (Based on Bruce et al. 1947, 144). (3) Ballyglass with postholes in black, hearth in stipple (After Ó'Nualláin 1972a, 51)

which includes the paired pits and postholes, is roughly 9.5m in length and may have been a ceremonial arena in front of the third barrier. The implied exclusivity in terms of the visibility of the ritual activity or its associated relics is something which may also be seen at certain henge monuments where the interior, and thus the primary ritual platform, are hidden from view by massive banks screening the actors in the interior from any audience outwith the monument (Topping 1992, 263). The layout of the western ritual sanctum in its arrangement of postholes and the irregular pit, would suggest that whatever was laid out in this area was done so on a vertical plane, creating a display which perhaps covered the whole of the west gable. This type of display, which may have been an assemblage of significant ancestral relics or hunting trophies, is well documented in ethnographic records (eg. Craig 1988). Such displays serve not only to perpetuate veneration of the ancestors, but can also be symbolic of – and differentiate between – the wild and domesticated resources exploited by the community. Consequently the ritual significance of such displays is vitally important to the community that has created them and is thus a symbolic reflection of that community.

The sheer scale of the Balbridie hall suggests that it was something beyond the ordinary in its regional context. If the hypothesis outlined above is correct in suggesting a ceremonial or ritual function for this hall, it follows that we may be seeing some form of cult house with a regional importance.

A second site which may exhibit ritual deposits on a smaller scale or perhaps more domestic level, was the generally well-preserved house at Ronaldsway on the Isle of Man (Bruce *et al.* 1947). Here a rectangular house 7.5m long and 4.1m wide contained a central hearth which had on its northeast edge – and aligned along the long axis of the house – a shallow pit covered by a slab. This pit contained a placed deposit of articulated long bones of oxen and a small flat based pot of crude construction and no decoration. No finds were recovered from the hearth itself. In addition, a series of centrally placed postholes have a relatively random placement with little symmetry, possibly implying that they were not required as roof supports but may have been used to create "screens to divide one part of the house from another" (Bruce *et al.* 1947, 145).

Perhaps the most important aspect of the house at Ronaldsway was the large amounts of pottery, tools and bones recovered: 11 axes, several small flint axes and chisels, assorted flint tools, five schist plaques (some decorated with geometrical designs), hammerstones and mauls, and various pots, some of which survived complete. Many of these artefacts "were uniform in character and unweathered" (Bruce *et al.* 1947, 143), – some appeared unused or resharpened – suggesting that they may not have seen normal levels of use in a domestic context. While many of these artefacts were ranged along the northern and eastern walls, the southern wall was noticeably devoid of artefacts (the western gable was disturbed by a mechanical excavator).

Bruce (Bruce *et al.* 1947, 143) suggested that the site may have been hastily abandoned. However, as so many of the artefacts seemed to have been little used, and appear to have very specific distributions within the house, they may have had a symbolic value which took them out of the domestic repertoire. Once abandoned, the memory of the ritual significance of the house would have probably saved the site from disturbance or reuse by immediately successive generations. As a caveat, it should be stressed that Ronaldsway was one of the few house to have been recovered with its occupation layer intact, and that had comparable survivals occurred it may not necessarily have been out of the ordinary.

At Ballygalley (Simpson 1993; this volume) a rectangular house 13.1m long and 5.1m wide included a semi-circular "annexe" at its northeast gable. Although the internal layout of the house was not unusual, the large artefact assemblages recorded at the site are of interest. Flaked stone artefacts accounted for several thousands of items recovered, including debitage and tools – predominantly scrapers, but also knives and axes. The site of a possible flint mine some 1.25km to the northeast of the house might have been expected to explain the presence of so much working debris; however, several imports including porcellanites from Tievebullagh 32kms away, mudstone from the River Bann 48kms distant, pitchstone from the Isle of Arran in Scotland, and two fragments of Group VI axes from Langdale, are also represented. These exotic imports imply, as the excavator has suggested (Simpson 1993, 62), that the site represents something other than a simple factory site. Although it has been argued that Ballygalley may have been part of an exchange network for prestige goods (Simpson 1993, 62), the fact that so many of these artefacts remained at the site suggests that it was either hurriedly abandoned and never returned to, or that a more complex interpretation is required. If Ballygalley were a cult house and the artefact assemblage had a ritual significance, then, as with Ballygalley, this may have protected it from disturbance. The fact that such a huge number of artefacts are represented could suggest that concepts of competitive material exhibitionism at a local or regional level were current. That tools could be created for a non-functional use and displayed at a cult house, thus being pointedly taken out of the economic sphere and in effect sacrificed in a non-destructive way which still allowed the sacrifice itself to remain on display to future generations (*cf.* Mauss 1988, 12–15), may explain the unusual nature of the Ballygalley assemblage.

Interestingly, at Ballygalley the house appears to have been deliberately demolished, the timbers removed, and the site buried beneath a sizeable deposit of cobbling (Simpson 1993, 60). The fact that the substantial artefact assemblage was not removed with the house timbers may imply that the demolition of the house was a part of the ultimate sacrifice, the destruction of the cult house and its deposits in an extravagant display of "catharsis". The event may equally denote a realignment of ritual practices.

At Trelystan, at a site near the summit of Long Mountain in Powys, excavations revealed two stake-built late Neolithic houses associated with Grooved Ware, which had been buried beneath two Bronze Age barrows producing Food Vessels from their earliest phases (Britnell 1982; and Gibson this volume). The two houses lay some 36m apart, and were both sub-circular in shape; House A 4.5m by 4.0m, and House B 4.2m by 3.9m. Both houses had their long axes aligned to the north, although this may not necessarily be significant as there was only 0.5m or less difference between the long axes and the short. However, there were strong similarities between both sites: both had central hearths, and both were associated with a series of pits of varying sizes. House A contained pits predominantly in an arc ranging from the southwest to the northeast, whereas House B had pits in an area stretching from the northeast to the south. Many of the pits held charcoal and black soil, some contained hazelnuts. Perhaps the most significant pit was Pit 13 at House B, which was 0.7m in diameter and 0.31m deep, and which produced not only charcoal and hazelnut shells, but sherds of Grooved Ware, flints, a small fragment of burnt bone, and some 10% of its volume was filled by fire-cracked water-worn pebbles. The excavator suggested that this may have been used for cooking, presumably in the method more normally associated with burnt mounds where the stones were heated on the nearby hearth.

Perhaps some of the most significant evidence which may indirectly attest to the ritual or ceremonial significance of such house structures is the later burial of the Trelystan houses by two Bronze Age barrows. This event could signify that a memory of these sites, and presumably that of the inhabitants or ancestors, was still current some 300–400 radiocarbon years after their abandonment when the barrows were built. The barrows do not overlie the houses centrally, but are somewhat askew, suggesting that the memory was vague, relating to the general area rather than the exact spot on which the houses were built. It would certainly seem to be too much of a coincidence that the barrows were located purely fortuitously on the former house sites.

A possible parallel for this type of scenario may be provided by the site at Grendon in Northamptonshire (Gibson 1985). Here although "overzealous removal of topsoil robbed all information regarding the sequence of construction" (Gibson 1985, 214), it would appear that there had been a square enclosure formed by a U-shaped ditch which was closed by a timber palisade and associated with Grimston Ware, which was subsequently enclosed by two ring-ditches. The enclosure has few obvious parallels, and although it may well have had a primarily funerary use and been allied ultimately to long barrows as suggested by the excavator, bearing in mind the difficulties encountered during excavation, it may be possible to view the site as a novel house structure, eventually encased within two concentric ring-ditches during the early Bronze Age. Indeed, the overall shape of the Grendon enclosure is not wildly different from the houses at Trelystan, and the alignment of the long axis is similar. In addition, it is difficult to be sure how much information may have been lost relating to postholes and other more ephemeral features which could have completed a more diagnostic plan. Although the U-shaped ditch of the square enclosure was found not to be a bedding trench, it did contain significant deposits of charcoal which could have been associated with a hearth as readily as with what would appear to have been a phase of destruction by fire of at least the timber façade which closed the U-shaped trench.

Perhaps the most obvious example of a stratified house is at Ballyglass (Ó'Nualláin 1972a) where a court cairn partly overlies the earlier house. This longhouse had a posthole arrangement in the northwest which suggests that the gable may have been open and that this area formed an elaborate entranceway or some covered activity area which required four regularly spaced verticals with a more random grouping of posts within it (Figure 11.3). If not a functional feature, this area may have had ritual or totemic relevance as a display area for cultic paraphernalia. The excavator suggested that the house had been purposefully demolished to create space for the tomb, perhaps perpetuating a sense of place by the construction of a more permanent structure in the form of the tomb, and thus "signing the landscape" for reference by future generations. It is interesting to note that a second site in Ballyglass township (Mayo 14; Shee Twohig 1990, 24) appeared to be associated with two timber buildings, of which one at least seems to have been overlain by another court tomb. The concept of houses for the dead has been explored elsewhere (*cf.* Fleming 1973), however, it may be pertinent to add that the veneration of specific ancestors is likely to only have had a direct significance to those generations which had first or second hand experience of the dead. Once beyond that cognitive level, it is more abstract ancestral veneration in direct connection with a specific location that will become significant, so that particular reference points in the landscape would develop over time which were allocated to the "ancestors" in general. As has been seen at Ballyglass (Mayo 13), Trelystan and possibly Grendon, after a time lapse of up to 300–500 years the locations could be converted to the local depository for the dead by the construction of a tomb, thus bringing the recently dead into direct contact with – and renewing the process of converting them into – the pantheon of abstract ancestors.

The role of mortuary houses and the large concentric structures seen at the great henges of Mount Pleasant and Durrington Walls, or sites such as Woodhenge and the Sanctuary, are of a completely different scale structurally to those sites referred to above. The mortuary houses by their very nature are generally closely associated with barrows and cairns, and in many cases are buried by (as at Gwernvale; see Britnell and Savory 1984), or incorporated into, burial monuments (as at Fussell's Lodge; see Ashbee 1966). The generally clear association between the mortuary houses and skeletal deposits, and the superimposition of or incorporation into burial sites gives these structures a defined role in the disposal of the dead.

In contrast, the concentric structures are much larger than the "domestic" sites discussed above, they are circular as opposed to the rectilinearity of the smaller sites, and their location within henges or forming an element of "ritual landscapes" suggests their role was more specialized and related to the ceremonial repertoire of the local communities. On a micro-level there is some evidence to suggest that certain sites such as the Southern Circle at Durrington Walls (Wainwright and Longworth 1971, 23–38) and Woodhenge (Cunnington 1929) had a basic design concept underpinning their structural layout which restricted and more importantly channelled access into their interiors (Thomas 1991, 49–52).

A similar feature may be present at Mount Pleasant, Site IV, Phase 1 (*cf.* Wainwright 1979, 9–31), where radial access routes appear to divide the concentric rings into quadrants, these access routes focusing on the centre of the structure. One important point at Mount Pleasant is that the southern radial route is noticeably blocked at the innermost circle by a prominent posthole, thus denying or hindering access into the centre from this direction, and emphasizing the need to confuse movement at this site, perhaps in a way not dissimilar to that suggested above for the large hall at Balbridie. It may be that the southern cardinal point was some form of immediate symbolic solar reference which needed to be highlighted by the placement of this additional post or other vertical feature.

CONCLUSION

Perhaps the main question to address is whether the structure and internal details of the Neolithic house symbolize and reflect a Neolithic world view in microcosm, or whether they relate to a series of functional requirements associated with a specific subsistence regime. The variations in dimensions of the houses of the Atlantic fringe of Europe illustrate not only chronological development, but may suggest that the symbolic/ functional requirements of domestic architecture in Britain and Ireland were largely different from mainland Europe. It is possible that settlement structure and size indirectly reflects the acceptance of the "Neolithic package" in Britain (*cf.* Kinnes 1988, 7) and Ireland, and that fewer traits were adopted, particularly in the case of extended longhouses, which are noticeable by their absence in Britain and Ireland. Despite possible data recovery bias, one is left with the impression that in terms of general settlement and house development the same symbolic or socio-economic constraints did not apply in Britain and Ireland as in mainland Europe. Large *Bandkeramik* type villages simply did not exist, and the settlement pattern was one of small discrete dispersed units which catered for various levels of ritual behaviour, domestic residence and specialized functions.

The longhouses associated with unusual structural traits or deposits discussed above comprise six from a corpus of 40 sites in Britain and Ireland, which is a significant 15%. However, the identification of the unusual may encompass only one level of ritual behaviour, should we naively expect a ritual differentiation to necessarily correlate with novel features? The distinction between secular and ritual may have been clouded, and the more "normal" house plans and deposits might equally reflect a different level of ritual behaviour from those with a distinctly unusual record. The preconceptions of ritual behaviour and structure engendered by contemporary beliefs may well inhibit the identification of Neolithic ritual behaviour simply by the expectation of a separate structure in the archaeological record. To reiterate the point made earlier, can the Neolithic house be seen simply as a residence and not also as a venue for ritual behaviour – should longhouses not be more appropriately seen as a domestic ritual monument?

Acknowledgements
My thanks go to Al Oswald who read and commented on a draft of this paper. Needless to state, opinions and errors remain the responsibility of the author.

Notes
1. The European examples were drawn from France, Belgium and Denmark.

Chapter 12

Life is not that simple: Architecture and cosmology in the Balinese house

Colin Richards

INTRODUCTION

Despite an acknowledgement by archaeologists that Neolithic societies constitute totally alien entities, there remains a tendency in interpretation towards ideas of "common sense" and "practicality". Often, however, it is forgotten that such conceptions are contingent and therefore "alien" to the society under investigation. Nowhere is this occurrence more exemplified than in the interpretation of domestic architecture. For instance, how often is it suggested that consistency in house orientation is due to factors such as prevailing wind direction, or that internal architecture is governed by available raw materials (eg. Startin 1978). Yes, these factors have to be taken into account, but in no way are they of the deterministic level which such interpretations would elevate them. This line of interpretation is actually quite inconsistently applied, for example, I have not come across the suggestion that the easterly orientation of earthen long barrows is due to prevailing winds from the southwest. It can only be assumed that this explanation is ignored because of the religious nature of the long barrow. Perhaps this is the basis of the problem where certain areas of material culture are still assigned as "ritual" and are seen as representing the "irrational", as opposed to the "domestic" with all its connotations of rationality. I suggest that if we uncritically use our common sense and rationality to interpret any part of the Neolithic it will always become "irrational".

In many traditional societies, categories such as directionality and orientation, form part of a complex system of classification and can express a host of associated meanings. Similarly, the architecture of the house and settlement may be based on a range of conceptions of order derived from cosmological principles (*cf.* Parker Pearson and Richards 1994). These themes are, of course, only realized through social practices and what is often neglected in archaeological studies is that the important aspect of architecture is the way in which it controls and governs movement. For example, when discussing entrance orientation it is often forgotten that its significance lies in the direction the subject moves to gain access or exit, hence, when an entrance to a building is easterly orientated, the subject moves west to gain admission. As orientation forms part of broader classifications, the movement of an individual in a particular direction carries many connotations including degrees of purity, pollution, sanctity, and so on.

It was through an appreciation of these ideas, gained from anthropological and ethnographic studies, which influenced my re-analysis of the architecture of Orcadian

Colin Richards

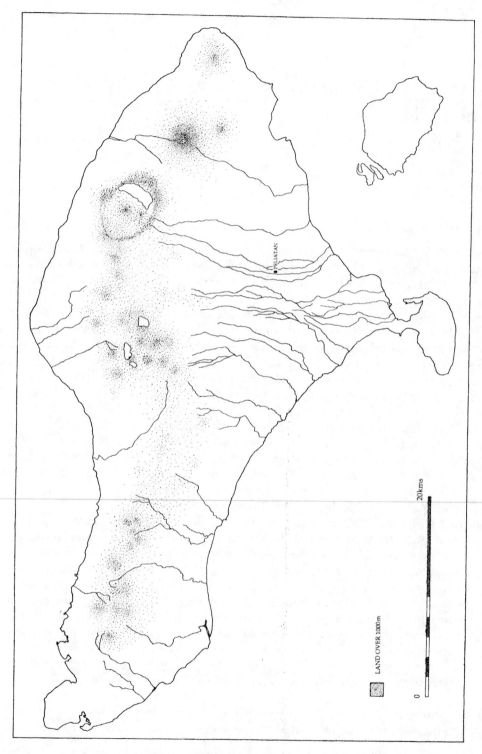

PELIATAN

LAND OVER 1000m

0

20kms

Figure 12.1: Map of Bali.

late Neolithic houses (Richards 1990a). Furthermore, it was the desire to witness and interpret the degree to which the cosmological principles of order manifest in architecture maintains a reflexive relationship with social practices which led to a short period of fieldwork in Bali, Indonesia. In the following account of life in the Balinese house, I hope to show both the importance of cosmology in architecture and the way it structures social practices within different temporal cycles.

THE HOUSE IN BALI

The Balinese conceive and order the world according to an elaborate cosmological system based upon opposed categories (Covarrubias 1986, 76). However, the central area or balancing point between such categories is an important and constantly realized principle which gives rise to a tripartite classification of the world. This structure is objectified in the natural features of the island (Figure 12.1). For example, the northern mountain range, particularly the highest peak, Gunung Agung, is identified as sacred, a place of deities and ancestral spirits; the navel of the world. In contrast, the ocean is recognized as an impure and dangerous place where the cremated bones of the dead are deposited and monsters and demons reside in its depths. In between, on the fertile slopes of the volcanoes live the Balinese, forever aware of their precarious and ambiguous central position.

The spatial distinctions between the mountains and the sea translate into cardinal directions, which, due to the majority of Balinese living to the south of the mountains, tend to coincide with north and south. The consistent path of movement of the sun introduces two further points on the horizon; east and west. Thus, sunrise and sunset combine with mountains and sea to create four cardinal directions around a central point.

Through my observations (see also Hobart 1978, 5–8), this forms the basis of a symbolic classification which is further complicated by the influence of Hindu symbolism which adds four more directions; southeast, southwest, northeast, and northwest. Thus giving a total of eight directions around a central point, each of which has associated deities, colours and many other qualities and meanings. This schema is frequently pictorially displayed on cloth and pottery and used as a holy symbol (Figure 12.2), and is often observed in ritual contexts. However, it is the ideas associated with the north – centre – south division which appears to predominate in a wide range of Balinese social practices. Particularly in the tangible areas of architecture and everyday activities.

The symbolic ordering of space, people, and things is constantly realized in the social practices of the Balinese. All aspects of daily life involve knowledge of orientation and classification; a constant sense of "place". Hence, it is a mistake to maintain a contrast between the architecture of the house or village as a microcosm, and the house or village as a response to practical needs (and see Geertz 1959). Apart from providing ontological status to acceptable behaviour in specific social situations, a particularly important aspect of Hindu life, the cosmological principles of order within any social context provide a potential which may be developed in practice, particularly in terms of authority and social position. By offering examples of how spatial symbolism is drawn on in various contexts

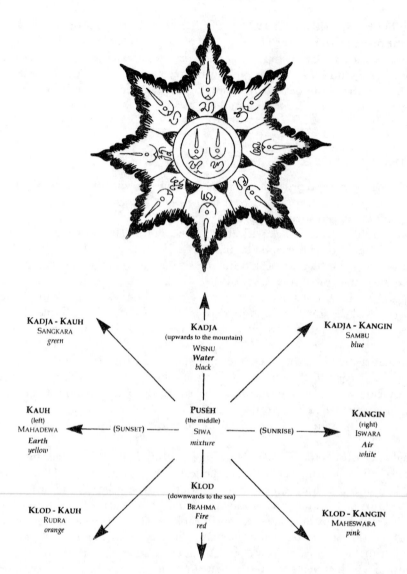

KADJA - KAUH
SANGKARA
green

KADJA
(upwards to the mountain)
WISNU
Water
black

KADJA - KANGIN
SAMBU
blue

KAUH
(left)
MAHADEWA
Earth
yellow

(SUNSET)

PUSÉH
(the middle)
SIWA
mixture

(SUNRISE)

KANGIN
(right)
ISWARA
Air
white

KLOD
(downwards to the sea)
BRAHMA
Fire
red

KLOD - KAUH
RUDRA
orange

KLOD - KANGIN
MAHESWARA
pink

Figure 12.2: Flower of the winds and the Balinese cardinal directions

of Balinese life I wish to show the significance of architectural order to everyday situations as well as larger communal rituals.

The Balinese house (see Howe 1983), is rectangular in shape and a surrounding wall encloses a number of small buildings (Figure 12.3). The wall can be built of brick, mud, or bamboo, according to the prosperity of the family. A single doorway provides access into the compound. Frequently, this entrance has an internal barrier wall known as the *aling-aling* which prohibits direct movement into the internal area and to a large degree restricts visual access (Figure 12.4). However, the presence of the *aling-aling* is attributed

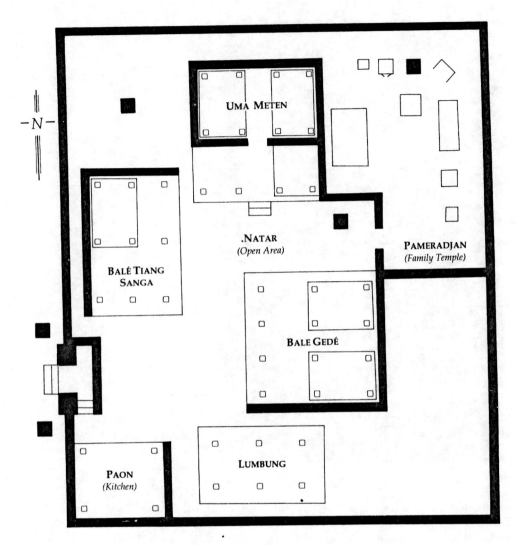

Figure 12.3: The Balinese house

to the defence of the house from evil spirits which are supposed to be unable to turn corners. The house compound is always orientated towards the sacred mountains and since the majority of the three million inhabitants of Bali live in the fertile, well irrigated south, the long axis of the enclosure assumes a north to south orientation. By virtue of its rectangular shape the side walls maintain an east and west aspect. A constant awareness of orientation and the auspicious nature of the directions north and east is a strong feature of Balinese life, to the extent of influencing the position of the head during sleep which should always be towards the northeast. Even with such an apparent concern with

Figure 12.4: Photograph of the view through the entrance to a Balinese house

orientation it is interesting to note that of a survey of a hundred houses in the Ubud – Peliatan – Bedulu area of central southern Bali, within a 5km radius, revealed a 70 degree variation in house alignment, centred on magnetic north. Such discrepancies, within a society with a keen sense of directionality, should provide the archaeologist with a realistic appreciation of the inconsistencies of orientation. This is particularly relevant to Neolithic studies where exact precision is often expected (and looked for in ridiculous detail) with regard to solar or lunar alignments.

The eight Balinese cardinal directions around a central point are translated into a symbolic division of space within the interior of the house compound dividing it into nine areas. Despite this complex classification of space, it appears to be the tripartite north – centre – south: east – centre – west divisions which exert the greater influence in structuring daily activities (*cf.* Hobart 1978). As we have seen the northern area of the compound enjoys a higher degree of ritual purity than the inauspicious southern region. However, this is not merely a two dimensional ordering since the orientation of the house combined with the overall topography of the island, frequently results in the northern area being physically, as well as symbolically, higher than the rest of the interior. Here the topography of the natural features of the island introduces the vertical dimension into the cosmological schema with the height of Gunung Agung representing the sacred and the depths of the ocean the impure. The flow of water from the mountains to the sea provides a metaphor for this aspect of purity/impurity (see Forge 1982).

Within the house this distinction is enhanced through the architecture of the buildings. For instance, the family temple situated in the northeast has a raised ground level, thus to gain entry one has to climb two or more steps. The height of the individual shrines and the absence of a constricting roof combine to give an impression of unlimited height. The absence of a roof is suggested to allow the deities and ancestors to descend on ritual occasions. The only structure situated in the northern area is the *una metin*, and in the houses examined, this building consistently had a higher floor level than other buildings within the compound. The *una metin* is the sleeping quarters of the head or elder of the family, and here we may equate age with spiritual acendency. As will be discussed later, this building is, on specific occasions, considered to be a place of great ritual purity.

In relation to the north, the middle area of the house is considered less auspicious although its pivotal position allows a certain flexibility with an east – west distinction coming into operation. It is suggested that in the spatial representation of the house, the middle area is directly analogous to the ambiguous central position of human beings in the Balinese conception and ordering of the natural world, complete with its own opposed principles of east-west / good-bad and so on; principles or qualities which the Balinese continually strive to keep in balance and harmony. As with many other societies, east tends to be associated with beginnings and rebirth, while west is associated with death and old age (Howe 1983, 142). In the eastern confines of the house compound lies the *Bale' Gede*. This building is separated from the westerly situated *Bale' Dauh* by the open and symbolically neutral central area, known as the *Natah*. The *Bale' Gede* is an open building having only a rear wall and is therefore well lit, as opposed to the *Bale' Dauh* which is walled and extremely dark inside. The auspicious and important nature of the *Bale' Gede* is revealed in its easterly position and in being physically linked to the family temple by its rear wall. Its floor level is almost the height of the *una metin* and it serves as the context for the majority of rites of passage in the life of a family member. In contrast the westerly *Bale' Dauh* is a place for non-inheriting sons and daughters and is also where the corpse is laid out and kept after the washing ceremonies.

The southern region of the compound is deemed impure by virtue of its lowly inauspicious direction (it is said to face the sea) this notion of impurity is manifest in the activities occurring within its confines. However, this is also an area involved with transformations, particularly natural to cultural, and these processes are predictably heavily sanctioned. The kitchen tends to be situated adjacent to the pigsty, in the southwestern corner. An immediate opposition is thus established with the family temple in the northeast. The Balinese for kitchen is *Paon* which is formed from *aon*, meaning ash of the hearth, hence, *Paon* is place of the hearth ash. The floor of the kitchen is generally at ground level, or if raised, remains the lowest floor level within the house (Figure 12.5). Internally, the fireplace is situated adjacent to the rear (southern) wall. In assuming this position it conforms to the general symbolic order which identifies fire with the deity

Figure 12.5: Photograph of the Paon (kitchen) in a Balinese house

Brahma, the colour red, and the direction south. Because of its transformatory qualities, there are many sanctions surrounding the use of fire. A special shrine made from the same clay as that used to form the hearth is always positioned nearby, this often receives offerings before the fire is used (Covarrubias 1986, 96–7). Whether for cooking, firing pottery, or smelting bronze, the position of the fire is always in the south of the compound or working area and its use is always surrounded by ritual observances.

Being an area of food preparation, the kitchen is a polluted area because of the spilling of blood onto the floor and the presence of dead animals. Indeed, for the Balinese, the conception of food substance is diametrically opposed to that of the insubstantial human spirit or essence, just as spatially the kitchen is opposed to the family temple in the northeast. Under these circumstances it is not surprising to learn that in Balinese body symbolism the head is associated with the family temple and the lower part of the body with the kitchen area.

It is important to stress that such oppositions are not clear cut, static "either or" distinctions, for instance, ideas of purity – impurity vary by degree and spatial symbolism is contingent on social practices. This is revealed in the strict prohibition placed on women entering the kitchen during menstruation and until three days after childbirth, since they are in a state of ritual pollution – *sebel*. However, the period of pollution after childbirth actually extends for 42 days and between 3 to 9 days the mother and baby (also in a similar state) are participants in one of the earliest rites of passage which significantly, takes place within the kitchen.

It is quite noticeable that it is women who are associated with the activities undertaken in the southern area. All food preparation and cooking within the house is normally undertaken by women either within or in close proximity to the kitchen. The rice barn is also situated in this area, normally positioned to the southeast. Although grown and tended by both sexes in the fields, when rice is brought into the house, it falls under the control of women who process and cook it. Similarly, the keeping of pigs, penned in the southern area, is the responsibility of the women who rear them and either sell them at market, keeping the profits themselves, or else use them for family ceremonies.

The ideas surrounding the symbolism of space within the house also effect the local environs. For instance, on the death of an individual, not only are the immediate family members of the "house" deemed to be in a state of ritual pollution but also the inhabitants of adjacent houses. However, the period of time that families in adjacent houses are "polluted" varies according to which direction they lie in relation to the house where a death has occurred. Hence, the inhabitants of the house situated to the south remain in a polluted state longer than those living in the house situated to the north.

Having described the architecture and symbolic organization of space within the Balinese house, I now wish to provide examples of how cosmological principles of order, manifest in architectural representation, structure social action. Hopefully, in doing so, the reflexive nature of spatial representation on the subject will be revealed in the constant reproduction and thus naturalization of strategies of authority. Different activities within different temporal cycles have been selected to illustrate this process; the first concerns the paths of movement taken by the subject when entering and moving within the house.

The Balinese village is always centred on a crossroads which correspond to the four cardinal points (Figure 12.6). The house entrance is not orientated towards any specific direction but is dictated by access to the adjacent road or track. This means that the entrance may face north, south, east, or west. As we have seen, directly inside the entrance is the barrier wall *aling-aling* which effectively prohibits forward movement, forcing one to turn either right or left in order to gain admittance to the house interior. This arrangement is absent, however, when the doorway faces north. Under these circumstances a long passage leads the subject down to the southwestern area of the compound.

It is this same rule of entry which determines the direction of movement through the entrances facing, east, west, and south (*cf.* Tan 1967, 454). When entering from the east one has to turn left at the *aling-aling*, conversely, when coming from the west one has to turn right. Admission from the south brings the east-west / right-left distinction into play and the subject turns to the west or left (Figure 12.7).

It can be seen that regardless of the direction of entry into the compound the subject is channelled into the southwest area of the house, thus ensuring a sequential passage from the dangerous and impure outside world into an internal area of transformation and impurity, before access is gained to other areas of the house. Hence symbolic order is both adhered to and reproduced in the path of movement into the interior. Moreover, it is noticeable that this route of entry, from front to back, places the visitor under the general scrutiny of the occupants, particularly the family elders, ideally situated at the rear in the *una metin*.

The situation and symbolic ordering of each building inside the house compound and

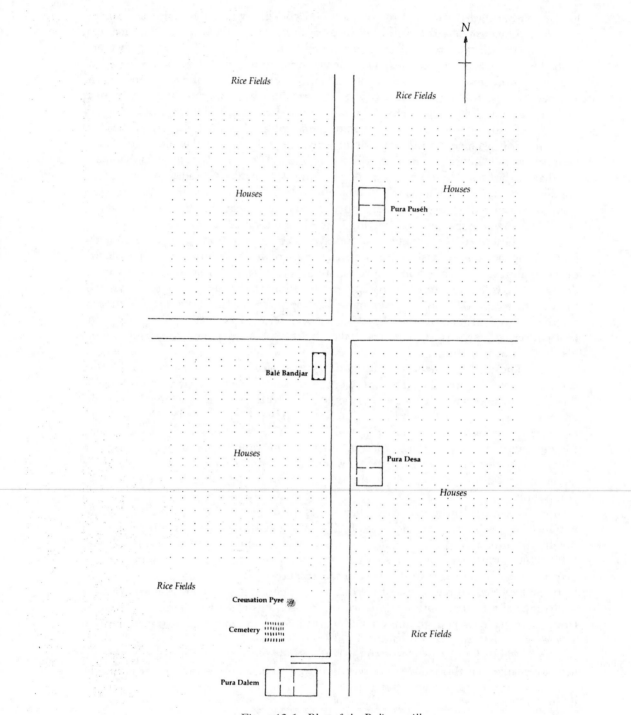

Figure 12.6: Plan of the Balinese village

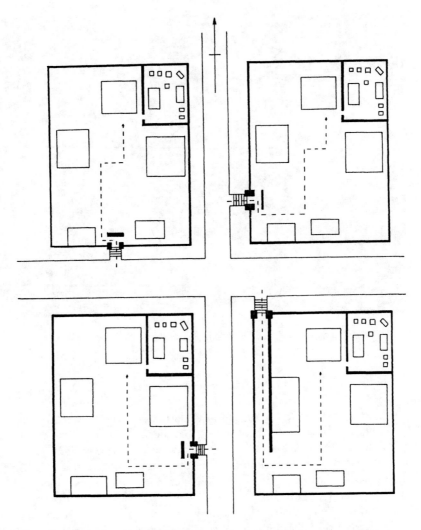

Figure 12.7: Movement within the Balinese house. (After Tan 1967)

its doorway orientation, dictates the direction of movement necessary to gain entry and exit. For example, by virtue of the position of the temple in the northeast corner; the most sacred internal area, its entrance must be positioned either in the south or west. Thus when entering the temple the subject is moving in the most auspicious of directions; east or north. This same rule effects movement into all the other buildings, clearly defining their symbolic status.

Moving to the daily cycle of activities which occur within the house, we find a similar pattern of events. At dawn the women and men rise together, the men go to the rice fields and generally the women venture out of the compound to collect water for the day.

Figure 12.8: The daily offerings within a Balinese house

On returning to the house, the women, enter the kitchen and light the fire for the day's cooking.

Food preparation for the entire day is undertaken early in the morning and takes about three hours. Only after the cooking has been completed do the women take offerings of rice to the other areas of the compound. Slowly moving northwards they place them at specific locations within the house, either on the ground or on the floors of the buildings, since these offerings are to appease the evil spirits which reside at a low level near the ground (Figure 12.8).

In these routine activities we again see the recreation of symbolic order in the temporal and spatial practices of daily life. It is only at later times of the day that family members undertake activities in the northern area of the compound and end the day sitting on the open fronts of their sleeping quarters.

The final series of activities to be examined are those of the life cycle rituals of the family (see Hobart 1978). Interestingly, birth takes place in the *una metin*, in the north of the house compound. If the child is female, the placenta is placed in a coconut and buried in a small pit to the left of the doorway, if male, it is buried to the right. Paradoxically, although the new born child is considered to be in a polluted state, *sebel*, the soul is still seen as being sacred. Thus, if the child dies within the first 42 days of its life it is not buried within the cemetery and the spirit does not require the purification ritual of cremation, since the soul is as yet untarnished. In another sense, this represents a sociological distinction as the child has taken on no human "social" role at this age. In providing the context of birth the *una metin* is both fulfilling its role as the most northerly and therefore most sacred dwelling, and in being the residence of the family elders who, after becoming grandparents, attain a higher degree of ritual purity. It is therefore, a context of juxtaposition, establishing links between the old with the new and re-establishing the cyclical nature of time and the generations.

The next rite of passage occurs at three days, when the child has to some degrees lost its sacred qualities but not its pollution. Appropriately this ceremony occurs to the south in the kitchen. After 105 days the ceremony of *nelubulan* takes place in the *Bale' Gede*. This marks the end of the period of pollution for the child and for the first time the *pemangku* (priest) may enter the house and perform the rituals. In moving north, to the context of the *Bale' Gede*, the child undergoes its first rites of passage, beginning a sequence of rituals which transfer it through all the stages of life, including, tooth-filing and marriage.

The *Bale' Gede* is also, if possible, the appropriate context of physical death. As pollution sets in the body is taken west, to a platform erected in the centre of the compound, and washed. The corpse is then taken further to the west where it is laid out in the *Bale' Dauh* with the head facing the west, in preparation for burial or immediate cremation. If burial is undertaken, the corpse is carried southwest to the cemetery, without ceremony, and buried in a grave to the southwest of the cremation mound. When a buried corpse is to be cremated the remains are exhumed and either immediately burnt on the pyre or returned to the house for preparation. In the latter situation or when the corpse has to be immediately cremated after death (as in the case of the death of a *pemangku*), a breach is supposed to be made in the wall of the house, since the main doorway may not be used to transfer the dead.

After the cremation and associated rituals the soul or essence is finally separated from the body as represented by the charred bones. The pure soul, as symbolized by an effigy, is taken in a northeasterly direction back to the house. After a brief spell on the upper shelf in the east of the *Bale Gede* it is finally placed in the ancestral shrine in the family temple. Thus, the circular journey from birth to death is finally completed and ready to begin again (Hobart 1978). As opposed to the passage of the soul, the cremated bones, the remains of the polluted body, are taken from the cremation area south, to be deposited in the sea.

CONCLUSION

In tracing the different rites of passage it is clear that cosmological order manifest in architectural representation structures human action, and that such action embodies spatiality and temporality. These procedures are endlessly reproduced in virtually every imaginable social situation. They are however dependant on interpretation and open to manipulation. In this way action is given an ontological status together within a complex process of naturalization. Sometimes subtle, sometimes not, for instance, it is no coincidence that the Brahmin cemetery is not only separate from that of the lower castes, but is positioned to the northeast. In Bali, even in death, there is no escape from architecture and cosmological principles of order.

In this account I have hopefully illustrated the influences of cosmological principles of order in the architecture of the Balinese house and the way this spatial representation structures social practices. Clearly, in the different temporal cycles discussed it would be a nonsense to attempt any division between "ritual" and "domestic" activities. Yet archaeologists still use this distinctly western mode of analysis in their interpretations, particularly in reference to the house and settlement as opposed to funerary and ceremonial monuments. Perhaps most striking is the fact that in Bali the routines of daily life occur within an architecture created through cosmological themes of order. Admittedly, Balinese culture is renowned for its highly symbolic qualities, however, who is to say that people in Neolithic Britain were any the less concerned with religion and cosmology within their daily lives?

Acknowledgements

I would particularly like to thank Jane Downes who undertook a concurrent study on Balinese cremation ritual, and the people of Peliatan, Bali for their kind help and patience. Thanks also to John Barrett and Malcolm Mcleod who commented on this paper.

Chapter 13

Houses in the Neolithic imagination:
An Amazonian example

Christine Hugh-Jones

INTRODUCTION

The Indian longhouses of Northwest Amazonia are a far cry from the Neolithic houses of temperate Europe, and the investigator has the inestimable advantage of not only watching and discussing the construction of houses but also of observing their use and bringing a wealth of other information learned from the inhabitants to bear on an analysis of the use and meaning of space. Even so, the contemporary anthropologist of these isolated Amerindian communities is also reconstructing a past of indeterminate distance because their traditional longhouses have all but disappeared in the 1990s and the social context and economic life intimately related to traditional architecture are changing fast. This account derives from fieldwork in 1968–70 when the majority of Tukanoan Indians of the river Pirá-Paraná (a strategic route from the black waters of the Vaupés to the white waters of the Caquetá system in southeast Colombia) still lived in longhouses similar to those described by Alfred Russell Wallace and photographed by Koch-Grünberg (Wallace 1889, 189–190; Koch-Grünberg 1909/10).

Traditionally, Northwest Amazon Indians are organized into "house" societies: there are no villages with significant juxtaposition of buildings, rather there is a village within a house and the relation of the whole to the nearby river and cultivations, and then to the forest beyond, is enhanced by the community's isolation from similar units which may be hours away by canoe or forest trail. The house serves all architectural functions – social and economic, ritual and secular – by sheltering a three-dimensional space for human activity but, besides this more concrete function, it provides the key to a symbolic system encompassing the entire Indian world and the mechanism of its continuity. It is this symbolic function that I shall explore here in order to let the Neolithic archaeologist reflect on the essential fabric of that metaphorical rope which ties his hands behind his back.

Like all human societies, Pirá-Paraná Indians have a broad ideological concern with the life-cycle, the reproduction of the physical and social person, and with the reproduction of society itself. To order and control the on-going creative process, powers beyond the individual must be harnessed and manipulated but the means to this end are set by the biological nature and material culture of the actors. Indians are obliged to move around in everyday space and use familiar objects to meet their physical and ideological needs. In the rhythm of Indian life, birth, growth, marriage, parenthood, and death are intertwined with the production of food, tobacco, and coca, utensils, ornaments, and houses. The spaces in which these activities and processes take place can be manipulated because they have multiple meanings. They make up a symbolic system composed of a Chinese box-like arrangement of spatial metaphors. The house is the middle box which contains the individual and is contained by the wider universe but, in spite of their different sizes, each box can stand for any other. Sadly, the space in this publication is not as fluid as that which provides my subject and therefore I hope the reader will accept that this brief presentation of formal static models stands for a much more comprehensive analysis of the ways in which spaces are defined and created by Indian activity – both physical and mental (see C Hugh-Jones 1979).

THE INHABITANTS

Pirá-Paraná Indians belong to a larger cultural group of Tukanoans and are divided into exogamous, patrilineal groups each of which, by and large, occupies a continuous area and has a distinct Eastern Tukanoan language. Within the exogamous group, of fifty to several hundred individuals, there are sub-groups arranged as a hierarchical set of siblings, the "older brothers" ideally living in downstream longhouses. A longhouse group is based on an extended patrilineal family with in-married wives, the daughters marrying out into other local groups. Daily life is governed by a division of labour between the sexes: men fell and burn the forest to provide gardens in which women plant, tend, and harvest bitter manioc – the staple – as well as other food crops. Men cultivate coca and tobacco and process the leaves. Men also build houses, make all weapons and wooden or basketry objects, hunt and do most of the fishing, while women process food – spending most of the day in gardening and manioc processing – cook and make all pottery. Both sexes gather plant and animal foods from the forest. The daily round is punctuated by ritual gatherings at which a number of longhouse groups visit a host community to drink manioc beer, use tobacco, coca and *yagé* (a hallucinogenic drink produced from *Banisteriopsis caapi*), chant about ancestral times, and dance decorated with feather ornaments and body paint. The occasion for these rituals may be the ritual exchange of food – smoked meat, fish or insects and preserved forest fruits – or it may be the playing of ancestral flutes, forbidden to women, which are the agents of male initiation and the embodiment of sacred power (see S Hugh-Jones 1979).

THE HOUSE

The longhouse is really a huge roof, gabled at one end and rounded at the other, supported by a structure of vertical posts, horizontal beams, and angled poles. The covering is made of palm leaves woven into overlapping horizontal slats whilst woven palm-leaf screens form the low perimeter walls and the internal family compartments. The gabled end is decorated with geometrical paintings on bark-cladding and contains the main, "men's" door. There is a "women's" door opposite to this in the rounded end and each of the family compartments clustered around the women's end of the house has a makeshift door out onto the cleared, sandy patio. The ground plan shows both bilateral symmetry

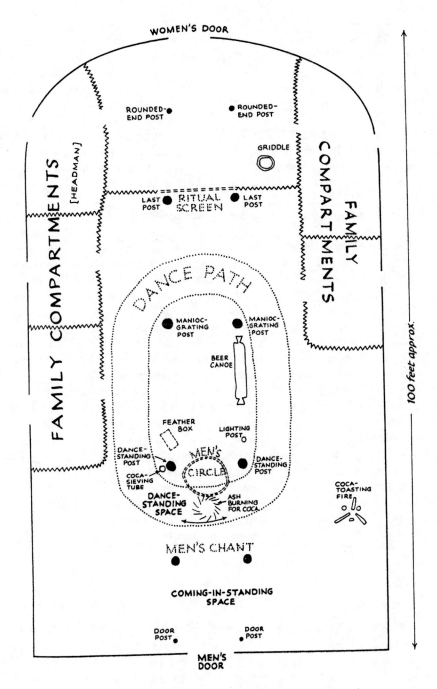

Figure 13.1: Groundplan of an Amazonian longhouse interior

and symmetry between the men's and women's ends but in neither case is this symmetry complete. The box of feather ornaments hangs from a roof beam on the "right" of the house (which we would call the "left" because we take our own, and not the house's, point of view) while the post for burning resin to give light at night is on the "left". The male and female ends are distinguished by shape and by the positions of activities, for instance the coca-tasting area and the site of the manioc-baking griddle (Figure 13.1).

The Indians say the house is man, "Roof-Father". The men's door is his mouth, surrounded by face-painting; the roof-supports are his rib-cage; the leaves his feathers; the box of ornaments his soul. In keeping with this body-model, during masked funerary rituals (no longer performed) the Dung-Beetles were posted at the women's door – the anus. The use of the main, men's door for the formal reception of visitors and gifts of food and of the women's door for waste-disposal fits this body-model and exemplifies an inequality between the sexes which are both different in kind and different in social value.

Besides having its own outside door, each family compartment has a central hearth. The family area as a whole is associated with the communal, women's end of the house and these two are combined and contrasted with the centre-front of the house when the ritual screen is erected during ceremonies at which women and children are prohibited. Although both sexes use the communal house-space in everyday life, the tendency for women to stay on the periphery, or towards the back-door, and for men to occupy the centre-front becomes an increasingly binding rule according to the formality of the occasion. At night, when visitors arrive, or during rituals, women use the centre-front of the house only for certain regulated activities and, conversely, during menstruation or following child-birth they are strictly confined to the periphery. In general, the use of space demonstrates the contrasts between male and female, public and private, community and domestic family unit, patrilineal continuity and female reproductive powers and also super imposes these pairs of opposed meanings, the one upon the other. In spatial terms these contrasts are arranged either as poles of a longitudinal structure – the male and female doors of the house – or in a concentric fashion with periphery contrasted to centre – family compartments and communal floor space. If the longitudinal model expresses formal relations between the sexes, the concentric one expresses the relationship between the longhouse group and its composite families, each dependent on the reproductive powers of the incoming wife. The relationship is acted out daily as each wife brings food from her compartment and sets it down for a communal meal in the centre of the house. The longitudinal and concentric models are elided in the structure of the house (Figure 13.2).

THE SOCIAL ORDER

The eliding or merging of these two models allows a complex and shifting play on the relationship between men and women and their separate roles in human reproduction and the reproduction of socially-defined groups. The house is not simply a building of wood and leaves; it is a community which is structured, or built, according to the same principles as the house which shelters it, but it is built over the generations, in time.

The preferred marriage rule among Tukanoan Indians is bilateral cross-cousin marriage with repeated exchange of sisters between the males of allied exogamous groups. From the point of view of the patrilineage, the male generations accumulate in one place ("like the leaves on the forest floor", Indians say) while women oscillate back and forth. Although a man's sister must marry out, her daughter will marry back again and bear children who are the direct patrilineal descendants of this man. Semen, bones and "soul" are intimately related as different aspects of male continuity and the enduring nature of bones is underlined by the belief that the sacred flutes are the bones of the ancestors. Semen and bones, the stuff of male growth and patrilineal development, are contrasted, in Indian ideology, with menstrual blood and the cyclical rhythm of its loss. Women are creatures of constant regeneration and decay, while the male descent line, with its seniority-order between both generations and sets of living siblings, accumulates and endures. Perhaps this is enough to suggest that, although the periphery of a concentric model is "female" as opposed to the centre, if the whole idea of moving to and fro between centre and periphery is contrasted to the idea of movement forward along a straight line, the models themselves may be contrasted as "female" and "male". A sexual differentiation between "round" and "straight" models leads directly into the inevitable womb / penis symbolism which, it is no surprise to learn, Indian ideology makes much of (see Figure 13.2). To take an example from everyday routine: men toast coca leaves in a rounded pot stirring them round with a long-handled vine hoop. The obvious phallic connotations of stirring a pot are reinforced by the nature of pottery and coca themselves. Pots are made, exclusively by women, from clay derived from the rotting flesh of a mythical anti-hero. Coca, a men's crop, is planted in long, straight rows which cut across a rounded field of manioc. These rows are the bones of a mythical hero. Such reproductive symbolism permeates the whole spectrum of human activity.

BEYOND THE LONGHOUSE

Looking beyond the house there is a surrounding patio (Figure 13.2). At the front it is spacious and clean, often used for ritual purposes; at the back it is meagre and scattered with fruits shells and debris. Beyond are cultivations and then the forest. From the men's door leads a path to the river port where canoes are kept and visitors arrive. The river, after a series of confluences, is said to flow into the Milk River from whose mouth in the East the ancestors came in the form of an Anaconda-Canoe to populate the centre of the earth. Indians say that longhouse communities on their branching river systems are like souls joined by an umbilical cord to their ancestral origin in the East; they liken these houses on their ancestral rivers to the small pink fruits, much used in shamanism, which grow on the branching stems of a common herbaceous plant (*Sabicea amazonensis*).

Tukanoan Indians like to live on the main rivers. The senior or "chief" sub-group of an exogamous group is the head of the Ancestral Anaconda and should occupy the mouth of the river; the "younger" groups should be placed in order of seniority – chiefs, dancers and chanters, warriors, shamans, servants – with the last-born subgroups of "servants" the furthest upstream. Although no Makú Indians live in the Pirá-Paraná area today, these groups are well known to Pirá-Paraná Indians as nomadic hunters who

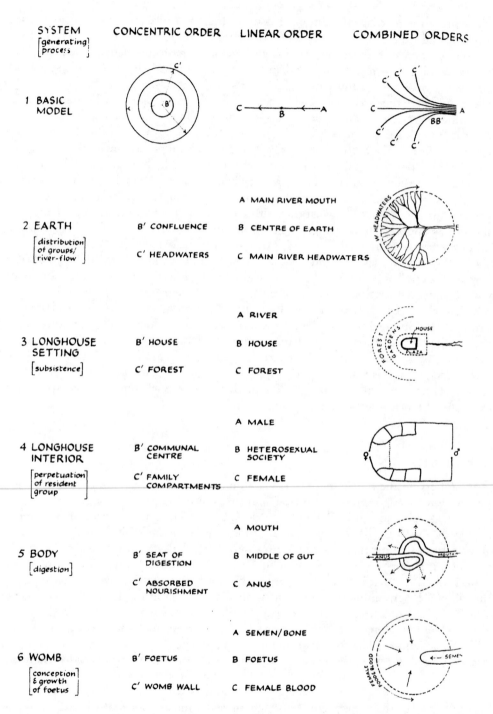

Figure 13.2: Models of horizontal time-space relationships

Figure 13.3: Anaconda model of Earth's River

exchange forest products and labour for cultivated food with neighbouring Tukanoans. They are universally regarded as inferior, incestuous people who inhabit headwater areas and behave like animals. Even further beyond the bounds of Tukanoan society are the forest spirits.

These beliefs and prescriptions suggest a model of the house poised between the creative ancestral source in the East and the dangerous headwaters on the western periphery, a model which contains a more formal and hierarchically-organized, linear dimension describing the "spiritual" aspect of social organization (Figure 13.3). The correspondence of these models with the ground-plan of the house, of which they are really just an extension in space, should be obvious.

THE VERTICAL DIMENSION

The models described so far have been set out in two-dimensional space but of course this is a gross simplification – as the box of feather ornaments tantalizingly suspended from the roof reminds us. While Indians can, and do, travel long distances in horizontal space, and tell of convincing encounters with alarming forest spirits in headwater swamps, the only encounters with ancestors in the East are the result of shamanic or hallucinogenic visions, dreams, or near-death experiences. The ancestral past is contacted by means of ritual where the dimensions of the universe are reduced to those of the house. Indians say the house becomes the universe: the central beam is the Sun's westerly path across the sky and the group of men chanting inside the men's door about the progression of the ancestral journey, with its transformation from water to land, are the ancestors themselves. They use spirit food or "drugs" (coca, tobacco, *yagé*, alcohol) instead of ordinary food. They undergo a mystical death from which they must be carefully revived afterwards by eating a series of shamanically-treated foods arranged from pure to most dangerous (predictably, the meat of large forest animals).

If the universe is represented by the house it should be no surprise to learn that the universe is also a human body. Indians say that the ancestral anacondas in the Milk River are like parasitic worms in the gut of the universe (Figure 13.2).

Even given the correspondence of house and universe, there are physical constraints on the use of vertical space which can only be overcome by a host of sliding-scale, multiple metaphors. The chanting men, for instance, are crowned with the feathers of birds which can fly above the trees and which represent the Sun's own feather crown. They are seated on stools which are mountains. The manipulation of underground space is more problematic, because ordinary human experience of it is limited to digging pits and graves and contact with underground or burrowing creatures. Besides being more problematic, it is less desirable because of the connotations of physical death and decay contained in the rotting flesh in the grave under the house and in the rotting placenta buried beyond the house at the site of child-birth.

In spite of the unpalatability of the whole notion, Indians do describe an underworld in myth. It is sometimes divided into two layers. A closer layer, associated with pits and graves, is the underworld equivalent of the attainable heights of trees and mountains; then there is a more distant layer which is the Sun's underworld river, continuous with his path across the sky, and with the great river system flowing downstream towards the East on this earth. We learn about the Sun's underworld layer in a myth about the origin of the vertical order of the world. In this myth, a hero first descends to the Sun's River and then returns to this earth. A halfway stage is provided, by a pit-fall tapir trap on the way down, and by a visit to a dance at the home of the underground Termite People on the way up. This myth specifies that the Sun canoes upstream ready to appear at dawn in the East. We learn about an alternative, more sinister, underground river in a different myth about a live woman who follows her dead husband to the River of the Dead. Disobeying instructions, she looks downstream and sees jostling corpses and grave ornaments floating off in the current. This woman is shown home by an agouti, a burrowing forest animal which enters cultivations to steal manioc. The myth about the woman shows that a downstream journey in the River of the Dead leads to the forest "west" of the longhouse while the myth about the Sun's River describes an upstream journey towards the East. The two journeys also serve to contrast a passive journey downstream associated with human decay and an active journey against the current, associated with the Sun's creative power.

It does not really matter whether the River of the Dead is the Sun's river (Indians disagree on this point) because both accounts emphasize the positive power of the East with respect to the negative, sinister powers of the West, a relationship which echoes that between the day and night, or life on earth and death in the grave. These parallels make it clear that there is a correspondence between the vertical axis of the universe and the longitudinal axis of the earth running from East to West (or from river mouth to forest headwaters) – a correspondence which extends to the longitudinal axis of the house with its sexually differentiated poles. The horizontal and vertical ordering of space are fundamentally similar, an anticlockwise rotation through 90 degrees transforming the East into the sky and the West into the underworld (Figure 13.4).

SO WHAT ?

This simplified sketch of the conception of space among the Tukanoan Indians, while it cannot begin to do justice to the richness of Indian symbolism, perhaps demonstrates the integration of the house itself with the social group it shelters. It took me many months of accompanying women to an fro with their manioc, pots of food and children and many years of struggling to make sense of piles of field-notes to appreciate the full significance of the rhythms of everyday domestic life. In a society where each person stands for the social order and each house stands for the universe, the most mundane

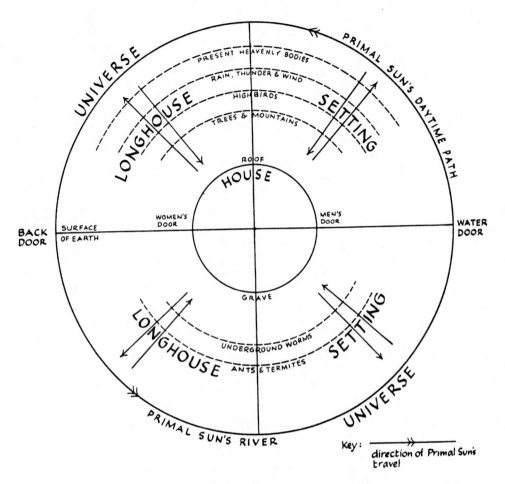

Figure 13.4: Model of vertical space-time relationships

activities have multiple levels of meaning. There are two major features of Tukanoan society that may make these models of space and social reproduction, with their theme of structural replication of body, house and universe, particularly powerful. Firstly, for most daily purposes each longhouse is a small social and economic world of its own. Secondly, the strict rule of exogamy lends the world outside the longhouse a very special power. The combination of these complementary features may lend themselves to model-making in a unique way; I would not expect such consistency in the ideology of space and time in a cognatic kinship system with local endogamy.

Of what use might all this be to an archaeologist who can find only the traces of house-structures and small hints about how they were used? I hope it will help to broaden the understanding of the relation between secular and religious or ritual functions of buildings and, beyond this, to stimulate the archaeological imagination to ask deeper questions about the social and intellectual life of people who build houses.

Ade-Rademacher, D, Bassler, T, Dresely, V, Rademacher, R, and Zimmer, S, 1987, Eine mittelneolithische Siedlung im "Hinterweil", Stadt Sindelfingen, Kreis Böblingen. *Archäologischen Ausgrabungen in Baden-Württemberg 1986*, 30–32

Adkins, K P, and Adkins, P C, 1991, A Neolithic settlement on the north bank of the River Blackwater. *Colchester Archaeological Group Annual Bulletin*, 34, 15–28

Angelova, I, 1981, Razkopki na selishtnata mogila Turgovishte, Turgovishte okrug. (Arkheologicheski otkritiya i razkopki za 1980). *26 Natsionalna Arkheologicheska Konpherentsiya*. Preslav. 18–19

Angelova, I, 1982a, Spasitelni razkopki na selishtnata mogila pri Turgovishte. (Arkheologicheski otkritiya i razkopki za 1981). *27 Natsionalna Arkheologicheska Konpherentsiya*. Mikhajlovgrad. 16–17

Angelova, I, 1982b, Tell Turgovishte. In H Todorova (ed), *Die kupferzeitliche Siedlungen in Nordostbulgarien*. Munich. Beck. 175–180

Angelova, I, 1986a, Eneolitnata selishtna mogila Turgovishte. *Interdistsiplinarni Izsledvaniya*, 14A, 33–44

Angelova, I, 1986b, Praistoricheski nekropol pri grad Turgovishte. *Interdistsiplinarni Izsledvaniya*, 14A, 49–66

Angelova, I, 1992. Predvaretel'ny rezultaty raskopok neoliticheskogo poseleniya Ovcarovo-gorata. *Studia Praehistorica*, 11–12, 41–50

ApSimon, A M, 1969, An early Neolithic House in Co Tyrone. *Journal of the Royal Society of Antiquaries of Ireland*, 99, 165–8

ApSimon, A M, 1976, Ballynagilly and the beginning and end of the Irish Neolithic. In S J de Laet (ed), *Acculturation and continuity in Atlantic Europe* (= Dissertationes Archaeologicae Gandenses 16). Bruges. De Tempel. 15–30

Armit, I, 1988, *Excavations at Loch Olabhat, North Uist 1988* (= Department of Archaeology, University of Edinburgh, Project Paper 10). Edinburgh. University of Edinburgh

Armit, I, 1992, The Hebridean Neolithic. In N Sharples and A Sheridan (eds), *Vessels for the Ancestors*. Edinburgh. Edinburgh University Press. 307–321

Ashbee, P, 1960, *The Bronze Age round barrow in Britain*. London. Phoenix House

Ashbee, P, 1966, The Fussell's Lodge long barrow. *Archaeologia*, 100, 1–80

Ashbee, P, 1984, *The earthen long barrow in Britain* (2nd Edition). Norwich. Geo Books

Asingh, P, 1987, Diverhoj – A Complex Burial Mound and a Neolithic Settlement. *Journal of Danish Archaeology*, 6, 130–154

Bailey, D W, 1990, The living house: Signifying continuity. In R Samson (ed), *The social archaeology of houses*. Edinburgh. Edinburgh University Press. 19–48

Bailey, D W, 1991, *The social reality of figurines from the Bulgarian Copper Age*. Unpublished PhD Dissertation. Cambridge. Cambridge University

Bailey, D W, 1993, Chronotypic tension in Bulgarian prehistory: 6500 – 3500 BC. *World Archaeology*, 25.2, 204–222

Bailey, D W, 1994, Reading prehistoric figurines as individuals. *World Archaeology*, 25.3, 321–331

Bailey, D W, (in press), Perspectives on Bulgarian prehistoric landscape: Continuity, sedentism and impermanence. In J Chapman and P Dolukanov (eds), *Landscape in Flux* (= Colloquenda Pontica).

Bakels, C C, 1987, On the adzes of the northwestern Linearbandkeramik. *Analecta Praehistorica Leidensia*, 20, 53–85

Bamford, H M, 1982, *Beaker domestic sites in the Fen Edge and East Anglia* (= East Anglian Archaeology 16). Norfolk. East Anglian Archaeology

Bamford, H M, 1985, *Briar Hill. Excavations 1974–1978* (= Northampton Development Corporation Archaeology Monograph 3). Northampton. Northampton Development Corporation

Banner, J, 1959, Anthropomorphe Gefässe der Theiss-Kultur von der Siedlung Kökénydomb bei Hódmezővásárhely (Ungarn). *Germania*, 37, 14–35

Barber, J, 1982, The investigation of some plough-truncated features at Kinloch Farm, Collessie in Fife. *Proceedings of the Society of Antiquaries of Scotland*, 112, 524–33

Barcham, R C, 1980, A lost radiocarbon date for Shetland. *Proceedings of the Society of Antiquaries of Scotland*, 110, 502–506

Barclay, G J, 1992, What's new in Scottish prehistory. *Scottish Archaeological Review*, 9, 3–14

Barclay, G J, 1993, *Balfarg: The prehistoric ceremonial complex*. Glenrothes. Fife Regional Council

Barclay, G J, and Tolan, M, 1990, The excavation of a terrace-edge enclosure at North Mains, Strathallan, Perthshire. *Proceedings of the Society of Antiquaries of Scotland*, 120, 45–54

Barclay, G J, and Russell-White, C J, (eds), 1993, Excavations in the ceremonial complex at Balfarg/Balbirnie, Glenrothes, Fife. *Proceedings of the Society of Antiquaries of Scotland*, 123, 43–210

Barfield, L H, and Hodder, M A, 1987, Burnt Mounds as saunas. *Antiquity*, 61, 370–379

Barker, C T, 1992, *The chambered tombs of south-west Wales* (= Oxbow Monograph 14). Oxford. Oxbow

Barnatt, J, 1995, Neolithic and Bronze Age radiocarbon dates from the Peak District: A review. *Derbyshire Archaeological Journal*, 115, 5–19

Barrett, J C, 1994, *Fragments from Antiquity: An archaeology of social life in Britain, 2900–1200 BC*. Oxford. Blackwell

Barrett, J C, Bradley, R J, and Green, M, 1991, *Landscape, monuments and society*. Cambridge. Cambridge University Press

Bell, M G, 1982, The effects of land-use and climate on valley sedimentation. In A Harding (ed), *Climatic change in later prehistory*. Edinburgh. Edinburgh University Press. 127–142

Beneš, J, 1991, Neolithische Siedlung in Hrdlovka-Liptice. Vorläufiger Bericht über die Forschung in den Jahren 1987–1989. *Archeologické Rozhledy*, 43, 29–46

Bengtsson, H, and Bergh, S, 1984, The hut sites on Knocknarea Mountain. In G Burenhult, *The archaeology of Carrowmore: Environmental archaeology and the megalithic tradition at Carrowmore, Co Sligo, Ireland* (= Theses and Papers in North-European Archaeology 14). Stockholm. Institute of Archaeology, University of Stockholm. 216–318

Bernhardt, G, and Hampel, A, 1992, Vorbericht zu einem ältestlinienbandkeramischen Siedlungs-platz in Frankfurt-Niedereschbach. *Germania*, 70, 1–16

Bersu, G, 1936, Rössener Wohnhäuser vom Goldberg, OA Neresheim, Württemberg. *Germania*, 20, 229–243

Bersu, G, 1937, Altheimer Wohnhäuser vom Goldberg, OA Neresheim, Württemberg. *Germania*, 21, 149–158

Bertemes, F, and Krastev, I, 1988, Die bulgarische-deutsche Ausgrabung in Drama, Bez. Burgas – Katalog. In A Fol and J Lichardus (eds), *Macht, Herrschaft und Gold*. Saarbruchen. Moderne Galerie des Saarland. 19–27

Bird-David, N, 1992, Beyond "the hunting and gathering mode of subsistence": Observations on the Nayaha and other modern hunter-gatherers. *Man* (NS), 27, 19–44

Boelicke, U, 1977, Das neolithische Erdwerk Urmitz. *Acta Praehistorica et Archaeologica*, 7/8, 73–121

Boelicke, U, 1982, Gruben und Häuser: Untersuchungen zur Struktur bandkeramischer Hofplätze. In *Siedlungen der Kultur mit Linearkeramik*. Nitra.

Boelicke, U, von Brandt, D, Lüning, J, Stehli, P, and Zimmerman, A, 1988, *Der bandkeramische Siedlungsplatz Langweiler 8. Gemeinde Aldenhoven, Kreis Düren*. Köln. Rheinland-Verlag

Bogucki, P, 1988, *Forest farmers and stockherders*. Cambridge. Cambridge University Press

Bogucki, P, and Grygiel, R, 1993, Neolithic sites in the Polish lowlands: Research at Brześć Kujawski, 1933 to 1984. In P Bogucki (ed), *Case studies in European prehistory*. Boca Raton, Florida. CRC Press. 147–80

Bökönyi, S, 1986, Environmental and cultural effects on the faunal assemblage at four large 4th millennium BC sites. *A Béri Balogh Múzeum Evkönyve*, 13, 69–88

Bourdieu, P, 1973, The Berber house. In M Douglas (ed), *Rules and meanings*. Harmondsworth. Penguin. 98–110

Bradley, R, 1970a, Where have all the houses gone? Some approaches to Beaker settlement. *Current Archaeology*, 2.10 (no. 21), 264–266

Bradley, R, 1970b, The excavation of a beaker settlement at Belle Tout, East Sussex, England. *Proceedings of the Prehistoric Society*, 36, 312–379

Bradley, R, 1978, A reconsideration of the late Neolithic site at Playden, East Sussex. In F Pryor, *Excavations at Fengate: Second report* (= ROM Archaeology Monograph 5). Toronto. Royal Ontario Museum. 219–223

Bradley, R, 1982, Belle Tout – Revision and reassessment. In P Drewett (ed), *The archaeology of Bullock Down, Eastbourne: The development of a landscape* (= Sussex Archaeological Society Monograph 1). Lewis. Sussex Archaeological Society. 62–71

Bradley, R J, 1987, Flint technology and the character of Neolithic settlement. In A Brown and M Edmonds (eds), *Lithic Analysis and later British prehistory* (= BAR British Series 162). Oxford. British Archaeological Reports. 67–86

Bradley, R, 1993, *Altering the earth*. Edinburgh. Society of Antiquaries of Scotland

Bradley, R J, and Chambers, R, 1988, A new study of the cursus complex at Dorchester on Thames. *Oxford Journal of Archaeology*, 7, 271–89

Brewster, T C M, 1969, Kemp Howe. *Archaeological Excavations 1968*. London. HMSO. 13

Britnell, W, 1981, Trelystan. *Current Archaeology*, 7.7 (no. 78), 201–5

Britnell, W, 1982, The Excavation of Two Round Barrows at Trelystan, Powys. *Proceedings of the Prehistoric Society*, 48, 133–201

Britnell, W, and Savory, H, 1984, *Gwernvale and Penywyrlod: Two Neolithic Long Cairns in the Black Mountains of Brecknock* (= CAA Monograph 2). Cardiff. Cambrian Archaeological Association

Brongers, J A, and Waltering, P J, 1978, *De Prehistorie van Nederlans*. Haarlem

Bruce, J R, Megaw, E M, and Megaw, B R S, 1947, A Neolithic site at Ronaldsway, Isle of Man. *Proceedings of the Prehistoric Society*, 13, 139–60

Burchard, B, 1973, The investigations of a Neolithic trapezoid-shaped building at Niedźwiedź, district of Miechow. *Sprawozdania Archeologiczne*, 25, 39–48

Burgess, C, 1984, The prehistoric settlement of Northumberland: A speculative survey. In R Miket and C Burgess (eds), *Between and beyond the Walls. Essays on the prehistory and history of North Britain in honour of George Jobey*. Edinburgh. John Donald. 126–175

Buttler, W, and Haberey, W, 1936, *Die bandkeramische Ansiedlung bei Köln-Lindenthal*. Berlin

Calder, C S T, 1950, Report on the excavation of a Neolithic temple at Stanydale in the parish of Sandsting, Shetland. *Proceedings of the Society of Antiquaries of Scotland*, 84, 185–205

Calder, C S T, 1956, Report on the discovery of numerous stone age house-sites in Shetland. *Proceedings of the Society of Antiquaries of Scotland*, 89, 340–397

Calder, C S T, 1961, Excavations in Whalsay, Shetland, 1954–5. *Proceedings of the Society of Antiquaries of Scotland*, 94, 28–45

Carsten, J and Hugh-Jones, S, (eds), 1995, *About the house: Levi-Strauss and beyond*. Cambridge. Cambridge University Press

Case, H J, 1961, Irish Neolithic pottery: Distribution and sequence. *Proceedings of the Prehistoric Society*, 27, 174–233

Case, H J, 1963, Notes on the finds and on ring-ditches in the Oxford region. *Oxoniensia*, 28, 19–52

Case, H J, 1973, A ritual site in north-east Ireland. In G Daniel and P Kjaerum (eds), *Megalithic graves and ritual*. Moesgård. Jutland Archaeological Society. 173–96

Catherall, P D, 1976, Excavations at Little Cheney, Dorset, 1974. In C Burgess and R Miket (eds), *Settlement and economy in the third and second millennia BC* (= BAR British Series 33). Oxford. British Archaeological Reports. 81–100

Caulfield, S, 1978, Neolithic fields – the Irish evidence. In H C Bowen and P J Fowler (eds), *Early land allotment* (= BAR British Series 48). Oxford. British Archaeological Reports. 137–43

Chapman, J, 1989, The early Balkan village. *Varia Archaeologica Hungarica*, 2, 33–53

Chapman, J, 1990, Social inequality on Bulgarian tells and the Varna problem. In R Samson (ed), *The social archaeology of houses*. Edinburgh. Edinburgh University Press. 49–92

Cheney, H J, 1935, A Neolithic occupation site at Playden near Rye. *Antiquaries Journal*, 15, 152–64

Chertier, B, 1980, Le site Neolithique de Larzicourt (Marne). Premiers resultats. *Prehistoire et Protohistoire en Champagne-Ardenne*. Chalons-sur-Marne. 51–67

Childe, V G, 1931, *Skara Brae: A Pictish Village in Orkney*. London. Kegan Paul

Childe, V G, 1949, *Prehistoric communities of the British Isles* (3rd Edition). London. W & R Chambers

Childe, V G, 1949, Neolithic house-types in temperate Europe. *Proceedings of the Prehistoric Society*, 15, 77–86

Childe, V G, 1950, *Ancient Dwellings at Skara Brae*. Edinburgh. HMSO

Childe, V G, and Grant, W G, 1939, A stone-age settlement at Braes of Rinyo, Rousay, Orkney (First report). *Proceedings of the Society of Antiquaries of Scotland*, 73, 6–31

Childe, V G, and Grant, W G, 1947, A stone-age settlement at Braes of Rinyo, Rousay, Orkney (Second report). *Proceedings of the Society of Antiquaries of Scotland*, 81, 16–42

Chowne, P, Healy, F, and Bradley, R, 1993, The excavation of a Neolithic settlement at Tattershall Thorpe, Lincolnshire. In R Bradley, P Chowne, R M J Cleal, F Healy and I Kinnes *Excavations on Redgate Hill, Hunstanton, Norfolk, and at Tattershall Thorpe, Lincolnshire* (= East Anglian Archaeology 57). Norwich. East Anglian Archaeology. 79–124

Clark, A, 1993, *Excavations at Mucking. Volume 1: The site atlas.* (= Historic Buildings and Monuments Commission for England Archaeological Report 20). London. English Heritage and The British Museum

Clark, J G D, 1937, Prehistoric houses. *Proceedings of the Prehistoric Society*, 3, 468–469

Clarke, A F, 1982, The Neolithic of Kent: A review. In P E Leach (ed), *Archaeology in Kent to AD 1500* (= CBA Research Report 48). London. Council for British Archaeology. 25–30

Clarke, D V, 1976a, *The Neolithic village at Skara Brae, Orkney, excavations 1972–3: An interim report*. HMSO. Edinburgh

Clarke, D V, 1976b, Excavations at Skara Brae: A summary account. In C Burgess and R Miket (eds), *Settlement and economy in the third and second millennia BC* (= BAR British Series 33). Oxford. British Archaeological Reports. 233–250

Clarke, D V, and Sharples, N, 1990, Settlement and subsistence in the third millennium bc. In C Renfrew (ed), *The prehistory of Orkney* (2nd Edition). Edinburgh University Press. Edinburgh. 54–82

Clarke, D V, Hope, R, Wickham-Jones, C, 1978, The Links of Noltland. *Current Archaeology*, 6.2 (no. 61), 44–6

Clayton, D, and Savory, H N, 1990, The excavation of a Neolithic hut floor on Cefn Glas, Rhondda, 1971–4. *Archaeologia Cambrensis*, 139, 12–20

Cleal, R M J, 1982, A re-analysis of the ring-ditch site at Playden, East Sussex. *Sussex Archaeological Collections*, 120, 1–17

Collins, A E P, 1952, Excavations in the Sandhills at Dundrum, Co. Down, 1950–51. *Ulster Journal of Archaeology*, 15, 2–26

Collins, A E P, 1978, Excavations on Ballygalley Hill, Co. Antrim. *Ulster Journal of Archaeology*, 41, 15–32

Cooney, G, and Grogan, E, 1994, *Irish prehistory: A social perspective.* Wordwell. Dublin

Cooney, G, and Grogan, E, (in press), People and place during the Irish Neolithic: Exploring change in time and space. In M Edmonds (ed), *Social life and social change: The Neolithic of north-western Europe.*

Coudart, A, 1989, Tradition, uniformity and variability in the architecture of the Danubian Neolithic. In J Rulf (ed), *Bylany Seminar 1987 – Collected papers.* Prague. Institute of Archaeology. 199–223

Coudart, A, 1992, Entre Nouvelle-Guinée et Néolithique européen: De la correspondance entre les variations de l'architecture domestique, la durabilité culturelle et la cohesion sociale du groupe. In *Ethnoarchéologie: Justification, problèmes, limites.* Juan-les-Pins

Covarrubias, M, 1986, *The Island of Bali.* London. KPL

Cowie, T G, 1979, Carwinning Hill. *Discovery and Excavation in Scotland 1978.* Edinburgh. The Scottish Group of the Council for British Archaeology. 28

Craig, B, 1988, Relic and Trophy Arrays as Art among the Mountain-Ok, Central New Guinea. In L Hanson and A Hanson (eds), *Art and identity in Oceania.* Bathurst. Robert Brown

Crone, A, 1993, Excavation and survey of sub-peat features of Neolithic, Bronze Age and Iron Age date at Bharpa Carinish, North Uist, Scotland. *Proceedings of the Prehistoric Society*, 59, 361–382

Cunnington, M E, 1929, *Woodhenge.* Devizes. Privately Printed

Cunnington, M E, 1931, The Sanctuary on Overton Hill near Avebury. *Wiltshire Archaeological Magazine*, 45, 300–35

Darvill, T, 1982, *The megalithic chambered tombs of the Cotswold-Severn region* (= VORDA Research Series 5). Highworth. VORDA

Darvill, T, 1987, *Prehistoric Gloucestershire.* Gloucester. Alan Sutton and Gloucestershire County Library

Darvill, T, and Grinsell, L V, 1989, Gloucestershire barrows: Supplement 1961–1988. *Transactions of the Bristol and Gloucestershire Archaeological Society*, 107, 39–105

Darvill, T, (in press), Landscapes and the archaeologist. In K Barker and T Darvill (eds), *The making of the English landscape: Changing perspectives – Papers presented to Christopher Taylor* (= Bournemouth University School of Conservation Sciences Occasional Paper 3). London. Archetype Publications

David, N, Sterner, J, and Gavua, K, 1988, Why pots are decorated. *Current Anthropology*, 29, 365–89

Davies, O, 1936, Excavations at Dún Rúadh. *Proceedings and Reports of the Belfast Natural History and Philosophical Society*, 1, 50–75

Davies, O, 1949, Excavations at the Horned Cairn of Ballymarlagh, Co. Antrim. *Ulster Journal of Archaeology*, 12, 26–42

Deetz, J F, 1977, *In Small Things Forgotten.* Garden City, New York. Anchor/Doubleday

de Grooth, M, 1987, The organization of flint tool manufacture in the Dutch Bandkeramik. *Analecta Praehistorica Leidensia*, 20, 27–51

Demoule, J-P, and Perlès, C, 1993, The Greek Neolithic: A new review. *Journal of World Prehistory*, 7, 355–416

Dent, J, (no date), *A Neolithic house site at Driffield* (= Humberside Archaeology Unit Note 25). Beverley. Humberside County Council

Dixon, P, 1988, The Neolithic settlements on Crickley Hill. In C Burgess, P Topping, C Mordant and M Madison (eds), *Enclosures and defences in the Neolithic of western Europe* (= BAR International Series 403). Oxford. British Archaeological Reports. (2 vols). 75–88

Dohrn-Ihmig, M, 1983, Ein Grossgartacher Siedlungsplatz bei Jülich-Welldorf, Kreis Düren, und der Übergang zum mittelneolithischen Hausbau. *Rheinische Ausgrabungen*, 24, 233–82.

Drewett, P, 1982, Later Bronze Age downland economy and excavations at Black Patch, East Sussex. *Proceedings of the Prehistoric Society*, 48, 321–400

Drewett, P, Rudling, D, and Gardiner, M, 1988, *The South East to AD1000*. London. Longman

Dubouloz, J, Ilett, M, and Lasserre, M, 1982, Enceinte et maisons chalcolithiques de Berry-au-Bac, La Croix-Maigret (Aisne). In *Le Néolithique de l'Est de la France* (= Société Archéologique de Sens, Cahier 1). Paris

Dubouloz, J, Lebolloch, M, and Ilett, M, 1988, Middle Neolithic enclosures in the Aisne Valley. In C Burgess, P Topping, C Mordant and M Madison (eds), *Enclosures and defenses in the Neolithic of Western Europe* (= BAR Supplemental Series 403). Oxford. British Archaeological Reports. (2 vols). 209–226

Dyer, J, 1964, A secondary Neolithic camp at Waulud's bank, Leagrave. *Bedfordshire Archaeological Journal*, 2, 1–12

Edmonds, M R, 1987, Rocks and risk: Problems with lithic procurement strategies. In A Brown and M Edmonds (eds), *Lithic analysis and later British prehistory* (= BAR British Series 162). Oxford. British Archaeological Reports. 155–80

Edmonds, M R, 1993, Interpreting causewayed enclosures in the past and the present. In C Tilley (ed), *Interpretative archaeology*. Oxford. Berg. 99–142

Ellis, P, 1986, A possible henge monument from aerial photographic evidence in Norton Fitzwarren parish. *Proceedings of the Somerset Archaeological and Natural History Society*, 130, 165

Engelhardt, B, 1983, Der Sallmannsberg bei Landshut, Niederbayern. *Das archäologische Jahr in Bayern 1982*, 26–32

Entwistle, R, and Grant, A, 1989, The evidence for cereal cultivation and animal husbandry in the southern British Neolithic and Bronze Age. In A Milles, D Williams and N Gardner (eds), *The beginnings of agriculture* (= BAR Supplemental Series 496). Oxford. British Archaeological Reports. 203–215

Eogan, G, 1963, A Neolithic habitation-site and megalithic tomb in Townleyhall Townland, Co. Louth. *Journal of the Royal Society of Antiquaries of Ireland*, 93, 37–81

Eogan, G, 1984, *Excavations at Knowth 1. Smaller passage tombs, Neolithic occupation and Beaker activity* (= Royal Irish Academy Monographs in Archaeology 1). Dublin. Royal Irish Academy

Eogan, G, 1991, Prehistoric and early historic culture change at Brúgh na Bóinne. *Proceedings of the Royal Irish Academy*, 91, 105–32

Eriksen, L B, 1988, Ornehus, St Heddinge s., Praesto a. *Journal of Danish Archaeology*, 7, 245

Eriksen, P, and Madsen, T, 1984, Hanstedgård. A settlement site from the Funnel Beaker Culture. *Journal of Danish Archaeology*, 3, 63–82

Evans, E E, 1939, Excavations at Carnanbane, County Londonderry: A double horned cairn. *Proceedings of the Royal Irish Academy*, 45, 1–12

Evans, E E, 1953, *Lyles Hill: A late Neolithic Site in County Antrim* (= Archaeological Research Publications 2). HMSO. Belfast

Fairweather, A D, and Ralston, I B M, 1993, The Neolithic timber hall at Balbridie, Grampian Region, Scotland: A preliminary note on dating and plant macrofossils. *Antiquity*, 67, 313–323

Field, N H, Matthews, C L, and Smith, I F, 1964, New Neolithic sites in Dorset and Bedfordshire, with a note on the distribution of Neolithic storage pits in Britain. *Proceedings of the Prehistoric Society*, 30, 352–381

Fleming, A, 1973, Tombs for the living. *Man* (NS), 8, 177–193

Forge, A, 1982, *Bali – down from the mountain* [30 minute colour film. Maker: Peter Ramsden]

Foster, S, and Stevenson, J B, (in preparation), Auchenlaich long cairn, Perthshire.

Gardiner, P J, Haldon, R, and Malam, J, 1980, Prehistoric, Roman and Medieval settlement at Stretton-on-Fosse: Excavations and salvage 1971–76. *Transactions of the Birmingham and Warwickshire Archaeological Society*, 90, 1–35

Gardiner, J P, 1984, Lithic distributions and settlement patterns in central southern England. In R J Bradley and J P Gardiner (eds), *Neolithic Studies* (= BAR British Series 133). Oxford. British Archaeological Reports. 15–40

Garton, D, 1986, *Lismore Fields, Buxton: 1986 Summary Report*. Nottingham. Trent and Peak Archaeological Trust. [Privately circulated report]

Garton, D, 1987, Buxton. *Current Archaeology*, 9.8 (no. 103), 250–253

Garton, D, 1991, Neolithic settlement in the Peak District: Perspective and prospective. In R Hodges and K Smith (eds), *Recent developments in the archaeology of the Peak District*. Sheffield. Department of Archaeology and Prehistory, Sheffield University. 3–22

Geertz, C, 1959, Form and variation in Balinese village structure. *American Anthropologist*, 61, 991–1012

Gibson, A, 1980, A reinterpretation of Chippenham Barrow 5, with a discussion of the Beaker-associated pottery. *Proceedings of the Cambridgeshire Antiquarian Society*, 70, 47–60

Gibson, A M, 1982, *Beaker domestic sites: A study in the domestic pottery of the late third and early second millennia BC* (= BAR British Series 107). Oxford. British Archaeological Reports. (2 vols)

Gibson, A, 1985, A Neolithic enclosure at Grendon, Northants. *Antiquity*, 59, 213–219

Gibson, A M, 1987, Beaker domestic sites across the North Sea: A review. *Les Relations entre le Continent et les Iles Britanniques a l'Age du Bronze* (= Supplement Revue Archaeologique de Picardie, Societe Prehistorique Francais). 7–16

Gibson, A, 1992, Approaches to the later Neolithic and Bronze Age settlement of Britain. *Colloque international de Lons-le-Saunier, 16–19 mai 1990*, 41–8

Gibson, A, 1993, Walton Basin Survey. *Archaeology in Wales*, 33, 55–56

Gibson, A M, 1994, Excavations at the Sarn-y-bryn-caled cursus complex, Welshpool, Powys, and timber circles of Great Britain and Ireland. *Proceedings of the Prehistoric Society*, 60, 143–223

Gibson, A, 1995, Walton. *Current Archaeology*, 12.11 (no. 143), 444–45

Gibson, A M, and Simpson, D D A, 1987, Lyles Hill, Co. Antrim. *Archaeology Ireland*, 1.2, 72–5

Gibson, A M, and Simpson, D D A, 1989, Lyles Hill, Toberagnee. In I Bennet (ed), *Excavations 1988*. Dublin. Wordwell and Organization of Irish Archaeologists. 9

Gimbutas, M, Winn, S, and Shimabuku, D, 1989, *Achilleion. A Neolithic settlement in Thessaly, Greece, 6400–5600 BC*. Los Angeles. Institute of Archaeology, University of California, Los Angeles

Gowen, M, 1987, Tankardstown, Co Limerick: A Neolithic house. *Archaeology Ireland*, 1.1, 6–10

Gowen, M, 1988a, Tankardstown South. In I Bennet (ed), *Excavations 1988*. Dublin. Wordwell and Organization of Irish Archaeologists. 24–6

Gowen, M, 1988b, *Three Irish gas pipelines: New archaeological evidence in Munster*. Dublin. Wordwell

Gowen, M, and Halpin, E, 1992, A Neolithic house at Newtown. *Archaeology Ireland*, 6.2, 25–27

Gowen, M, and Tarbett, C, 1988, A third season at Tankardstown. *Archaeology Ireland*, 2.4, 156

Green, F, 1991, Mesolithic structures in the Test Valley: Bowman's Farm. *Past*, 11, 1–2

Green, F J, and Lockyear, K, 1992, Plant remains from buried soils, Romsey, Hants. In J P Pals, J Buurman and M van der Veen (eds), *Festschrift for Professor W van Zeist* (= Review Palaeobotany Palynology 73). Amsterdam. Elsevier Science Publishers. 57–70

Greenfield, E, 1960, The excavation of Barrow 4 at Swarkeston, Derbyshire. *Derbyshire Archaeological Journal*, 80, 1–48

Griffith, F, 1995, Watching brief at Haldon Belvedere. *Devon Archaeological Society Newsletter*, 62 (September 1995), 3

Grogan, E, 1980, *Houses of the Neolithic period in Ireland and comparative sites in Britain and on the Continent.* Unpublished MA Dissertation. National University of Ireland

Grogan, E, 1988, Possible reconstructions of the (Tankardstown South) house. In M Gowen, *Three Irish gas pipelines: New archaeological evidence in Munster.* Dublin. Wordwell. 42

Grogan, E M, 1992, Neolithic Settlements. In M Ryan (ed), *The illustrated archaeology of Ireland.* Dublin. 59–64

Grogan, E, and Eogan, G, 1987, Lough Gur excavations by Seán P. Ó Ríordáin: Further Neolithic and Beaker habitations on Knockadoon. *Proceedings of the Royal Irish Academy* 87C, 299–506

Grygiel, R, 1986, The household cluster as a fundamental social unit of the Lengyel Culture in the Polish lowlands. *Prace I Materiał y Muzeum Archeologiczneyo I Etnograficzneyo W Łodzi, Seria Archeologiczna,* 31

Günther, K, 1976, *Die jungsteinzeitliche Siedlung Deiringsen/Ruploh in der Soester Börde.* (Boden altertümer Westfalens 16)

Haggarty, A, 1991, Machrie Moor, Arran: Recent excavations at two stone circles. *Proceedings of the Society of Antiquaries of Scotland,* 121, 51–94

Halpin, C, 1987, Irthlingborough Bronze Age barrow excavation 1986. In B Dix (ed), The Raunds area project: Second interim report. *Northamptonshire Archaeology,* 21, 3–30

Halstead, P, 1989, The economy has a normal surplus: Economic stability and social change among early farming communities of Thessaly, Greece. In P Halstead and J O'Shea (eds), *Bad year economics: Cultural responses to risk and uncertainty.* Cambridge. Cambridge University Press. 68–80

Hampel, A, 1989, *Die Hausentwicklung im Mittelneolithikum Zentraleuropas.* Bonn

Harding, A F, and Lee, G E, 1987, *Henges and related sites of Great Britain* (= BAR British Series 175). Oxford. British Archaeological Reports

Hartnett, P J, and Eogan, G, 1964, Feltrim Hill, Co. Dublin: A Neolithic and early Christian Site. *Journal of the Royal Society of Antiquaries of Ireland,* 94, 1–37

Healey, F, 1988, *Spong Hill Part VI: 7th to 2nd Millennia BC* (= East Anglian Archaeology 39). Norwich. East Anglian Archaeology

Healy, F, Cleal, R M J, and Kinnes, I, 1993, Excavations on Redgate Hill, Hunstanton, 1970 and 1971. In R Bradley, P Chowne, R M J Cleal, F Healy and I Kinnes *Excavations on Redgate Hill, Hunstanton, Norfolk, and at Tattershall Thorpe, Lincolnshire* (= East Anglian Archaeology 57). Norwich. East Anglian Archaeology. 1–77

Hegedűs, K, and Makkay, J, 1987, Vésztő-Mágor. A settlement of the Tisza culture. In P Raczky (ed), *The late Neolithic of the Tisza region.* Budapest/Szolnok. Szolnok County Museums. 85–103

Henshall, A S, 1963, *The chambered tombs of Scotland. Volume 1.* Edinburgh. Edinburgh University Press

Herity, M, and Eogan, G, 1977, *Ireland in prehistory.* London. Routledge and Kegan Paul

Hermann, F-R, and Jockenhövel, A, 1990, *Die Vorgeschichte Hessens.* Stuttgart

Herne, A, 1988, A time and a place for the Grimston bowl. In J Barrett and I Kinnes (eds), *The archaeology of context in the Neolithic and Bronze Age: Recent trends.* Sheffield. Department of Archaeology and Prehistory. 9–29

Hobart, M, 1978, The path of the soul: Legitimacy of nature in Balinese conceptions of space. In G B Milner (ed), *Natural symbols in southeast Asia.* London. SOAS

Hodder, I, 1982a, *Symbols in action.* Cambridge. Cambridge University Press

Hodder, I, 1982b, Sequences of structural change in the Dutch Neolithic. In I Hodder (ed), *Symbolic and structural archaeology.* Cambridge. Cambridge University Press. 162–177

Hodder, I, 1984, Burials, houses, women and men in the European Neolithic. In D Miller and C Tilley (eds), *Ideology, power and prehistory.* Cambridge. Cambridge University Press. 51–68

Hodder, I, 1990, *The Domestication of Europe.* Oxford. Blackwell

Hodder, I, 1992, The domestication of Europe. In I Hodder, *Theory and practice in archaeology*. London and New York. Routledge. 241–53

Hodgson, K S, 1939, Some excavations in the Bewcastle district. *Transactions of the Cumberland and Westmoreland Antiquarian and Archaeological Society*, 40, 154–66

Höhn, B, 1991, Siedlungen der Michelsberger Kultur in der Wetterau. In V Rupp (ed), *Archäologie der Wetterau: Aspekte der Forschung*. Friedberg. 137–44

Holgate, R, 1988, *Neolithic settlement of the Thames Basin* (= BAR British Series 194). Oxford. British Archaeological Reports

Horváth, F, 1987, Hódmezűvásárhely-Gorsza. A settlement of the Tisza culture. In P Raczky (ed), *The late Neolithic of the Tisza region*. Budapest/Szolnok. Szolnok County Museums. 31–46

Houlder, C, 1968, The henge monuments at Llandegai. *Antquity*, 42, 216–221

Howe, L E A, 1983, An introduction to the cultural study of traditional Balinese architecture. *Archipel*, 25, 137–57

Hugh-Jones, C, 1979, *From the Milk River: Spatial and temporal processes in northwest Amazonia*. Cambridge. Cambridge University Press

Hugh-Jones, S, 1979, *The Palm and the Pleiades*. Cambridge. Cambridge University Press

Hunter, J R, Dockrill, S J, Bond, J M, and Smith, A N, (eds), (in press), *Archaeological Investigations on Sanday, Orkney.*

Ilett, M, 1987, The early Neolithic of north-eastern France. In C Scarre (ed), *Ancient France 6000–2000 BC*. Edinburgh. Edinburgh University Press. 6–33

Ilett, M, Constantin, C, Coudart, A and Demoule, J-P, 1982, The late Bandkeramik of the Aisne Valley: Environment and spatial organization. *Analecta Praehistorica Leidensia*, 15, 45–61

Ilett, M, and Coudart, A, 1983, Cuiry-lès-Chaudardes. In *Les Fouilles Protohistoriques dans la vallée de l'Aisne*, 11, 23–42

Ivanov, T G, 1981, Arkheologicheski prouchvaniya v selishtnata mogila i nekropol pri s Radingrad, v Razgradski okrug. (Arkheologicheski otkritiya i razkopki za 1980). *26 Natsionalna Arkheologicheska Konpherentsiya*. Preslav. 21–23

Ivanov, T G, 1982, Tell Radingrad. In H Todorova (ed), *Die kupferzeitliche Siedlungen in Nordostbulgarien*. Munich. Beck. 166–174

Ivanov, T G, 1984, Monogoslojnoe poselenie u s. Radingrad, Razgradskogo rajona. *Studia Praehistorica*, 7, 81–98

Jessop, R, 1930, *The archaeology of Kent*. London. Methuen

Jochim, M A, 1990, The late Mesolithic in southwest Germany: Culture change or population decline. In P M Vermeersch and P van Peer (eds), *Contributions to the Mesolithic in Europe*. Leuven. Leuven University Press. 183–91

Jope, E M, 1952, Porcellanite axes from factories in north-east Ireland: Tievebulliagh and Rathlin. *Ulster Journal of Archaeology*, 15, 31–55

Kalicz, N, and Raczky, P, 1987a, The late Neolithic of the Tisza region: A survey of recent archaeological research. In P Raczky (ed), *The late Neolithic of the Tisza region*. Budapest/Szolnok. Szolnok County Museums. 11–30

Kalicz, N, and Raczky, P, 1987b, Berettyóújfalu-Herpály. A settlement of the Herpály culture. In P Raczky (ed), *The late Neolithic of the Tisza region*. Budapest/Szolnok. Szolnok County Museums. 105–25

Kazdová, E, 1990, On the relations of the Stroked Pottery and the Moravian Painted Ware settlements. In J Rulf (ed), *Bylany Seminar 1987 – Collected papers*. Prague. Institute of Archaeology. 87–94

Keefer, E, 1988, *Hochdorf II: Eine jungsteinzeitliche Siedlung der Schussenrieder Kultur* (= Forschungen und Berichte zur Vor- und Frühgeschichte in Baden-Württemburg 27). Stuttgart

Keeley, L H, and Cahen, D, 1989, Early Neolithic forts and villages in NE Belgium: A preliminary report. *Journal of Field Archaeology*, 16.2, 157–176

Kelly, R L, 1992, Mobility / sedentism: Concepts, archaeological measures, and effects. *Annual Review of Anthropology*, 21, 43–66

Kempfner-Jorgensen, L, and Watt, M, 1985, Settlement sites with middle Neolithic houses at Grodby, Bornholm. *Journal of Danish Archaeology*, 4, 87–100

Kent, S, 1992, The current forager controversy: Real versus ideal views of hunter-gatherers. *Man* (NS), 27, 45–70

Kinnes, I, 1975, Monumental function in British Neolithic burial practices. *World Archaeology*, 7.1, 16–28

Kinnes, I, 1985, Circumstance not context: The Neolithic of Scotland as seen from the outside. *Proceedings of the Society of Antiquaries of Scotland*, 115, 15–57

Kinnes, I A, 1988, The cattleship Potemkin: The first Neolithic in Britain. In J C Barrett and I A Kinnes (eds), *The archaeology of context in the Neolithic and Bronze Age: Recent trends*. Sheffield. Department of Archaeology and Prehistory, University of Sheffield. 2–8

Koch-Grünberg, T, 1909/10, *Zwei Jahre unter den Indianern*. Berlin. Wasmuth. (2 vols)

Korek, J, 1987, Szegvár-Tűzköves. A settlement of the Tisza culture. In P Raczky (ed), *The late Neolithic of the Tisza region*. Budapest/Szolnok. Szolnok County Museums. 47–60

Kotsakis, K, 1995, The use of habitational space in Neolithic Sesklo. In J-C Decourt, B Helly and K Gallis (eds), *La Thessalie, Colloque international d'archéologie: 15 années de recherches (1975–1990), bilans et perspectives, Lyon, 1990*. Athens. Tameio Arhaiologikon Poron Kai Apallotrioseon. 125–30

Kreuz, A M, 1990, *Die ersten Bauern Mitteleuropas – eine archäobotanische Untersuchung zu Umwelt und Landwirtschaft der ältesten Bandkeramik*. Leiden. Leiden University Press

Kulczycka-Leciejwiczowa, A, 1988, Erste Gemeinschaften der Linienbandkeramikkultur auf polnischem Boden. *Zeitschriften für Archäologie*, 23, 137–182

Lane, P, 1986, Past practices in the ritual present: Examples from the Welsh Bronze Age. *Archaeological Review From Cambridge*, 5, 181–92

Larsson, M, 1985, *The early Neolithic Funnel-Beaker Culture in South-West Scania, Sweden* (= BAR International Series 264). Oxford. British Archaeological Reports

Leaf, C S, 1936, Two Bronze Age barrows at Chippenham, Cambridgeshire. *Proceedings of the Cambridgeshire Antiquarian Society*, 36, 134–155

Leaf, C S, 1940, Further excavations in Bronze Age barrows at Chippenham, Cambridgeshire. *Proceedings of the Cambridgeshire Antiquarian Society*, 39, 29–68

Leeds, E T, 1936, Round barrows and ring-ditches in Berks. and Oxon. *Oxoniensia*, 1, 7–23

Lenneis, E, 1989, Zum Forschungstand der ältesten Bandkeramik in Österreich. *Archäologisches Korrespondenzblatt*, 19, 23–36

Lewis, J M, 1974, Excavations at Rhos-y-clegyrn prehistoric site, St Nicholas, Pembs. *Archaeologia Cambrensis*, 123, 13–42

Lichardus, J, 1974, *Studien zur Bükker Kultur*. Saarbrücker Beiträge zur Altertumskunde 12.

Lička, M, 1990a, Besiedlung der Kultur mit Stichbandkeramik in Mšeno, Bezirk Melnik – Teil 1. *Acta Musei Nationalis Pragae 44*.

Lička, M, 1990b, Grundrisse von Doppelhäusern aus der Stichbandkeramik. In J Rulf (ed), *Bylany Seminar 1987 – Collected Papers*. Prague. Institute of Archaeology. 227–31

Liddell, D M, 1931, Report of the excavations at Hembury Fort, Devon. Second season, 1931. *Proceedings of the Devon Archaeological and Exploration Society*, 1.3, 90–120

Lieberman, D E, 1993, The rise and fall of seasonal mobility among hunter-gatherers. The case of the southern Levant. *Current Anthropology*, 34, 599–631

Liversage, G D, 1958, Excavations at Dalkey Island, Co. Dublin, 1956–1959. *Proceedings of the Royal Irish Academy*, 66, 53–233

Liversage, G D, 1960, A Neolithic site at Townleyhall, Co. Louth, *Journal of the Royal Society of Antiquaries of Ireland*, 90, 49–60

Louwe Kooijmans, L, 1974, *The Rhine/Meuse Delta: Four Studies in its Prehistoric Occupation and Holocene Geology*. Oudheidkundige Mededelingen uit het Rijksmuseum van Oudheden 53–4. Leiden

Loveday, R, The Barford ritual complex: Further excavations (1972) and a regional prespective. In A Gibson (ed), *Midlands prehistory* (= BAR British Series 204). Oxford. British Archaeological Reports. 51–84

Lloyd, J E, 1928, Hendref and Hafod. *Bulletin of the Board of Celtic Studies*, 4, 224–225

Lückerath, C, 1986, *Funf Häuser der Bischheimer Siedlung von Creglingen-Frauental*. Unpublished MA dissertation. Frankfurt/Main

Lüning, J, 1981, *Eine Siedlung der mittelneolithischen Gruppe Bischheim in Schernau, Ldkr*. Kitzingen. Materialhefte zur Bayerischen Vorgeschchte, Reihe A, Band 44

Lüning, J, 1982. Siedlung und Siedlungslandschaft in bandkeramischer und Rössener Zeit. *Offa*, 39, 9–33

Lüning, J, 1988, Zur Verbreitung und Datierung bandkeramischer Erdwerke. *Archäologisches Korrespondenzblatt*, 18, 155–158

Lüning, J, Kloos, U, and Albert, S, 1989, Westliche Nachbarn der bandkeramischen Kultur: Die Keramikgruppen La Hoguette und Limburg. *Germania*, 67, 355–421

Lynch, F, 1972, Ring-cairns and related monuments in Wales. *Scottish Archaeological Forum*, 4, 61–80

Lynch, F, 1989, Wales and Ireland in prehistory: A fluctuating relationship. *Archaeologia Cambrensis*, 138, 1–19

Lynch, F, no date, *The Neolithic "house" at Llandegai, Caernarfonshire, North Wales*. Bangor. Privately circulated discussion paper

Macalister, R A S, Armstrong, E C R, and Praeger, R L, 1912, Report on the exploration of Bronze-Age cairns on Carrowkeel Mountain, Co. Sligo. *Proceedings of the Royal Irish Academy*, 29, 311–47

Madsen, T, and Jensen, H J, 1982, Settlement and land use in early Neolithic Denmark. *Annalecta Praehistorica Leidensia*, 15, 63–86

Makkay, J, 1978, Excavations at Bicske 1: The early Neolithic – the earliest Linear Band Ceramic. *Alba Regia*, 16, 9–60

Makkay, J, 1986, Bauopfer in der Lengyel-Kultur und seine Beziehungen zu der Bauopferformen der Körös-Kultur und der Linearbandkeramik. In B Chropovsky and H Friesinger (eds), *Internationales Symposium über die Lengyel-Kultur*. Nitra and Vienna

Mallory, J P, 1990, Trial excavations at Tievebulliagh, Co. Antrim. *Ulster Journal of Archaeology*, 53, 15–28

Mallory, J, and Hartwell, B, 1984, Donegore. *Current Archaeology*, 8.9 (no. 92), 271–5

Marolle, C, 1989, Le village Michelsberg des Hautes Chanvières à Mairy (Ardennes): Étude préliminaire de principales structures. *Gallia Préhistoire*, 31, 93–117

Marshall, A, 1981, Environmental adaptation and structural design in axially-pitched longhouses from Neolithic Europe. *World Archaeology*, 13.1, 101–121

Marshall, D N, 1978, Excavations at Auchategan, Glendaruel, Argyll. *Proceedings of the Society of Antiquaries of Scotland*, 109, 36–74

Mauss, M, 1988, *The Gift*. London. Routledge

McInnes, I J, 1971, Settlements in later Neolithic Britain. In D D A Simpson (ed), *Economy and settlement in Neolithic and Beaker Britain and Europe*. Leicester. Leicester University Press. 113–130

McPherron, A, and Srejović, D, 1988, *Divostin and the Neolithic of Central Serbia*. (Ethnology Monographs 10). Pittsburgh. Department of Anthropology, The University of Pittsburgh

Megaw, J V S, 1976, Gwithian, Cornwall: Some notes on the evidence for Neolithic and Bronze Age settlement. In C Burgess and R Miket (eds), *Settlement and economy in the third and second millennia BC* (= BAR British Series 33). Oxford. British Archaeological Reports. 51–80

Megaw, J V S, and Simpson, D D A, 1979, *Introduction to British Prehistory*. Leicester. Leicester University Press

Mercer, R J, 1980, *Archaeological Field Survey in Northern Scotland*. Edinburgh. Department of Archaeology University of Edinburgh

Mercer, R J, 1981, Excavations at Carn Brea, Illogan, Cornwall, 1970–3. A Neolithic fortified complex of the third millennium bc. *Cornish Archaeology*, 20, 1–204

Mercer, R J, 1983, *Excavations at Spott Dod Near Dunbar, 1983: Interim report*. Edinburgh. Privately circulated paper

Michaelsen, K K, 1988, Oster Nibstrup, Brondersleus, Hjorring a. *Journal of Danish Archaeology*, 7, 246–7

Midgley, M, 1992, *TRB Culture: The first farmers of the European plain*. Edinburgh. Edinburgh University Press

Miles, D, and Palmer, S, 1990, Claydon Pike and Thornhill Farm. *Current Archaeology*, 11.1 (no. 121), 19–23

Milisauskas, S, 1986, *Early Neolithic settlement and society at Olszanica*. Ann Arbor. Museum of Anthropology, University of Michigan

Milisauskas, S, and Kruk, J, 1993, Archaeological investigations on Neolithic and Bronze Age sites in southeastern Poland. In P Bogucki (ed), *Case studies in European prehistory*. Boca Raton, Florida. CRC Press. 63–94

Milojcić, V, Boessneck, J, and Hopf, M, 1962, *Die deutschen Ausgrabungen auf der Argissa-Magula in Thessalien, I: Das präkeramische Neolithikum sowie die Tier- und Pflanzenreste*. Bonn. Rudolf Habelt

Modderman P J R, 1970, Linearbandkeramik aus Elsloo und Stein, *Analecta Praehistorica Leidensia*, 3, 1–218. (3 vols)

Modderman, P J R, 1977, Die neolithische Besiedlung bei Hienheim, Ldkr. Kelheim. 1. Die Ausgrabungen am Weinberg 1965 bis 1970. *Analecta Praehistorica Leidensia*, 10

Modderman, P J R, 1988, The Linear Pottery Culture: Diversity in uniformity. *Berichten van de Rijksdienst voor het Ouheidkundig Bodemonderzoek*, 38, 63–139

Modderman, P J R, 1989, Comments on "Theses on the Neolithic site of Bylany". In J Rulf (ed), *Bylany seminar 1987*. Prague. Institute of Archaeology. 341–2

Moffett, L, Robinson, M A, and Straker, V, 1989, Cereals, fruit and nuts: Charred plant remains from Neolithic sites in England and Wales and the Neolithic economy. In A Milles, D Williams and N Gardner (eds), *The Beginnings of Agriculture* (= BAR International Series 496). Oxford. British Archaeological Reports. 243–61

Mogey, J M, 1941, The "Druid Stone", Ballintoy, Co. Antrim, *Ulster Journal of Archaeology*, 4, 49–56

Moore, H, 1986, *Space, text and gender: An anthropological study of the Marakwet of Kenya*. Cambridge. Cambridge University Press

Moore, J W, 1964, Excavations at Beacon Hill, Flamborough Head, East Yorkshire. *Yorkshire Archaeological Journal*, 41, 191–202

Mordant, C, and Mordant, D, 1992, Noyen-sur-Seine: A Mesolithic waterside settlement. In B Coles (ed), *The wetland revolution in prehistory*. Exeter. WARP and The Prehistoric Society. 55–64

Morgan, F de M, 1959, The excavation of a long barrow at Nutbane, Hants. *Proceedings of the Prehistoric Society*, 25, 15–51

Mortimer, J R, 1905, *Forty year's researches in British and Saxon burial mounds of East Yorkshire*. London. A Brown and Sons

Musson, C, 1970, House-plans and prehistory. *Current Archaeology*, 2.10 (no. 21), 267–275

Musson, C R, 1971, A study of possible building forms at Durrington Walls, Woodhenge and The Sanctuary. In G J Wainwright and I H Longworth, *Durrington Walls: Excavations 1966–1968* (= Reports of the Research Committee of the Society of Antiquaries of London 29). London. Society of Antiquaries. 363–377

Neal, D, Wardle, A, and Hunn, J, 1990, *Excavation of the Iron Age, Roman and Medieval Settlement at Gorhambury, St. Albans* (= Historic Buildings and Monuments Commission for England Archaeological Report 14). London. English Heritage

Němejcová-Pavúková, V, 1986, Vorbericht über die Ergebnisse der systematischen Grabung in Svodín in den Jahren 1971–1983. *Slovenská Archeológia*, 34, 133–176

Nielsen, F O, and Nielsen, P O, 1985, Middle and late Neolithic Houses at Limensgard, Bornholm. *Journal of Danish Archaeology*, 4, 101–114

Nikolov, V, 1989, Das frühneolithische Haus von Sofia-Slatina. Eine Untersuchung zur vorgeschichtlichen Bautechnik. *Germania*, 67, 1–49

Nikolov, V, 1992, Die Untersuchungen der frühneolithischen Siedlung Slatina (Sofia) in den Jahren 1985–1987. *Studia Praehistorica*, 11–12, 68–73

O'Kelly, M J, 1982, *Newgrange. Archaeology, art and legend*. London. Thames and Hudson

O'Kelly, M J, 1983, The Excavation. In M J O'Kelly, R M Cleary, and D Lehane, *Newgrange, Co Meath, Ireland: The late Neolithic/Beaker Period Settlement* (= BAR International Series 190). Oxford. British Archaeological Reports. 1–57

O'Kelly, M J, Lynch, F, and O'Kelly, C, 1978, Three passage-graves at Newgrange, Co. Meath. *Proceedings of the Royal Irish Academy*, 78C, 249–352

O'Neil, H E, 1966, Sale's Lot long barrow, Withington, Gloucestershire, 1962–65. *Transactions of the Bristol and Gloucestershire Archaeological Society*, 85, 5–35

Ó Nualláin, S, 1972a, A Neolithic house at Ballyglass near Ballycastle, Co. Mayo. *Journal of the Royal Society of Antiquarians of Ireland*, 102, 49–57

Ó Nualláin, S, 1972b, Ballyglass, Co. Mayo. In T Delaney (ed), *Excavations 1972*. Belfast. Association of Young Irish Archaeologists. 20–2

Ó Ríordáin, S P, 1954, Lough Gur excavations: Neolithic and Bronze Age houses on Knockadoon. *Proceedings of the Royal Irish Academy*, 56C, 297–459

Orme, B J and Coles, J M, 1983, Prehistoric woodworking from the Somerset Levels: 1. Timber. *Somerset Levels Papers*, 9, 19–43

O'Sullivan, A, 1991, *Prehistoric Woodworking Techniques: The evidence from excavated trackways in the raised bogs of Co. Longford*. Unpublished MA Dissertation. National University of Ireland

Oswald, A, (ed), 1969, Excavations for the Avon/Severn Research Committee at Barford, Warwickshire. *Transactions of the Birmingham and Warwickshire Archaeological Society*, 83 (1966–7), 1–64

Oswald, A, 1991, *A doorway on the past: Round-house entrance orientation and its significance in Iron Age Britain*. Unpublished PhD Dissertation. Cambridge University

Parker Pearson, M, and Richards, C, (eds), 1994, *Architecture and order: Studies in social space*. London. Routledge

Pavlů, I, 1990, Early Linear Pottery culture in Bohemia. In D Srejović and N Tasić (eds), *Vinča and its world*. Belgrade. Serbian Academy of Sciences and Arts. 133–41

Pavlů, I, Rulf, J, and Zapatocka, M, 1986, Theses on the Neolithic site of Bylany. *Památky archeologické*, 57, 288–412

Pavlů, I, and Zápotocká, M, 1983, *Bylany Katalog, Sekce A*. Prague

Pavúk, J, 1981, *Umenie a zivot doby kamennej [Art and Life of the Stone Age]*. Tatran

Pavúk, J, 1982, Zweites Jahr der Rettungsgrabung in Zlkovce. *Archeologické vyskumy a nálezy na slovensku vroku 1981*, 221–222

Pavúk, J, 1984, Viertes Jahr der Grabung auf der Siedlung der Lengyel-Kultur in Žlkovce. *Archeologické vyskumy a nálezy na slovensku vroku 1983*, 176–177

Pavúk, J, 1986, Linearkeramische Großbauten aus Čataj. *Slovenská Archeológia*, 34, 365–382

Pavúk, J, 1991, Lengyel-culture fortified settlements in Slovakia. *Antiquity*, 65, 348–357

Payne, G F, 1880, Celtic remains discovered at Grovehurst, in Milton-next-Sittingbourne. *Archaeologia Cantiana*, 13, 122–26

Pearson, G W, and Stuiver, M, 1986, High-precision calibration of the radiocarbon time scale, 500–2500BC. *Radiocarbon*, 28, 839–862

Pearson, G W, Pilcher, J R, Baillie, M G L, Corbett, D M, and Qua, F, 1986, High-precision ^{14}C measurement of Irish oak to show the natural ^{14}C variation from AD 1840 to 5210 BC. *Radiocarbon*, 28, 911–934

Peltenburg, E J, 1982, Excavations at Balloch Hill, Argyll. *Proceedings of the Society of Antiquaries of Scotland*, 112, 142–214

Petrasch, J, 1990, Mittelneolithische Kreisgrabenanlagen in Mitteleuropa. *Berichte der* Römisch-Germanischen Kommission, 71, 409–564

Piggott, S, 1935, A note on the relative chronology of the English long barrows. *Proceedings of the Prehistoric Society*, 1, 115–126

Piggott, S, 1940, Timber circles: A re-examination. *Archaeological Journal*, 96, 193–222

Piggott, S, 1954, *The Neolithic cultures of the British Isles*. Cambridge. Cambridge University Press

Piggott, S, 1982, *Scotland before history*. Edinburgh. Edinburgh University Press

Pleinerová, I, 1984, Häuser des Spätlengyelhorizontes in Březno bei Louny. *Památky Archeologické*, 75, 7–49

Pollard, A, 1992, *Beckton Farm. Glasgow University Archaeology Research Division Project 73*. Glasgow

Pollard, J, 1992, The Sanctuary, Overton Hill, Wiltshire: A re-examination. *Proceedings of the Prehistoric Society*, 213–226

Pollard, J, 1995, The Durrington 68 timber circle: A forgotten late Neolithic monument. *Wiltshire Archaeological and Natural History Magazine*, 88, 122–126

Powell, T G E, 1973, The excavation of a megalithic chambered cairn at Dyffryn Ardudwy, Merioneth, Wales. *Archaeologia*, 104, 1–49

Pryor, F M, 1974, *Excavation at Fengate, Peterborough, England: The first report* (= Royal Ontario Museum, Archaeology Monograph 3). Toronto. Royal Ontario Museum

Pryor, F M, 1976, A Neolithic multiple burial at Fengate, Peterborough. *Antiquity*, 50, 232–3

Pryor, F M, 1978, *Excavation at Fengate, Peterborough, England: The second report* (= Royal Ontario Museum Archaeology Monograph 5). Toronto. Royal Ontario Museum

Pryor, F M, 1988, Etton, near Maxey, Cambridgeshire: A causewayed enclosure on the fen-edge. In C Burgess, P Topping, C Mordant, and M Madison (eds), *Enclosures and defences in the Neolithic of Western Europe* (= BAR International Series 403). Oxford. British Archaeological Reports. (2 vols). 107–126

Pryor, F M, 1991, *Flag Fen*. London. Batsford and English Heritage

Pryor, F M, French, C, and Taylor, M, 1985, An interim report on excavations at Etton, Maxey, Cambridgeshire, 1982–84. *Antiquaries Journal*, 65, 275–311

Pucher, E, 1987, Viehwirtschaft und Jagd zur Zeit der ältesten Linearbandkeramik von Neckenmarkt (Burgenland) und Strögen (Niederösterreich). *Mitteilungen der Anthropologischen Gesellschaft in Wien*, 117, 141–155

Quitta, H, 1958, Die Ausgrabungen in der bandkeramischen Siedlung Zwenkau-Harth, Kr. Leipzig. In W Krämer (ed), *Neue Ausgrabungen in Deutschland*. Berlin. 68–74

Raczky, P, 1987, Öcsöd-Kováshalom. A settlement of the Tisza culture. In P Raczky (ed), *The late Neolithic of the Tisza region*. Budapest/Szolnok. Szolnok County Museums. 61–83

Raduncheva, A, 1976, *Vinitsa. Eneolitno Selishte i Nekropol*. (= Razkopki i Prouchvaniya 6). Sofia. Bulgarian Academy of Sciences, Institute of Archaeology

Rahtz, P A, and ApSimon, A M, 1962, Neolithic and Beaker sites at Downton, near Salisbury, Wiltshire. *Wiltshire Archaeological Magazine*, 58, 116–141

Rahtz, P A, and Greenfield, E, 1977, *Excavations at Chew Valley Lake, Somerset* (= Department of the Environment Archaeological Reports 8). London. HMSO

Ralston, I B M, 1982, A timber hall at Balbridie Farm. *Aberdeen University Review*, 168, 238–249

Rapoport, A, 1990, Systems of activities and systems of settings. In S Kent (ed), *Domestic architecture and the use of space*. Cambridge. Cambridge University Press. 9–20

RCAHMS, 1994, *South-east Perth: An archaeological landscape*. Edinburgh. HMSO

Rennie, E B, 1984, Excavations at Ardnadam, Cowal, Argyll, 1964–1982. *Glasgow Archaeological Journal*, 11, 13–39

Rennie, E B, 1986, Dunloskin. *Discovery and Excavation in Scotland 1986*. Edinburgh. Scottish Group of the Council for British Archaeology. 26–7

Reynolds, N, 1980, Dark Age timber halls and the background to excavation at Balbridie. *Scottish Archaeological Forum*, 10, 41–60

Richards, C, 1990a, The late Neolithic house in Orkney. In R Samson (ed), *The social archaeology of houses*. Edinburgh. Edinburgh University Press. 111–124

Richards, C, 1990b, The late Neolithic settlement complex at Barnhouse Farm, Stenness. In C Renfrew (ed), *The Prehistory of Orkney* (2nd Edition). Edinburgh. Edinburgh University Press. 305–316

Richards, C, 1991, Skara Brae: Revisiting a Neolithic village in Orkney. In W S Hanson and E A Slater (eds) *Scottish archaeology: New perceptions*. Aberdeen. Aberdeen University Press. 24–43

Richards, C, 1992, Barnhouse and Maeshowe. *Current Archaeology*, 11.11 (no. 131), 444–448

Richards, C, and Thomas, J, 1984, Ritual activity and structured deposition in late Neolithic Wessex. In R Bradley and J Gardiner (eds), *Neolithic studies* (= BAR British Series 133). Oxford. British Archaeological Reports. 189–218

Ritchie, A, 1983, Excavation of a Neolithic farmstead at Knap of Howar, Papa Westray, Orkney. *Proceedings of the Society of Antiquaries of Scotland*, 113, 40–121

Ritchie, J N G, 1974, Excavation of the stone circle and cairn at Balbirnie, Fife. *Archaeological Journal*, 131, 1–32

Ritchie, J N G, 1976, The Stones of Stenness, Orkney. *Proceedings of the Society of Antiquaries of Scotland*, 107, 1–60

Ritchie, J N, and MacLaren A, 1973, Ring-cairns and related monuments in Scotland. *Scottish Archaeological Forum*, 4, 1–17

Robertson-Mackay, R, 1987, The Neolithic causewayed enclosure at Staines, Surrey: Excavations 1961–63. *Proceedings of the Prehistoric Society*, 53, 23–128

Roche, H, 1989, Pre-tomb habitation found at Knowth, Co. Meath, spring 1989. *Archaeology Ireland*, 3.3, 101–3

Rosman, A and Rubel, P G, 1971, *Feasting with mine enemy: Rank and exchange among Northwest Coast societies*. Prospect Heights. Waveland Press

Rudd, G T, 1968, A Neolithic hut and features at Little Paxton, Huntingdonshire. *Proceedings of the Cambridgeshire Antiquarian Society*, 61, 9–13

Rynne, E, and Ó h Éailidhe, P, 1965, A group of prehistoric sites at Piperstown, Co. Dublin. *Proceedings of the Royal Irish Academy*, 64C, 61–84

Saville, A, 1990, *Hazleton North: The excavation of a Neolithic long cairn of the Cotswold-Severn Group* (= Historic Buildings and Monuments Commission for England Archaeological Monograph 13). London. English Heritage

Savory, H N, 1952, The excavation of a Neolithic dwelling and a Bronze Age cairn at Mount Pleasant Farm, Nottage, (Glam.). *Transactions of the Cardiff Naturalist's Society*, 89, 9–25

Savory, H N, 1959, The excavation of a Bronze Age cairn at Sant-y-Nyll, St Brides-Super-Ely (Glam.). *Transactions of the Cardiff Naturalist's Society*, 89, 9–25

Savory, H N, 1972, Copper Age cists and cist-cairns in Wales: With special reference to Newton,

Swansea and other multiple-cist cairns. In F Lynch and C Burgess (eds), *Prehistoric Man in Wales and the West*. Bath. Adams and Dart. 117–140

Savory, H N, 1980, The Neolithic in Wales. In J A Taylor (ed), *Culture and environment in prehistoric Wales* (= BAR British Series 76). Oxford. British Archaeological Reports. 207–232

Scott, W L, 1951, Eilean an Tighe: A pottery workshop of the second millennium BC. *Proceedings of the Society of Antiquaries of Scotland*, 85, 1–37

Selkirk, A, 1972, Waulud's Bank. *Current Archaeology*, 3.7 (no. 30), 173–177

Sharples, N M, 1984, Excavations at Pierowall, Westray, Orkney. *Proceedings of the Society of Antiquaries of Scotland*, 114, 75–125

Shee-Twohig, E, 1990, *Irish megalithic tombs*. Princes Risborough. Shire Archaeology

Shell Chemicals UK Ltd, 1993, *Archaeological studies along the North Western Ethylene Pipeline*. London. Shell UK

Shepherd, I A G, 1976, Preliminary results from the Beaker settlement at Rosinish, Benbecula. In C B Burgess and R F Miket (eds), *Settlement and economy in the third and second millennia BC* (= BAR British Series 33). Oxford. British Archaeological Reports. 209–20.

Sheridan, A J, 1986, Porcellanite artifacts: A new survey. *Ulster Journal of Archaeology*, 49, 19–32

Sheridan, A J, Cooney, G, and Grogan, E, 1992, Stone axe studies in Ireland. *Proceedings of the Prehistoric Society*, 58, 389–416

Sherratt, A G, 1980, Water, soil and seasonality in early cereal cultivation. *World Archaeology*, 11.3, 313–330

Sherratt, A G, 1982, Mobile resources: Settlement and exchange in early agricultural Europe. In C Renfrew and S Shennan (eds), *Ranking, resource and exchange*. Cambridge. Cambridge University Press. 13–26

Shotton, F W, 1978, Archaeological inferences from the study of alluvium in the lower Severn / Avon valleys. In S Limbrey and J G Evans (eds), *The Effect of Man on the Landscape: The Lowland Zone* (= CBA Research Report 21). London. Council for British Archaeology. 27–32

Siklódi, C, 1983, An early Copper Age settlement at Tiszaföldvar. *Szolnók Megyei Múzeumi Évkönyr*, 1982–3, 11–31

Simonsen, J, 1983, A late Neolithic house site at Tastum, northwestern Jutland. *Journal of Danish Archaeology*, 2, 81–89

Simpson, D D A, 1971, Beaker houses and settlements in Britain. In D D A Simpson (ed), *Economy and settlement in Neolithic and early Bronze Age Britain and Europe*. Leicester. Leicester University Press. 131–152

Simpson, D D A, 1976, The later Neolithic and Beaker settlement at Northton, Isle of Harris. In C B Burgess and R F Miket (eds), *Settlement and economy in the third and second millennia BC* (= BAR British Series 33). Oxford. British Archaeological Reports. 221–231

Simpson, D D A, 1993, Ballygalley. *Current Archaeology*, 12.2 (no. 134), 60–2

Simpson, D D A, (in press), The Neolithic settlement site at Ballygalley, Co. Antrim. In C Mount (ed), *Annus Archaeologia, Archaeological Research 1992*. Dublin. Organization of Irish Archaeologists

Simpson, D D A, Conway, M, and Moore, D, 1990, The Neolithic Settlement Site at Ballygalley, Co. Antrim. Excavations 1989, Interim Report. *Ulster Journal of Archaeology*, 53, 40–49

Simpson, D D A, Conway, M G, and Moore, D G, 1994, Ballygalley, Co. Antrim. In I Bennett (ed), *Excavations 1993*. Dublin. Organization of Irish Archaeologists / Wordwell. 1–2

Šiška, S, 1986, Grabungen auf der neolithischen und äneolithischen Siedlung in Šarišske Michal'any. *Slovenská Archeológica*, 34, 439–454

Šiška, S, 1989, *Kultúra s vychodnou lineárnou keramikou na Slovensku* [Die Kultur mit östlicher Linearkeramik in der Slowakei]. Bratislava

Skov, T, 1982, A late Neolithic house site with Bell Beaker pottery at Stendis, northwestern Jutland. *Journal of Danish Archaeology*, 1, 39–44

Slater, E A, 1991, Sir Lindsay Scott: Forty years on. In W S Hanson and E A Slater (eds), *Scottish archaeology: New perceptions*. Aberdeen. Aberdeen University Press. 1–23

Smith, I F, 1965a, *Windmill Hill and Avebury. Excavations by Alexander Keiller 1925–1939*. Oxford. Clarendon Press

Smith, I F, 1965b, Excavation of a bell barrow, Avebury G55. *Wiltshire Archaeological and Natural History Magazine*, 60, 24–46

Soudský, B, 1969, Étude de la maison néolithique. *Slovenská Archeológia*, 17, 5–96

Speck, F G, 1940, *Penobscot man: The life history of a forest tribe in Maine*. London. Oxford University Press

Startin, W, 1978, Linear pottery culture houses: Reconstruction and manpower. *Proceedings of the Prehistoric Society*, 44, 143–60

Stehli, P, 1989, Merzbachtal – Umwelt und Geschichte einer bandkeramischen Siedlungskammer. *Germania*, 67, 51–76

Stone, J F S, 1933, Excavations at Easton Down, Winterslow, 1931–1932. *Wiltshire Archaeological Magazine*, 46, 225–242

Stone, J F S, 1934, Three "Peterborough" dwelling-pits and a double-stockaded early Iron Age ditch at Winterbourne Dauntsey. *Wiltshire Archaeological Magazine*, 46, 445–53

Strathern, M, 1980, No nature, no culture: The Hagen case. In C P MacCormack and M Strathern (eds), *Nature, culture and gender*. Cambridge. Cambridge University Press. 174–222

Strathern, M, 1988, *The gender of the gift*. Berkeley. University of California Press

Stuiver, M, and Reimer, P J, 1993, Extended 14C database and revised CALIB radiocarbon calibration program. *Radiocarbon*, 35, 215–230

Sturdy, D, 1972, A ring-cairn in Levens Park, Westmorland. *Scottish Archaeological Forum*, 4, 52–55

Sweetman, D P, 1976, An earthen enclosure at Monknewtown, Slane. *Proceedings of the Royal Irish Academy*, 76C, 325–72

Tan, R Y D, 1967, The domestic architecture of South Bali. *Bijdragen tot de taal-,Land-,en volkenk*, 123, 442–74

Theocharis, D, 1973, *Neolithic Greece*. Athens. National Bank of Greece

Thomas, J, 1987, Relations of production and social change in the Neolithic of North-West Europe. *Man* (NS), 22, 405–430

Thomas, J, 1988, Neolithic explanations revisited: The Mesolithic – Neolithic transition in Britain and South Scandinavia. *Proceedings of the Prehistoric Society*, 54, 59–66

Thomas, J, 1991, *Rethinking the Neolithic*. Cambridge. Cambridge University Press

Thomas, J, 1993, Discourse, totalisation and "the Neolithic". In C Tilley (ed), *Interpretative Archaeology*. Oxford. Berg. 357–94

Thomas, J S, 1996, *Time, culture and identity*. London. Routledge

Thorpe, O W and Thorpe, R S, 1984, The distribution and sources of archaeological pitchstone in Britain. *Journal of Archaeological Science*, 11, 1–34

Todorova, H, 1976a, *Ovcharovo*. Sofia. Izdatelstvo Septembri

Todorova, H, 1976b, Eneolitnata arkhitectura v Bulgariya. *Izvestiya na Bulgarskoto Istorichesko Druzhestvo*, 30

Todorova, H, 1982, Tell Poljanica. In H Todorova (ed), *Die kupferzeitliche Siedlungen in Nordostbulgarien*. Munich. Beck. 144–165

Todorova, H, 1986, *Kamenno-mednata Epokha v Bulgariya*. Sofia. Izdatelstvo Nauka i Izkustvo

Todorova, H, Ivanov, S, Vassilev, V, Hopf, M, Quitta, H and Kohl, G, (eds), 1975, *Selishnata mogila pri Golyamo Delchevo*. (= Razkopki i Prouchvaniya 5). Sofia. Bulgarian Academy of Sciences, Institute of Archaeology

Todorova, H, Vasilev, V, Ianushevich, Z, Kovacheva, M and Vulev, P, (eds), 1983, *Ovcharovo* (= Razkopki i Prouchvaniya 8). Sofia. Bulgarian Academy of Sciences, Institute of Archaeology

Topping, P, 1992, The Penrith Henges. *Proceedings of the Prehistoric Society*, 58, 249–264

Tringham, R E, 1991a. Houses with faces: The challenge of gender in prehistoric architectural remains. In J M Gero and M W Conkey (eds), *Engendering archaeology: Women and prehistory*. Oxford. Blackwell. 93–131

Tringham, R E, 1991b, Men and women in prehistoric architecture. *Traditional Dwellings and Settlements Review*, 3.1, 9–28

Tringham, R E, 1994, Engendered places in prehistory. *Gender, place and culture*, 1.2, 169–203

Tringham, R, and Krstic, D, (eds), 1990, *Selevac: A Neolithic village in Yugoslavia* (= Monumenta Archaeologica 15). Los Angeles. Institute of Archaeology, UCLA

Tringham, R, Brukner, B, Kaiser, T, Borojevic, K, Bukvic, L, Stehli, P, Russell, N, Stevanovic, M and Voytek, B, 1992, Excavations at Opovo, 1985–1987: Socioeconomic change in the Balkan Neolithic. *Journal of Field Archaeology*, 19, 351–86

Tringham, R E, Bruckner, B, and Voytek, B, 1985, The Opovo Project: A study of socio-economic change in the Balkan Neolithic. *Journal of Field Archaeology*, 12, 425–444

Uenze, H-P, 1992, Eine Altheimer Grubenhütte im Chamer Erdwerk von Piesenkofen, Gde. Obertraubling, Ldkr. Regensburg. In K Schmotz and M Zápotocká (eds), *Archäologische Arbeitsgemeinschaft Ostbayern / West- und Südböhmen. 1. Treffen 23. bis 25. April 1991*. Deggendorf. Resümées der Vorträge

van Andel, T H, Gallis, K, and Toufexis, G, 1995, Early Neolithic farming in a Thessalian river landscape. In J Lewin and J C Woodward (eds), *Mediterranean Quaternary river environments*. Rotterdam. Balkema. 131–43

van Berg, P, 1989, Architecture et geometrie de quelques villages rubanés récents du Nord-Ouest. *Helinium*, 29, 13–41

van de Velde, P, 1990, Bandkeramik social inequality – a case study. *Germania*, 68, 19–38

Vasilev, V K, 1985, *Izsledvane na Phaunata ot Selishtna Mogila Ovcharovo* (= Interdistsiplinarni Izsledvaniya 13). Sofia. Bulgarian Academy of Sciences, Institute of Archaeology

Veit, U, 1993, Burials within settlements of the LBK and SBK cultures of central Europe: On the social construction of death in early Neolithic society. *Journal of European Archaeology*, 1, 107–140

Vine, P M, 1982, *The Neolithic and Bronze Age cultures of the middle and upper Trent Basin* (= BAR British Series 105). Oxford. British Archaeological Reports

Vladar, J and Lichardus, J, 1968, Erforschung der Frühäneolithischen Siedlung in Branč. *Slovenská Archeológia*, 16, 263–352

Voss, K L, 1965, Stratigrafische Notizen zu einen Langhaus der Trichterbecherkultur bei Wittenwater, Kr. Uelzen. *Germania*, 43, 343–51

Vyner, B, 1984, The excavation of a Neolithic cairn at Street House, Loftus, Cleveland. *Proceedings of the Prehistoric Society*, 50, 151–196

Wainwright, G J, 1971, The excavation of a late Neolithic enclosure at Marden, Wiltshire. *Antiquaries Journal*, 51, 177–239

Wainwright, G J, 1973, The excavation of prehistoric and Romano-British settlements at Eaton Heath, Norwich. *Archaeological Journal*, 130, 1–43

Wainwright, G J, 1979, *Mount Pleasant, Dorset: Excavations 1970–1971* (= Reports of the Research Committee of the Society of Antiquaries of London 37). London. Society of Antiquaries

Wainwright, G J, 1989, *The henge monuments*. London. Thames and Hudson

Wainwrght, G J, and Donaldson, P, 1972, Ritual shafts and wells: A Neolithic settlement near Norwich. *Antiquity*, 46, 231–234

Wainwright, G J, and Longworth I H, 1971, *Durrington Walls: Excavations 1966–1968* (= Reports of the Research Committee of the Society of Antiquaries of London 29). London. Society of Antiquaries

Wallace, A R, 1889/1972, *Travels on the Amazon and Rio Negro*. London. (Reprinted: New York. Dover)

Wallace, P F, 1992, *The Viking Age buildings of Dublin*. Dublin

Walshe, P T, 1941, The excavation of a burial cairn on Baltinglass, Co. Wicklow. *Proceedings of the Royal Irish Academy*, 46C, 221–36

Ward, A, 1987, The excavation of Great Carn. *Archaeology in Wales*, 27, 39–40

Warren, S H, Piggott, S, Clark J G D, Burkitt, M C, and Godwin, M E, 1936, Archaeology of the submerged land-surface of the Essex coast. *Proceedings of the Prehistoric Society*, 2, 178–210

Webley, D P, 1958, A cairn cemetery and secondary Neolithic dwelling on Cefn Cilsanws Vaynor (Breck.). *Bulletin of the Board of Celtic Studies*, 18, 79–88

Wheeler, H, 1972, A late Neolithic site at Willington, Debyshire. *Antiquity*, 46, 314–16

Wheeler, H, 1979, Excavation at Willington, Derbyshire, 1970–1972. *Derbyshire Archaeological Journal*, 99, 58–220

Whittle, A W R, 1977, *The earlier Neolithic of southern England and its continental background* (= BAR International Series 35). Oxford. British Archaeological Reports

Whittle, A, 1985, *Neolithic Europe: A survey*. Cambridge. Cambridge University Press

Whittle, A, 1988, *Problems in Neolithic archaeology*. Cambridge. Cambridge University Press

Whittle, A, Keith-Lucas, M, Milles, A, Noddle, B, Rees, S, and Romans, J C C, 1986, *Scord of Brouster* (= OUCA Monograph 9). Oxford. Oxford University Committee for Archaeology

Wijnen, M, 1982, *The early Neolithic I settlement at Sesklo: An early farming community in Thessaly, Greece*. Leiden. Leiden University Press

Wilkinson, T J, and Murphy, P, 1985, *The Hullbridge Basin Survey 1985. Interim report 6*. Chelmsford. Archaeology Section, Essex County Council

Wilkinson, T J, and Murphy, P, 1986, *The Hullbridge Basin Survey 1986. Interim report 7*. Chelmsford. Archaeology Section, Essex County Council

Wilkinson, T J, and Murphy, P, 1987, *The Hullbridge Basin Survey 1987. Interim report 8*. Chelmsford. Archaeology Section, Essex County Council

Williams, A, 1953, Clegyr Boia, St David's (Pembrokeshire): Excavation in 1943. *Archaeologia Cambrensis*, 102, 20–47

Willock, E H, 1936, A Neolithic site on Haldon. *Proceedings of the Devon Archaeological Exploration Society*, 2, 244–63

Willock E H, 1937, A further note on the Neolithic site on Haldon. *Proceedings of the Devon Archaeological Exploration Society*, 3, 33–43

Wilson, P J, 1988, *The domestication of the human species*. New Haven and London. Yale University Press

Windell, D, 1989, A late Neolithic "ritual focus" at West Cotton, Northamptonshire. In A Gibson (ed), *Midlands Prehistory* (= BAR British Series 204). Oxford. British Archaeological Reports. 85–94

Woodman, P C, 1985, *Excavations at Mount Sandel 1973–7, County Londonderry* (= Northern Ireland Archaeological Monograph 2). Belfast. HMSO (N. Ireland)

Zápotocká, M, 1986, Die Unterschiede und Übereinstimmungen zwischen der Lengyel-Kultur und der Gruppen mit stichverzierter Keramik: Die Interpretationsmöglichkeiten. *A Béri Balogh Ádám Múzeum Évkönyve*, 13, 265–272

Zeeb, A, 1990, *Die Hausbefunde der mittelneolithischen Siedlung von Nördlingen-Baldingen im Nördlinger Ries*. Unpublished MA Dissertation. Frankfurt/Main

Zimmerman, W H, 1979, Ein Hausgrundriß der Trichterbecherkultur von Flögeln-Im Örtjen, Kreis Cuxhaven. In H Schirnig (ed), *Großsteingraber in Niedersachen*. Hildesheim. 247–53

Printed in the United Kingdom
by Lightning Source UK Ltd.
883